UNDERSTANDING WATER POLO

A GUIDE TO THE GAME OF WATER POLO FOR PLAYERS, PARENTS AND FANS

By: Dante Dettamanti

ACKNOWLEDGEMENTS

I want to acknowledge the hundreds of players who I have coached and been associated with during 36 years as a head coach and assistant coach, from the Olympians and the All-Americans, to the last substitute who sat on the bench. The players from UC Davis, UCLA, Occidental College, Hawaii, UC Santa Barbara, Stanford, Sacred Heart Prep, the USA National teams and the USA World University Games teams, have all played a part in my coaching career. You have to have talented players to succeed as a coach, and I have coached some of the best. It goes without saying that I couldn't have achieved the success in coaching that I have had without them. I learned as much from the players over the years as I have from other coaches and coaching books. Being associated with the great players that I have met over the years has made the coaching experience well worthwhile. To see them go out into the real world and achieve success as doctors, lawyers, businessmen, scientists, writers, coaches, and even astronauts, makes me proud to have played a small part in their lives. The wins and championships can directly be attributed to them; but are secondary to what they have achieved after their playing days were over.

About the Author

Dante Dettamanti: Coach Dettamanti has produced winning and championship water polo teams at all levels. He was an engineering graduate and MVP and all-league swimmer and water polo player at UC Davis. After a stint as a 1st Lieutenant and US Army Airborne-Ranger, he returned to UCLA for a Master's degree in Exercise Physiology. While at UCLA he became a graduate assistant coach under the legendary coach Bob Horn. The school won the first ever NCAA Championship ever held in 1969. From there he went on to Occidental College, where he transformed a water polo program that had been the league doormat, into league champions in both swimming and water polo. After coaching at Oxy for 4 years, he went on to UC Santa Barbara and turned the water polo program around; again producing a league champion team and a NCAA top-four finish in just three years time.

It was at Stanford University though, that Dettamanti came into his own as a winning coach. In 25 years at Stanford, his teams played in the NCAA Championship final game a total of 14 times, producing eight NCAA Championships and six second-place finishes. He became only the second collegiate coach in NCAA history to record over 600 career wins, and the only collegiate coach to win NCAA Championships in four different decades, the 70's, 80's 90's, and 2000's. His eight National championships tie the NCAA record for the most in NCAA history, along with the legendary Pete Cutino of Cal-Berkeley. NCAA records include a .800 winning percentage at Stanford, a 52 game undefeated streak over a three year period in the 80's, and two undefeated seasons (28-0 in 1981 and 36-0 in 1985).

He has been named League "Coach of the Year" ten times and NCAA "Coach of the Year" six different times. Dettamanti has also had great success at the International level. He coached the USA World University Games teams to Gold and Silver medals in 1979 and 1981; the highest finish ever for a USA National team. Dettamanti gained valuable International coaching experience as the Assistant National Team Coach at the 1990 FINA Cup and at the 1991 FINA World Championships under Olympic Coach Bill Barnett; and as an USA assistant at the 2001 World Championships, under US Olympic and top International coach, Ratko Rudic.

Dettamanti has not only produced winning teams, but also top international players. Fourteen of his players have gone on to play for the USA Olympic Team, including Olympic team standouts Jody Campbell (1980, 84, 88), Wolf Wigo (1996, 2000, 2004) and Tony Azevedo (2000, 2004, 2008). Several of his players have gone on to become successful coaches at the high school and college levels; and several have gone on to become nationally ranked referees as well. Dettamanti is an excellent athlete in his own right. He was one of the original pioneers in the sport of triathlon, placing 6th overall in the prestigious Hawaii Ironman in 1981, along with competing in many other marathons and triathlons during the early 80's when the sport was just getting off the ground.

Table of Contents

Introduction

Appendix A: Numbering systems

Appendix B: Water polo terminology

CHAPTER   PAGE

1. Introduction to the game of water polo_____ 12

2. Understanding the rules and how referees call

   the game_____ 17

3. What it takes to become a good water polo player_ 33

   Appendix C: The commandments of water polo__ 44

4. Playing water polo in college _____ 45

5. Getting in shape to play water polo_____ 57

6. Exposing diet and exercise myths_____ 87

7. Strategies used in the game_____ 99

8. Essential defensive skills_____ 128

9. Passing and shooting skills_____140

10. Playing and defending the 2-meter position_____155

11. Extra-man offense and defense_____ 171

12. Counterattack skills _____189

13. Goalkeeper tactics and training_____ 206

INTRODUCTION

UNDERSTANDING WATER POLO

By

Dante Dettamanti
Head Water Polo Coach
Stanford University
1977-2001

Water polo is one of the most difficult games in the world to play, referee and especially for the casual fan, to understand. This book is written for everyone who is involved in the game as a player, parent and fan. It is most frustrating for a person watching the game for the first time to understand what is going on. Even people who have watched water polo for years sometimes don't understand the game. Partly this is because of the changes in the rules of the game, and the interpretations of those rules by the referees.

There is also some confusion in the game because it is the only team sport that is played in the water. Many things go on under the water that is not apparent to the parent or fan, and sometimes not even apparent to the referee. Remember when watching a game, that the referee cannot see the actual foul that is occurring under water, only the result of the foul.

Water polo, along with many other sports, is constantly being tinkered with by rule-makers in order to make the game more exciting. Because of the constant changes in the rules, the style of game that is played today is much different from the game that was played fifty years ago when I started playing. The way that the referees call the game is also changing, and confusing at the same time. This book is an attempt to clarify what is going on, and to give people an idea of why teams do things a certain way; and why referees make the calls that they do.

This book also contains all of the fundamentals of playing the game that will be useful to the young water polo player. If you are a parent of a water polo player, and want to know what is happening to you daughter or son in the water; then this is the book for you. Your children can read the book to find out how to play the game, and improve themselves as players; and parents can learn what their children are actually doing in the water, and why the referee blows the whistle when he does.

The young player, who might be interested in playing at the college level, will be interested in the chapter on "Playing Water Polo in College". Parents can also learn about the process that their young student/athlete will have to go through in order to get into and play at the college of their choice. It really is a book for the entire family, and for people who just love to watch the game. Water Polo is truly an exciting game to play and watch. It is even more fun when you know what is going on in the water.

There are many parts of the book that will help the young player to learn and improve his/her game, including chapters on "Getting in Shape to Play Water Polo", "What it Takes to Become a Good Water Polo Player" and exposing "Myths about Training and Diet" for water polo players. Chapters on position skills, extra-man skills, counterattack skills, passing and shooting skills, and how to play different positions like hole-man, defender, driver and goalkeeper will help the player to improve his/her game.

It will help parents and fans to understand the game if they understand game tactics and strategies, what the team and players are trying to do, and why they are using different tactics during different parts of the game. Tactics of water polo are covered in the chapter on " Strategies Used in the Game". Are you confused about referee's calls? Everyone should have a better understanding of what the referee is calling after reading the chapter "Understanding the Rules and How Referees Call The Game".

Appendix A describes the numbering system used to describe both the extra-man and frontcourt offensive and defensive systems that are utilized in the book. Appendix C at the end of chapter 3 describes the "The Commandments of Water Polo", a list of important skills and fundamentals of the game that are essential to becoming a successful player. A player who follows the fundamentals described in Appendix C will be way ahead of the game when it comes to competing against other players and teams. Appendix B, describing water polo terminology, may help out parents and fans who are unfamiliar with the words and terminology used by water polo players and coaches.

My reason for writing this book is to help increase the popularity of a great game, to help educate the player and parents about how to play the game, and to make it more enjoyable for the fan to watch the game. Hopefully it will give everyone a better "understanding" of the game of water polo.

Appendix A: Numbering systems

In the early years of water polo, field players were simply referred to as backs and forwards. As the game progressed, the positions in the field of water polo had names like "Wing," "Flat," "Point," and "Hole." To this day, there are still coaches from coast to coast that still refer to these positions by name. The most common names that are still in use in today's game are center forward/hole man/hole set/2-meter position/center for the offensive player at the center position; and center defender/2-meter defender/2-meter guard/hole guard for the defender of the center position. These terms will be interchangeable throughout the text when referring to these two positions. Other terminology used in the text refers to the two outside players in front of the center forward as "drivers", the two players on each side of the goal as "wings", and the player at the top outside position as the "point". All players besides the center forward are considered to be in "perimeter" positions, while the center forward is in the "hole" position.

A specific number, 1 through 6, is issued to each position in the water for frontcourt positions. This allows for easier in-pool communication between players as well as between coaches and players. It does not discriminate between hand dominance; but rather it relates to location in the pool relative to the goal. See Diagram A-1 below for the numbering system and names that will be used in the manual for frontcourt offense and defense positions. Offensive players are marked with a "0" and defensive players are marked with an "X." Diagram A-2 below shows the numbering system for the 6 on 5 extra-man.

Diagram A-1 Front court offense (3-3 set-up) and defense positions

G goalie

01 X1 right wing   X6 06 hole   left wing X5 05

X2   X3   X4 defenders

02 right-hand driver   03 point driver   04 left-hand driver

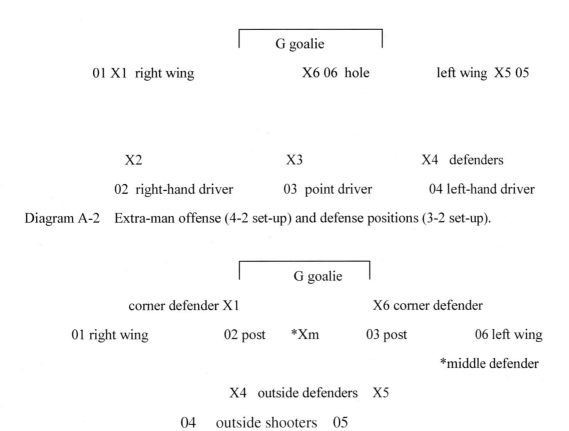

Diagram A-2 Extra-man offense (4-2 set-up) and defense positions (3-2 set-up).

G goalie

corner defender X1   X6 corner defender

01 right wing   02 post   *Xm   03 post   06 left wing

*middle defender

X4 outside defenders X5

04 outside shooters 05

Appendix B:
Water Polo Terminology

Attacker- Any player, but the center forward, who is facing the goal and in position to attack forward and towards the goal. Also know as a "driver". Attackers usually play on the half-circle (perimeter) that forms around the center forward.

Ball control- The team on offense "controls", or keeps the ball under their control for a period of time, without turning it over to the defensive team.

Ball under- A player in control of the ball cannot take the ball underwater when he is under attack. Under attack means that the defender is playing on the shoulder of the player with the ball. The penalty for "ball-under" is a minor foul and turnover of the ball to the defensive team.

Ball side- The same side that the ball is on. An attacker going towards the goal on the left side of the pool tries to swim between the defender and the ball on the right side of the pool. He is swimming on the "ball side" of the defender. Coaches will tell a driver to drive "ball side" so he can receive the pass directly without the ball having to go past the defender.

Cherry picker- A defensive player who "hangs back" by himself, uncovered in the backcourt, while the rest of his teammates are playing defense in the frontcourt.

Contra-foul- An international term for an offensive foul; a foul against the team on offense.

Counterattack- The fast break of water polo. The team on defense "counters" the attacking team when the ball changes hands from offense to defense. Also known as the "counter".

Crashing- When a defensive player leaves his man on the perimeter, "crashes" back, and then attempts to steal the ball from the center forward.

Direct shot after foul- Any player in control of the ball, who is fouled outside of a line that is five-meters from the goal, may take a direct shot at the goal after he is fouled.

Double-post- Two players, each one playing in front of a goal post; instead of the normal single center-forward playing in front of the center of the goal.

Drawing the foul- A player in possession of the ball who tries to "draw the foul" from the referee and be awarded a free pass or direct shot on goal.

Driver- Any offensive player, who facing the goal, "drives" toward the goal in order to gain offensive advantage. See "attacker" above.

Dry pass- A pass to a player who receives the ball in his hand (dry) rather than in the water (wet).

Dumping the ball- When a team on offense, and running out of time on the shot clock, decides to toss (dump) the ball into a corner of the pool; rather than shoot the ball at the goal or loose it from a shot-clock violation.

Eggbeater- An alternating breaststroke kick used exclusively in water polo and synchronized swimming to elevate a player above the surface of the water.

Extra-man- When a defensive player is excluded from the water, the offensive team has an extra player (six against five) for 20 seconds, or until a turnover or goal is scored. The offensive team has a "man-up" or "extra-man". The defensive team has one player less and is playing a "man-down". Also called a "6 on 5".

Five-meter- Term used when a player inside the 5-meter line, in control of the ball and facing the goal, is fouled and awarded a penalty shot. The penalty (free) shot is taken from the five-meter line.

Fronting- When a defensive player plays in front of the offensive player instead of his normal position between his man and the goal. A strategy commonly used to "front" the center forward, usually in conjunction with a "pressing" defense.

Free man- On the counterattack, the player who has broken "free" down the pool and has not been covered by a defensive player.

Foul and drop- A tactic used by the defense in the scoring area in front of the goal. The defender fouls the player with the ball, and then drops back to double team the center forward in order to deny him the ball.

Foul to prevent a goal- A defensive tactic used in the scoring area within 5-meters in front of the goal. The defender will purposely foul an attacker with the ball. In so doing, the attacker will only be rewarded with a free pass, and will loose his opportunity to shoot at the goal.

Helping the ball- A player receiving the pass from a teammate can "help" his teammate to complete the pass by swimming towards him. Swimming will create a better target for the passer, rather than sitting and waiting for the ball to arrive.

Hole man- The offensive player, with his back to the goal, who takes a position directly in front of the goal. Usually the hole man is the centerpiece of the offense. Also known as the "center forward", the "center", the "hole-forward" or the "2-meter" player.

Hole guard- The defensive player who guards the other team's hole-man. Also known as the "2-meter defender", the "hole guard" or the "hole defender".

Kick-out- When a player commits a major foul, he is "kicked out" of the game and must go into a penalty area just outside the corner of the pool, behind his own goal, for a period of 20-seconds; or until a goal is scored or his team gains possession of the ball. In International play a "kick-out" is called an "exclusion".

Knock down- When a defensive player swims directly at an offensive player who is about to shoot or pass the ball, in essence forcing him backwards or "knocking" him down. Knocking-down does not imply physical contact; but it is the physical presence of the defensive player moving at the offensive player that forces him to fall backwards as if he were knocked down.

Ladder back- When a defensive player leaves the player he is guarding and falls back to guard another player, his teammate falls back or "ladders-back" to cover the area that was vacated by the first defensive player. Both players fall back in a series of sequential steps, as in "ladder-steps".

Man to man- A pressure or pressing defense in which a player guards an offensive player closely, usually making physical contact. Often called a man-to- man press.

Man-up- When the counterattacking team has a man advantage over the other team, they are a "man-up". This can be anything from a 2 on 1 to a 6 on 5 one-man advantage. "Man-up" is different from the "extra-man" 6 on 5 offense, which is created by a player being kicked-out.

Match hands- A player in a zone defense will hold try to block a shot by "matching hands" with the player shooting the ball. If the offensive player is shooting with his right hand, the defender will hold up his left hand, directly opposite the shooting hand. For a left-handed shooter, the defender will hold up his right hand.

Mismatch- A mismatch is created when a player of superior size and ability is being guarded by a smaller defender. This situation often occurs at the 2-meter position.

Passing-lane- The open lane that is created between a player passing the ball, and his teammate who is receiving the ball. For a pass to be successful, the path of the ball must follow along the passing lane. A defensive player can intercept the pass by stepping into the lane.

Perimeter- Any player who is situated in the half-circle formation of five players located in front of and around the center-forward, is playing on the "perimeter" of the front court offense. Players can shoot, drive or pass the ball into the center forward from the perimeter. These players are known as drivers or attackers.

Pocket- When playing the 6 on 5 extra-man offense, the two wing players can play near the 2-meter line, or move out into the "pocket" areas on the 4-meter line.

Posting up- When an attacker or non-2-meter player takes his defender to an area in front of one of the goalposts, instead of his normal area on the perimeter, it is called "posting-up".

Press- A style of defense where players create pressure by guarding all offensive players closely, in a man-to-man press.

Press without foul- A pressing style defense where the defender guarding the player with the ball tries not to foul him. Not fouling allows the clock to continue running, and doesn't give up an easy free pass to the player with the ball.

Set the goalie- A player with the ball and facing the goal must get the goalie to "lock" on him before passing to a teammate on the other side of the pool. He "sets" the goalie by looking at him, and then making the goalie think that he will shoot by bringing his arm forward and faking the shot.

Shoot off the pass- A player who receives a dry pass from a teammate, and immediately shoots the ball, is shooting directly "off the pass", rather than hesitating or faking before he shoots.

Shot clock- After taking possession of the ball, a team must take a shot on goal within a specified time period (30 seconds); or loose possession of the ball to the other team.

Slough- A player who drops off (sloughs-off) of the player he is guarding, and places himself in a position in front of another player; effectively keeping the ball from being passed to him. A slough is different from a crash in that it occurs before the ball is passed, rather than after it is passed. A slough denies the ball to a player, while a crash steals the ball from a player already in possession of the ball.

Turnover- Any manuever that causes the ball to change hands from the offensive to the defensive team is a "turnover". A turnover can be caused by a bad pass, an offensive foul, ball under, a steal, or even a shot on goal that does not go in the goal.

Transition- A team going from offense to defense, or defense to offense, is in "transition" from one to the other.

Wet pass- Any pass where the ball lands on the water is a "wet" pass.

Zone defense- A defense where players guard an area in front of the offensive player, rather than pressing him closely as in a man-to-man defense.

CHAPTER 1
INTRODUCTION TO THE GAME OF WATER POLO

Water polo has often been described as "soccer in the water" or "ice hockey in the water", because of the similarities of the three different games. Water polo does closely resemble soccer and ice hockey, and also basketball in some tactics and strategy; but basketball does not have a goalie or a large netted goal situated on the field of play. All four sports move the ball by passing or dribbling, players play both offense and defense, and all four have a counterattack or fast break. Other similarities with soccer are that fouls in the field of play are rewarded with a free kick (soccer) or free pass (water polo) for the offended player. As in soccer, a foul in front of the goal that may have prevented a chance to score is rewarded with a penalty kick (soccer) or penalty shot (water polo) directly at the goal.

Another similarity with ice hockey is that certain kinds of over aggressive fouls result in the offending player having to leave the field of play for a period of time, and the team having to play a player "short" during that period. This is called a "power play" in hockey and the "extra-man" in water polo. The closest similarity of water polo with basketball is that both sports position their biggest player near the goal (basket), with his back to the goal. The other players try to feed the ball to the "center" (basketball) or "hole-man" (water polo) so that he can try to score, draw a foul, or pass to the other players. Perimeter players (drivers-water polo, guards-forwards-basketball) can either drive toward the goal (basket) or shoot from the outside.

Both basketball and water polo also have "man to man" and "zone" styles of defense. Both sports also have shot clocks that limit the amount of time a team can keep the ball on offense without shooting the ball. The biggest differences between water polo and the other sports is that it is played in the water, and not on land. This results in a little slower paced game than land sports; but on the other hand a game that requires great stamina and physical exertion to play. Water polo players have to be in tremendous physical condition to swim up and down the pool at a fast pace, while dragging another player along with them. The biggest difference in water polo is that players can foul underwater; making it difficult for the referee to see the actual foul. This makes water polo unique from all land sports. It also makes it the most difficult sport in the world to referee.

HOW WATER POLO GOT ITS NAME
There are several versions to the story of how the game came to be called water polo. The "water" part is obvious. During aquatic festivals in the late 1800's in England and other Commonwealth countries, a rugby style game with a submersible ball was played in a harbor to entertain spectators. Since the ball was made of rubber from the East Indies, the Indian name for ball, "pulu", was probably translated into English as "polo".

The game really had no connection with horse polo; except there may have been a game played at around the same time in which players paddled around on barrels floating in the water; with wooden hobbyhorse's heads attached to the barrels. Today, most non-English speaking countries in the world call the game "water-ball" instead of water "polo". "Pallanuoto" in Italian and "Vasserball" in German are examples of water polo described as "water-ball".

Early versions of the game had no rules and it was very rough indeed. Players where allowed to take the ball underwater, and keep it there as long as they could hold their breath. The opposing players could just about do anything they wanted to try and dislodge the ball from the grip of the player with the ball. Along the way rules changed; or where added to speed up the game and bring it up above the surface of the water. The Europeans were instrumental in changing the game, probably basing the rules on the game of soccer. The ball was moved down the field of play by passing or swimming, and a goal was scored by placing the ball in a net at the end of the playing course.

The United States, however stubbornly stuck to the "wrestling in the water" style of play, probably because it was very physical and exciting to watch. In the late 1800's, this style of "water ball" was played between Athletic Clubs in New York, Boston, Saint Louis and other Eastern cities. Water polo and soccer were both introduced as the first team sports in the Olympic games. At the 1904 Olympic games in Saint Louis, the United States insisted on playing the wrestling style of water polo. As a result, the Europeans boycotted the games and club teams from the USA "won" the unofficial gold, silver and bronze medals.

COLLEGIATE WATER POLO
Water polo in the United States and England has long been affiliated with colleges and Universities. The University of Pennsylvania began a program as early as 1897, while Cambridge and Oxford started the oldest collegiate rivalry in the sport in 1891. Men's water polo was revived on the West Coast in the late 1920's and early 30's; as newer colleges and universities were the beneficiaries of more modern pools that created the opportunity to play a more mobile swimming style of play. As part of the resurrection, the American universities devised a set of rules that were similar to basketball, in that personal fouls were recorded. A player was only allowed five fouls before he fouled out of the game. Again, this was in direct conflict with the European game, which did not record personal fouls.

The Olympic games adopted the rules of the European "club" system of water polo, forcing players from the United States to change their style of play whenever they went to the Olympics. It wasn't until the early 70's that the USA finally adopted European/International (FINA) rules that everyone else in the world played. The result was an Olympic Bronze medal in 1972, and Silver medals in 1984, 1988 and 2008 for the USA. The United States has still to win the coveted Olympic Gold medal.

An official NCAA Collegiate championship for men was initiated in 1969, with UCLA declared as the first Championship team. California, with its Mediterranean climate and abundance of pools, has been the "hot bed" of collegiate water polo in this country. Seven California colleges have won all thirty-nine men's championships between them. The University of California, Berkeley and Stanford University have won the most National titles with twelve and ten respectively. There are approximately 50 colleges and universities that sponsor men's varsity water polo in this country, while 80 to 100 sponsor "club" level water polo.

Women's water polo was officially added as an NCAA sport in 2001, with UCLA again claiming the first national championship and winning six of the eight titles contested through 2008. With a stimulus from Title 9, women's water polo has surpassed the men's programs; with about 80 colleges sponsoring the sport at the varsity level. The Sydney 2000 Olympic games were the first contested in women's water polo. Australia was declared the gold medal winner, beating the United States in the gold medal game. The USA is the only country to medal in all three of the Women's Olympic games held.

Outside of the academic school year, there are hundreds of clubs that play water polo at all age levels, under the auspices of USA Water Polo Inc, the official governing body of the sport in our country. All of our club and International competitions, including the Olympic games, are supported and directed by USA Water Polo. At the 2008 Olympic games in Beijing, China, the United States became the first country in the history of the sport to place both its men's and women's teams in the medal round of competition. Both teams finished with silver medals.

HOW THE GAME IS PLAYED

Water polo is played with seven players on a side, six field players and one goalkeeper. The object of the game is to move the ball down the pool and into position in front of the goal as quickly as possible. If another player is guarding a player with the ball, he will try and pass the ball down the pool to one of his teammates. If he is not being guarded, he will usually swim the ball down the pool. If he is holding the ball in his hand, he may be tackled/impeded by the defensive player. If he is tackled/impeded when in possession of the ball, but the ball is not in his hand, the referee blows the whistle to indicate a foul and a resulting "free" pass is awarded to the offended player. He may pass the ball anywhere in the pool; or he may immediately shoot at the goal if he is fouled in a position that is outside 5-meters from the goal. He may only pass the ball if he is fouled in a position that is inside 5-meters from the goal. He may not shoot the ball from that position inside the 5-meter line.

The team on offense will put their biggest and strongest player in front of the goal, with his back to the goal. All the other players form a half circle around the "center-forward" or "hole-man". Their job is to shoot the ball from their positions in the half-circle, or pass the ball into the hole-man. Because of the hole-man's position directly in front of the goal, and because of his size and strength, he has an excellent opportunity to score a goal from this position. If the defensive player guarding the hole-man tries to foul him to prevent him from scoring, that player may be excluded from the game for 20 seconds; and his team must play a "man-short" during that time period. The six against five (6 on 5 extra-man) offense that is used when a team has a man advantage has become an essential part of scoring in water polo and an important part of the game. An exclusion foul may also be called for various other offenses that will be discussed in the referee/rules chapter.

THE MOST PHYSICALLY DEMANDING GAME IN THE WORLD

In 1991, water polo was ranked by a panel of physiology experts from all over the United States, as the "best overall sport" in terms of physiological demands placed on the athlete. A lot of exertion is required to swim at all-out bursts of speed for distances of 5-25 meters at a time, and then immediately turn around and swim in the other direction. Extra effort is required because the player's head must always be held in a position out of the water, even while swimming, in order to be able to see the ball and positions of other players. Opposing players are constantly trying to sink or hold the player that is swimming, and at the same time he must control a ball that is in his possession.

In the course of the hour-long game, players will probably swim a total of 1200 to 1500 meters, the equivalent of a metric mile in the water. In between these fast-paced swims, players constantly have to stop and propel themselves high out of the water, using their legs for support and without using the bottom of the all-deep pool. At times during the game, especially during the extra-man situation, players have to hold themselves in this high-vertical position for periods of 20-30 seconds, with a hand out of the water and with only their legs for support. Players are constantly going from horizontal to vertical positions in the water and then back to horizontal again. In addition, there is a certain amount of holding and maneuvering between players that require them to be in top condition to play the game.

WHY PLAY THE GAME?

Water polo is a physically demanding and mentally challenging sport; but at the same time it is a lot of fun to play. A young athlete can get into great physical condition by playing the sport; and at the same time enjoy the benefits of playing a team game that involves a ball, scoring goals and the challenge of preventing an opponent from scoring. Water polo is a game that captures a number of different facets of some of the more popular sports in world culture. It combines the dual skills of swimming and ball handling, the physicality and power play opportunities of hockey, the fast break opportunities and passing of basketball, and the penetration and goalie play of soccer. Playing in the water has the added advantage of "softening" the physical contact between players. As a result injuries are rare and less debilitating than almost all other land-based sports.

In addition, there are the added benefits and life lessons that the young athlete can learn from playing a team sport, and from the interactions with teammates and coaches. Examples of lessons that can be learned and applied to life outside the pool include working hard to achieve a common goal, working together as a team, unselfish play, helping teammates, playing your best, communicating with others, overcoming adversity, respect for others, winning and losing with dignity, good sportsmanship and discipline.

PLAYING IN COLLEGE

The opportunity to play water polo at the college level is available to the high school player who wants to continue in the sport at a higher level. Athletic scholarships are available for water polo, but there are only a limited number available to men. Although 50 Universities offer men's varsity water polo, only about 15-20 of these schools offer scholarships; and they are limited to 4 1/2 full scholarships per team. There are more scholarships available for women at the college level. Not only are there more women's teams at the college varsity level (80), but more schools offer athletic scholarships; and more are available for each team (eight per team) as opposed to the men's limit of four and one-half per team.

In order to play for a varsity team at the college level a player must be one of the top players on their high school teams. In order to qualify for a scholarship, a player must be one of the best in the country at the high school level. Many colleges across the country offer club water polo for players who do not wish to play at the top level; but simply play for the enjoyment of the sport. For more information about applying for college and playing at the college level see Chapter 4, "Playing Water Polo in College".

WATER POLO IS AN OLYMPIC SPORT

Water polo offers the opportunity for athletes to achieve the highest level of play in the world, the Olympic games. Along with soccer, water polo is the oldest team sport in the Olympic games. Only a very few athletes achieve the goal of playing in the Olympics; but the opportunity is there for those that have the talent and aspirations to achieve that goal. International competition is available at most age levels in this country. The path to the USA Olympic Team starts at the Cadet (14 years old), Youth (16 years old), and Junior (18 years old) National programs that are sponsored by USA Water Polo, Inc. Tryouts are available at zone (area) competitions held around the United States. Interested athletes should contact www.usawaterpolo.org for more information.

CLUB AND PROFESSIONAL WATER POLO

Club competition is available in this country; but is usually affiliated with high schools and colleges. There are a few college sponsored summer teams that do allow older players outside of college. Two of the non-college affiliated private clubs that still compete in the USA are the famous New York Athlete Club and the San Francisco Olympic Club. Unfortunately, and until recently, there have been very few places to play water polo in the United States after an athlete's college playing days were over. Master's water polo has now become a great way to keep playing after the age of twenty-five. Competition for male and female players is sponsored by US Water Polo for all age groups and is rapidly gaining popularity across the country. World Master's Championships, sponsored by FINA, are held every two years for players 25-80 years old.

Even though the United States does not offer professional water polo, most European countries do offer this opportunity. Some of our top players, both men and women, travel abroad after they graduate from college, and try to hook up with one of the many clubs that play water polo in Europe, Australia and New Zealand. It is a great way to see another part of the world, and continue playing water polo at the same time.

CHAPTER 2
UNDERSTANDING THE RULES AND HOW REFEREES CALL THE GAME

The way the rules of water polo are called by referees can be confusing at times. But, don't blame the referees! They are just applying the rules the way that they are written and interpreted by FINA, the international governing body of all aquatic sports. More specifically the rules of water polo come directly from the Technical Water Polo Committee (TWPC), a subcommittee of FINA that governs the sport around the world. Every country in the world must follow FINA rules if they want to belong to the water polo community of nations.

Some countries will modify the rules during school or age group competition, but when they play in International tournaments, they must play by FINA rules. The United States at one time had a completely different set of rules for colleges and high schools during the Fall school season: and then would play FINA rules during the summer club season. This was confusing to players on our National Teams who had to adjust to playing under different sets of rules. At the present time, the school rules in the USA are almost identical to FINA rules, except for a few minor exceptions like number of time-outs per game, etc.

WHY ARE THE RULES CONFUSING?
Part of the reason why the rules can be confusing is because of the way that the game is played: and the fact that the game is played in the water where many of the fouls are hidden from the referee's view. The rules of water polo are unique; but generally follow the rules of soccer, probably the land game that is closest to water polo in the way that it is played. For years soccer and water polo were the only two court sports (the other two being basketball and hockey) in which the penalty for a foul in the field of play was the awarding of a free pass (kick) to the offended player. The only exception was in the scoring area in front of the goal. A foul in that area, that would have taken away a good opportunity to score a goal, was awarded with a penalty shot (kick) directly at the goal.

EXCLUSION FOULS
There is a difference however in the two sports, namely the exclusion foul for certain infractions. In this respect water polo is more similar to ice hockey, than to soccer. Certain rule infractions that took away a "good" opportunity to score a goal resulted in the offending player being excluded from the game for a period of time, while his team had to play without him, or a player "short". An example of this rule in water polo is when a player is swimming down the pool by himself, without any defenders in front of him. If a defender following behind, pulls him back by the leg; he is excluded from the game because he has taken away the players "good" opportunity to score. The resulting "power play" in ice hockey and the "extra-man" in water polo has become a very important part of the game for both sports. A high percentage of the goals scored during a game are when the teams have an extra man during the power play.

RULES UNIQUE TO WATER POLO

There are exceptions to the rules that are unique only to water polo. Because the result of a normal foul was only a free pass awarded to the offended player, many defensive teams would foul a player that was trying to shoot the ball. This effectively took away his "shot on goal", because he was required to take a free pass rather than shoot the ball. In recent years, the TWPC decided to try and stop this tactic and create more shots on goal, with a rule that allows the player to shoot directly at the goal after he is fouled, as long as he is 5-meters or further from the goal.

The jury is still out on the effectiveness of this rule, because teams are still allowed to foul inside 5-meters to prevent a shot on goal. A shot outside 5-meters is still not a high percentage shot compared to a shot inside 5-meters. In addition, the defender is allowed to hold his arm up in front of the shooter, and block the shot, making it even a lower percentage shot.

PROTECTING THE PLAYER AT 2-METERS

Where water polo really parts ways with the other sports is the way that fouls are called in the prime position in water polo, the "hole" or "2-meter" position in front of the goal. Fouls are called in a certain way when they occur in the prime scoring area directly in front of the goal; compared to the same foul that occurs somewhere else in the pool being called in a different way. The center forward or hole man in water polo that occupies the 2-meter position, has always been given certain protection in regard to fouls called against him. This is mainly because of his position in front of and close to the goal, and his opportunity to score a goal from that position.

It is an interpretation of the rules that the player at 2-meters has a better chance to score from that position than from anywhere else in the pool. Taking away his opportunity to score will result in a more severe penalty, than will fouling a player who is further away from the goal. This can be confusing to spectators, because a foul in the middle of the pool results in only a free pass, while the same foul at 2-meters results in an exclusion from the game of the offending player. All of these "cornerstone" rules of water polo will be explained further on in the chapter.

WHY ARE THERE SO MANY WHISTLES?

People who see the game of water polo for the first time always ask this question. It can best be answered by looking at what happens after the whistle blows. Water polo, along with soccer, is the only team sport in the world in which a whistle initiates action, rather than stops the action. When a whistle blows in most other sports, a foul of some kind has just occurred; and the action of the game completely stops while the penalty is being assessed.

In water polo and soccer, in all penalty situations but a penalty shot or penalty kick, a free pass is awarded to the player who has been fouled. At the same time, players away from the ball are free to move around and jockey for position. The result of the foul is to help the ball advance down the pool or field, and at the same time keep the game flowing and moving forward. A whistle may interrupt the game itself; but the actual play is not interrupted. Notice when watching a soccer or water polo game, that there is constant movement in the game; while games such as basketball and football are constantly stopped for assessment of penalties.

Whistles are used more in water polo than other sports because of the nature of the game, and the fact that it is played in the water rather than on land. In soccer and basketball, a player with the ball can easily maneuver around a defender who is guarding him. A soccer player may also pass the ball while he is moving, keeping the flow of the game moving forward towards the goal. In water polo it is very difficult for a player with the ball to maneuver around a defender in the water, and it is also more difficult to pass the ball under pressure from the defender. As a result of defensive pressure, the ball gets stopped on its way down the pool, much more in water polo than in other sports like soccer and basketball.

HELPING THE BALL DOWN THE POOL
Because water polo also has a 30-second "must-shoot" clock, it is imperative that the ball gets down the pool quickly so that a team has time to score a goal. The player with the ball tries to "draw a foul" so that he can make an easier "free" pass down the pool. In many cases the referee is only too happy to oblige by blowing the whistle and awarding a free pass; all in the interests of "helping" the ball move down the pool. Because of the necessity of getting the ball into the frontcourt, many times referees will respond to any kind of defensive pressure with a whistle. Remember though, that players cannot be holding the ball if they wish to be awarded a foul and "free" pass.

If the defender wants to avoid committing a foul, he must show both hands to the referee when the offensive player lets go of the ball. This is where the confusing part comes in. In the interest of helping the ball down the pool, some referee's will call a foul even if the defender has both hands up. Everyone watching the game has puzzled looks on their face and ask, "why is the referee calling a foul when it doesn't look like the defender is committing a foul"? Still confused? So am I, and I've been involved in this game for 50 years. (See picture 2-A on next page)

Picture 2-A: This is not a foul; but it sometimes is called a foul by the referee in the interest of "helping the ball" to get down the pool.

DIFFERENCES WITH SOCCER

The biggest difference in the games has to do with the "shot" clock in water polo. A water polo team must shoot the ball within 30 seconds, or lose possession of the ball. Because of the shot clock, the ball must get into the scoring area in front of the goal as quick as possible. Hence, you see the use of the whistle to help advance the ball. Without a shot clock in soccer, the ball gets stuck at mid-field; mainly because there is no urgency to get the ball into the scoring-area. The result is a lower scoring game than water polo. It is difficult to score a lot of goals when the ball is at mid-field for 50% of the game.

Soccer also has an offside rule, which doesn't allow the ball to be passed to a player who gets ahead of his defender down the field. There would be much more scoring and counterattacking if there wasn't an offside rule in soccer. Water polo also has off sides; but it is only 2-meters from the front of the goal, and it only prevents an offensive player without the ball from camping right in front of the goal to wait for the ball to be passed to him. Consequently, water polo has more scoring on the counterattack than in soccer. A player can beat his defender down the pool and receive the ball without being called for off sides.

DIFFERENCES WITH BASKETBALL

The question is often asked, "They have a shot clock in basketball; but why don't you hear a lot of whistles helping the ball get down the court." One reason is because it is not necessary to help the ball down the court. It is much easier and faster to get the ball down the court on dry land than it is in the water. Another reason is because basketball defenders are reluctant to foul a player who is not shooting the ball, because it is recorded as a "personal" foul against the defender; one of five personals allowed before he fouls out of the game. It is much easierto have the foul called in water polo because it doesn't count against a player, and the penalty is only a minor one, a free pass.

Water polo in the United States high school and collegiate levels used to have "personal" fouls; but because of the lack of a shot clock, and the reluctance of players to commit fouls, the ball was stuck at mid-court a lot of the time. For many reasons, mainly because the rest of the water polo world did not have personal fouls, they were discontinued in the 70's.

PLAYING IN THE WATER CHANGES THE GAME

The combination of a 30-second shot clock and playing in the water has a lot to do with the way the game is played and officiated. It all has to do with getting the ball down the pool. In water polo, it takes 10 to 12 seconds to swim the ball down the pool and into the scoring area. This is about 1/3 to 1/2 of your possession time just to get the ball into scoring position. Compare this to a land sport like basketball, which takes about 5 seconds, or 1/10 of possession time to get the ball down the court. Consequently, water polo teams prefer to pass the ball rather than try to swim the ball down the pool; mainly because it takes less time.

Once again, this brings up the need for free passes being awarded by the referee. It is much easier to pass the ball with a free pass. In addition, drawing the foul and subsequent free pass also stops the clock. Every time the whistle blows, the clock is stopped until the player makes the pass. This also gives the offensive team more time to get the ball down the pool; but results in more whistles being blown.

FOULS OCCUR UNDERWATER (AT LEAST THE ONES THAT THE REFEREE CANNOT SEE)

Water polo is the only sport in the world in which the referee cannot see the foul, because it usually happens under water. Since most of the player's body is under the surface of the water, this is where most of the grabbing and holding takes place. The referee may not see the actual foul that occurs under water; but he sees the "result" of the foul. Push down on a player's shoulder and the result is that he will sink under water. Pull back on a player's leg and the result is that he will fall backwards.

Unfortunately, it is easy for a player to "fake" as if he is being fouled. If a player fakes the foul, and the defenders hand is underwater, then the referee has to call the foul. The only way for the defender to avoid being called for a foul is to show the referee both of his hands. Sometimes that doesn't even work. (See picture 2-A above). As long as referees award fouls for "fakes", players will continue faking to draw a foul and free pass.

ISN"T THAT CHEATING?

People who don't know about the game will usually claim that holding underwater is cheating; and that those players shouldn't be coached to play that way. Actually, it is part of the tactics and maneuvering between players that is an "accepted" part of the game. Coaches like to describe this part of the game as proper "technique". If players refuse to play in this way, they will usually find themselves at a disadvantage when playing against players who do play that way.

As a consequence, everybody does it, and a coach has to coach this type of play; or his team will be at a disadvantage. The player with the best "technique" will usually win the one on one battle. There is even more holding under-water in the women's game because of more suit material and straps to grab on to.

DRAWING A FOUL

Do you ever wonder why players act as if they are being mortally wounded whenever they are being fouled? If that is your son or daughter being fouled, relax! It's not as bad as it looks. Remember the referee does not see the actual foul, only the result of the foul. If I am swimming in a forward direction and someone grabs my leg and pulls me backwards, that is the result of the foul.

It is amazing how players can "act" as if they are being pulled back, even when they are actually not. This type of thing occurs all of the time. Most players over-dramatize when they are being fouled, as if they were being nominated for an Academy Award performance. Sometimes they will do so even when they are not being held, mainly because the referee cannot tell the difference.

So the next time you see a players head snap back as an opposing player swims away from them, remember that the player has probably not been kicked in the head. Someone is just trying to draw the referee's attention to a foul, whether it was a foul or not! Now do you see what I mean about water polo being the most difficult sport to officiate? How would you like to be a referee and have to determine if a player is "acting" or not?

WHY COMMITT A FOUL?

Fouling in water polo is unique to the sport, and another reason why you hear a lot of whistles being blown. Water polo players foul a lot because there is no personal penalty for fouling. For years players could not shoot at the goal after they were fouled; only pass the ball. Penalties for fouling are only assessed for "over-aggressive" fouling, which occurs rarely in the game.

Players commit fouls for two reasons. First, under the old rules, players fouled to prevent a goal. Since the penalty for fouling was only a free pass for the offended player, "fouling to prevent a goal" became a common tactic; especially in the scoring area within 7-8 meters from the goal. The second reason for fouling was to enable the defender to foul, and then drop back and "double team" the center forward (hole man) after committing the foul. Since most teams rely on getting the ball into their hole man; this effectively stopped the other teams offense.

As a coach, I would rather see my players press, and hold both hands up so that the referee will not call the foul and stop the clock. However, holding both hands up to avoid the foul takes a lot more work, especially with the legs. Consequently the players get a little lazy and take the easy way out and just foul the player. I don't like this kind of water polo because it creates more annoying whistles by the referee calling the foul. It also allows the opposing team to gain more time to score a goal.

If the clock is constantly stopped every time the whistle blows, it effectively gives the offense more time and more scoring opportunities in front of the goal. It is up to the coach to teach his players how "not to foul" when playing a pressing defense.

NEW RULE: SHOT AFTER FOUL OUTSIDE 5-METERS

Rule-makers thought that they could increase scoring and make the game more exciting by eliminating the "foul to prevent a goal" tactic; and also help the ball get into the hole-man by eliminating the "foul and drop" tactic. They did this by changing the rules to allow the person who was fouled to shoot the ball after the foul; thinking that defenders would be reluctant to foul if the player was allowed to shoot. At first the rule stated that any person fouled outside of 7-meters from the goal could shoot the ball. Players were reluctant to shoot from this distance, because it was quite a ways from the goal. So the rule-makers changed the distance to 5-meters.

Surely the players would be taking a lot of shots from only 5-meters out! Think again! Because the defender could hold up an arm in front of the shooter after the foul, it makes the shooter think twice about shooting; for fear of having the shot blocked. While it has not helped to increase scoring, it has been effective in eliminating the "foul and drop" defense. Defenders could not drop back and cover the 2-meter player after they committed the foul, and at the same time still put their arm up to defend the shot. They would rather attempt to block the shot than drop back and double team the center forward.

Coaches countered this rule by dropping back into a zone defense, instead of being in a pressing defense; thus avoiding a potential foul by pressing too tight. Playing back in a zone completely eliminated the outside foul, and also effectively kept the ball from going into the hole man. As in other sports, it is a never-ending battle between coaches and rule-makers to try and outwit each other. In this case the coaches won; but water polo lost. Zone defenses take movement and counterattacks out of the game, making it more of a static and less exciting game. Back to the drawing boards!

HOW IS THE SHOT AFTER FOUL RULE EXECUTED?

First of all, the foul must occur outside of the 5-meter line that is located 5 meters from in front of the goal. The player who has been fouled has about 3-seconds to take the free pass, or he has the option of immediately take the shot on goal. Of course this depends on the definition of "immediately". The player who has been fouled is given a very small amount of time to pick up the ball, and at the same time glance at the goal. He may then shoot the ball "immediately", or pass the ball, or put the ball in play by dropping it out of his hand.

The game clock and the shot clock both stop when the whistle blows indicating a foul, and starts again when the ball leaves the players hand by either passing, shooting or dropping the ball. The defender is allowed to hold up one arm in front of the passer/shooter in order to block the pass or shot; but he must be about a shoulder width away from the passer before he can hold up his arm.

SOMETIMES IT'S A KICKOUT; SOMETIMES IT'S NOT?

Most fouls that occur in water polo do not result in a "kick-out" or "exclusion" against the offending player. These are the so-called "minor" fouls, or what some people like to call "common" or "ordinary" fouls. For a minor foul, a player commits an infraction, the referee calls a foul by blowing his whistle, and a free pass is awarded. That's it, end of story!

But, wait a minute! This time the referee excluded the offending player from the water. What gives? Apparently that player has just committed a "major" foul instead of a "minor" foul. How can you tell the difference? All fouls look alike. There are several ways to commit a major foul, and they all result in the offending player being excluded (kicked-out) from the water for 20 seconds. The difference between "minor" and "major" is described below.

WHAT KINDS OF MINOR FOULS ARE THERE?

Examples of minor fouls are taking the ball under water, touching the ball with two hands, delaying the game by not putting the ball in play right away (about 3-seconds) after being awarded a free pass, jumping off the bottom or the wall of the pool, pushing off another player to gain an advantage, an offensive player being inside the 2-meter line in front of the goal without the ball (off-sides), and impeding a player who is not holding the ball. A free pass is awarded to the player who is closest to the ball when the foul occurs. If the player who is fouled is not the closest player to the ball, then his teammate who is closest to the ball will take the free pass. Free pass means passing the ball without interference in his throwing motion.

WHAT EXACTLY IS A MAJOR FOUL?

Most major fouls are for holding, sinking or pulling back a player NOT in possession of the ball. (For possession to occur, the ball has to physically be in the palm of the hand). The most common major foul occurs when the defender fouls the center forward from the other team, right in front of the goal. Another major foul, but less common occurs when a player has been beaten by his opponent and is following him down the pool. If he pulls him back or impedes his forward progress, he will be excluded. Other examples of major fouls include interfering (not allowing) a player to take the free pass or shot that he has been awarded, blocking the ball with two hands up at the same time, and leaving or coming back into the pool incorrectly after being excluded. (See Picture 2- B on next page)

Picture 2-B: This is a major foul when committed on the hole man in front of the goal. It is a minor foul anywhere else in the pool. Why? Because of the "advantage" rule. (See below)

WHAT HAPPENS TO THE PLAYER WHO IS KICKED OUT?
The player who is excluded has to leave the pool by the most direct route, without interfering with play and without climbing out of the pool; and go to a penalty area in the corner of the pool. He must stay there for a period of 20 seconds (including the time it takes to get there); or until the offensive team has scored a goal, his team gains possession of the ball, or the 20-second time period elapses.

When the 20-second period is over, the desk will wave a flag corresponding to his hat color, indicating that he can enter. If he comes back in too early or launches himself off the wall, he will be penalized by another kick-out. If a shot is taken before the 20 seconds has expired, the excluded player may come back in only if his team (defending team) gains possession of the ball or a goal is scored. Once a player has accumulated three major fouls during the course of the game, he may not play for the rest of the game. A red flag is waved by the desk indicating that a player has accumulated three fouls.

A 5-METER PENALTY SHOT IS ALSO A MAJOR FOUL
A free shot on the goal is awarded to a team if a defensive player commits any foul inside the 5-meter line that would have prohibited a goal from being scored. This includes the goalie pulling the goal down, a player jumping off the bottom to block a shot, or a player blocking the ball with two hands. These fouls count as one of three major fouls that will exclude a player from the rest of the game. The most common situation for issuing a penalty shot occurs when a player who is facing the goal, inside 5-meters, in possession of the ball and trying to score, is fouled from behind by a defender. (See Picture 2-C on next page).

Picture 2-C: This will be called a 5-meter penalty foul, when the player in possession of the ball lets go of the ball.

Anyone on the team can take the penalty shot. The player taking the shot will line up on the 5-meter line (a penalty shot is typically called a "5-meter" because the foul has to occur inside the 5-meter line, and the penalty is taken from the 5-meter line), with the ball, and facing the goal. The goalie must remain on the goal line, and cannot go in front of the goal until the whistle blows to initiate the shot. When the referee blows the whistle, the player must shoot directly at the goal without any interrupted motion or fake. It is OK to bring the ball back and then forward before taking the shot, as long as the motion is continuous and not interrupted. If the goalie blocks the shot back into the field of play, the ball will be live and anyone can play the rebound.

WHY IS A PENALTY SHOT AWARDED TO THE CENTER FORWARD WHO IS INSIDE THE 5-METER LINE, BUT NOT FACING THE GOAL?
The center-forward or any other player with the ball may start out facing away from the goal; but if he picks up the ball and turns toward the goal and goes past a 90 degree angle to the goal, then he is in position to receive the penalty shot call from the referee; even though he is not technically facing the goal. The player has to let go of the ball in order for the call to be made.

IT SEEMS THAT EVERY TIME THE BALL IS PASSED INTO THE CENTER FORWARD, THE DEFENDER IS EXCLUDED FROM THE GAME FOR 20-SECONDS.
The reason for excluding the defender who is guarding the center forward is because in the sport of water polo, the center forward is considered the player with the best opportunity to score a goal. This is because of his position directly in front of and the closest player to the goal. Teams will position their biggest and strongest player in that position. Their number one priority is to pass the ball to the center-forward, so he can try to score a goal or draw an exclusion foul. The reason the defender is "kicked-out" is because the referee has determined that he has been fouled in order to "prevent" him from scoring.

WHY CAN'T THE REFEREE JUST CALL AN ORDINARY FOUL ON THE CENTER DEFENDER; OR CALL NOTHING AT ALL?

This occurs because of the "advantage" rule in water polo, WP RULE 7.3 as stated below:
"The referee shall refrain from declaring a foul if, in their opinion, such declaration would be an advantage to the offending player's team (the defending team). The referees shall not declare an ordinary (minor) foul when there is still a possibility to play the ball."

This is a difficult rule for people who are not familiar with the game to understand. It is sometimes even difficult for coaches and referees to understand. Referees will take classes that cover the interpretation of this rule alone. However, it remains the "cornerstone" rule of water polo and is the reason why certain calls by the referee are made or not made. An explanation follows: If the referee only calls an ordinary foul against the center defender, he not only takes away the center forward's "chance to score" from directly in front of the goal, but he also will help out, or give the "advantage" to the team that committed the foul. How so?

If the team on defense knows that the referee will only call an ordinary foul whenever they foul the center forward, they can stop him from shooting simply by fouling. This takes them "off the hook" because they don't have to worry about the center forward trying to score, and the resulting penalty will only be a free pass by the center forward. If, however they are exclude from the game every time they foul the center-forward, they will have to except the consequences of playing with one player less for 20 seconds; and also have a major foul recorded against the center-defender. (See Picture 2-A above).

OPPORTUNITY TO SCORE

The second part of this rule has to do with the chance to play the ball. As long as the center forward has the "chance" or "opportunity" to score a goal, and he is trying to shoot the ball; the referee should not blow the whistle. He must allow the player the time to "play" the ball, or until the defender fouls him to prevent him from playing the ball. An "exclusion" should then be called against the defender.

There are certain situations where the referee many not exclude the defender, and may simply call an ordinary foul; or make no call at all. This occurs when the center forward has lost his "prime" position directly in front of the goal; or the ball that is passed into him is out of his reach. By loosing position or receiving a "bad" pass, the center forward has lost his "advantage" or "opportunity" to score a goal. He is no longer protected by the "advantage" rule. It is up to the referee to award an ordinary foul, or not blow the whistle, if there is no foul. The referee should not blow the whistle at all if the center forward has the ball in his hand and/or is attempting to shoot.

STEAL FROM ANOTHER DEFENDER

Another situation in which the referee might not blow his whistle when the ball lands on the water in front of the center-forward, is when it is stolen by a defensive player who is swimming in from another position. This is a legitimate steal, and the foul should not be called on the 2-meter guard unless he is holding the center forward, and preventing him from playing the ball. To show that he is not holding, the 2-meter guard must put both hands in the air as the steal is being made by a teammate. (See Picture 2-C and 2-D below)

Picture 2-C: This is an exclusion on the defender   Picture 2-D: This is not an exclusion

ANOTHER EXPLAINATION

An easier way to explain the advantage rule is as follows: Suppose two players are swimming down the pool and stop in front of the goal. One player has the ball in his hand and is about to shoot. His teammate, who is playing on the other side of the goal, is being sunk under water by a defensive player. The referee can refrain from calling a foul against the defender who is sinking the player on the other side of the goal.

Awarding a foul to the player without the ball would take away the "opportunity" of the player with the ball to take the shot; and would also give the advantage to the "offending" (defensive team). Instead of a possible goal being scored, an ordinary foul awarded to the player without the ball results in only a free pass, and not a shot by the player with the ball. This is definitely an advantage to the defensive or "offending" team.

WHY ISN'T THE PLAYER WHO HAS BEEN FOULED ALLOWED TO TAKE THE "FREE" PASS EVERY TIME?

This is because of a new rule that was put in several years ago in order to speed up the game. It states that if a foul occurs anywhere in the pool, and the foul occurs in a position that is AHEAD of the ball, then the free pass is taken by the player closest to the ball; even if he was not the player who was fouled. Under the old rules, if a player was fouled, but the ball was knocked away; then the ball had to be returned to player who was fouled so that he could take the free pass. Returning the ball to the fouled player often slowed down the game, and kept the ball from being quickly passed to an open player who might be in position to shoot. (See Diagram 2-1 on the next page).

Under the new rule, the player closest to the ball when the foul occurs, takes the free pass. It does not have to be returned to the "point of the foul". This avoids a lot of confusion and speeds up the game. Anyone close to the ball can take the free throw, as long as the ball is not ahead of the spot where the foul occurs. If the foul is on the 4-meter line, but the ball is knocked ahead to the 2-meter line, then it must be returned to the player at 4-meters. Confusing? Yes it can be! (See Diagram 2-2 on the next page).

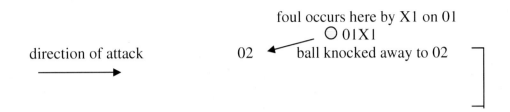

foul occurs here by X1 on 01

direction of attack

Diagram 2-1: Foul by X1, ball is knocked away, closest player to ball (02) takes free throw. Under the old rules, the ball would have to be returned to 01 for free throw.

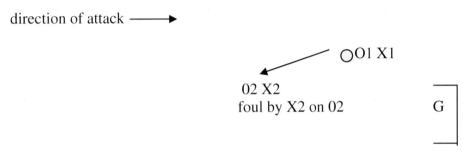

direction of attack

Diagram 2-2: Foul by X2 on 02 while ball is in possession of 01. Ball must go to 02 for free pass, because the ball was ahead of the foul when the foul occurred.

WHY IS THERE SO MUCH WRESTLING ALLOWED BETWEEN THE 2-METER OFFENSIVE AND DEFENSIVE PLAYERS BEFORE THE BALL ARRIVES?

This is another one of the confusing rules that usually occurs in front of the goal. Actually, this is because of the above stated rule in which the free pass is taken by the player closest to the ball. Imagine a situation that occurs all of the time as the ball is being passed down the pool. As the center forward (without the ball) tries to get position in front of the goal, the defender fouls him in an attempt to keep him getting into that position. The referee is reluctant to call a foul on the defender, because it does not advance the ball to the center forward, or award him a free pass. This is because the free pass is taken wherever the ball is located when the whistle blows. In this case the ball is on the perimeter and stays on the perimeter. (See Diagram 2-3 on next page).

The referee will not call a foul at 2-meters while the ball is not present. Why call a foul when that player (the 2-meter player) is not awarded a free pass? The referee cannot call an exclusion on the defender because the ball is not present, and the 2-meter player doesn't have an advantage or opportunity to score. So, nothing is called! The result is grabbing and holding by both players. (See Picture 2-E on the next page).

Picture 2-E: This is not called a foul at the 2-meter position because the ball is not present. Calling a foul does not advance the ball, nor give the 2-meter player (dark hat) a free pass.

The rule-makers are trying new interpretations of the rules in order to help clean up the "wrestling" at 2-meters. If one of the two players initiates the contact, and gains an advantage over the other by fouling, then the foul could be called against that player. This foul will be called as an offensive foul against the center-forward; or an exclusion foul against the defender. If both players are holding each other "equally", and neither one fouls to gain position over the other, then nothing is called by the referee.

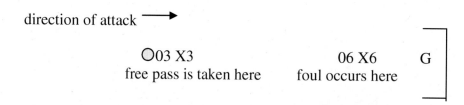

direction of attack ⟶

◯O3 X3   O6 X6   G
free pass is taken here   foul occurs here

Diagram 2-3: If a foul is called on X6 while the ball is in possession of O3, the ball would stay at O3. Consequently this foul is not called because it does not advance the ball to O6.

WHAT'S WITH ALL THE POINTING AND WAVING?
This is just the referee's way of telling the players what is going on. We used to have blue and white flags to indicate which team had possession of the ball. Now the referee just points with his hand. For instance, if he calls a normal foul, he will blow the whistle once and point in the direction that the team in possession of the ball is going. The free pass is then taken by the closest player to the ball. (See Diagram 2-1 above)

However, if the referee calls an offensive foul against the team with the ball, then the ball must turn over to the other team. So the referee simply points in the other (opposite) direction with one hand and usually points to the spot in the water that he wants the free pass to be taken from.

An offensive foul such as this may occur away from the ball; but because of the change in direction of the teams, the foul may now be behind the ball, so it has to be returned to the point of the foul before the free pass is taken. (See Diagram 2-4 below)

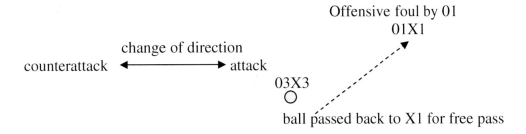

Diagram 2-4: Change of direction causes foul to be behind the ball
is passed back to X1, who takes the free pass

HAND SIGNALS
Sometimes you will also see the referee give a signal with his hands indicating the reason why he called the foul. For instance, for "ball under" he will put his palm down on an imaginary ball and push downwards with his hand. The referee will show a player grabbing another player by grabbing his wrist with his hand. He will make a kicking motion with his leg when indicating a "push-off" foul by a player. A good referee will always signal what he is calling so that everyone knows what the call is for.

A major foul that results in an exclusion from the game is usually called a little differently then a normal foul. The referee will blow the whistle several times, point his hand at the player who committed the foul, and then wave his hand in a sweeping motion indicating that the player should leave the pool. Some referee's will blow the whistle as they point their hand and then blow the whistle again as they "wave" the player out. A "double" whistle usually indicates an exclusion.

As the player starts leaving the water, the referee will turn towards the scoring table, and use his thumb and fingers to indicate the hat number of the excluded player. A clenched fist indicates the number ten. The number twelve is indicated by a clenched fist on the left hand (10), plus the thumb and first finger of the right hand (2). (10 + 2 = 12). A 5-meter penalty foul is indicated by blowing the whistle and extending the referee's arm in front of him; holding all five fingers of the extended hand straight up, similar to a traffic cop halting traffic.

DOES THE REFEREE FAVOR ONE TEAM OVER ANOTHER?
It may seem that way, especially to the parents and fans, especially when they see a big discrepancy in the number of fouls or the number of exclusions called against their team, versus the number called against the opposition. Believe me, the referee is not purposely calling more fouls on your team because he likes the other team better. It is just a matter of circumstance that one team may have many more fouls than another.

The most logical explanation is that one team is probably committing more fouls than the other team. It may seem that a similar situation is called differently at one end of the pool than the other end; but usually there are subtle differences that might not warrant a call. Usually the referee has the best view of a situation; even a better view than the fans, coaches and players. What may look like a foul to a fan sitting in the stands, may not be a foul to the referee who is right on top of the situation.

BALANCING THE FOULS BETWEEN TEAMS

As mentioned above, at the end of the game one team may have many more "exclusion" (major) fouls than the other team. There are many fans, and even some coaches, who will look at this and claim that the discrepancy in numbers means that the referee favors one team over the other. As far as I know, there is nothing in the rulebook that says there must be an equal number of major fouls awarded to each team. Balancing the number of fouls is NOT one of the referee's duties.

There are many reasons why there can be a discrepancy in fouls between teams. One team may just play a more physical style than the other. Taking the exclusion and playing a man-down, rather than allowing a goal, is a common and legitimate tactic of some teams, especially in Europe. One team may have a dominant center forward, and the only way to keep him from scoring is to commit a major foul. One team may be pressing, while the other team may be playing a zone defense that results in less fouls. One team may have a great counterattack that may force defenders who are caught behind to reach out and grab, resulting in an exclusion.

YOU SEE WHAT YOU WANT TO SEE

There is an old axiom about watching the game and criticizing the call. Remember that when you favor one team over the other, the call by the referee will look completely different to you; the opposite of what it may look like to someone who favors the other team. "You see what you want to see"; or to put it another way, you see what favors your team. Remember this before you criticize the referee's call. The referee is making the call from a completely neutral point of view. His job is to apply the rules fairly and without prejudice. It doesn't matter whether the call affects your team or the other team, as long as it is fairly called and according to the rules. You may not like the call; but that is the way things are in the world of sport, especially sports that require judgment calls by an official.

CHAPTER 3
WHAT IT TAKES TO BECOME A GOOD WATER POLO PLAYER

BASIC SKILLS NEEDED TO PLAY THE GAME

SWIMMING SKILLS

It is essential in a sport that is played in the water that a participant knows how to swim well. The same holds true with running and a land sport. The biggest difference is that running is a skill that occurs naturally for human beings, while humans need to learn how to swim. Freestyle, or the crawl stroke, is the stroke used most often in water polo. A player must learn to swim freestyle well and learn to swim it fast. There are differences between the freestyle that is used in water polo and the freestyle used in competitive swimming. The head and eyes must be held out of the water during the entire game. This is in order for the player to see where his teammates and opponents are positioned, where the ball is, to hear the whistle and see which way the referee is pointing, and to be able to communicate with his teammates.

Other differences with swimming are that the stroke is shorter and the turnover is quicker. The hand enters the water slightly to the outside of the shoulders and is not extended in front of the body as far. Water polo players are more like sprint swimmers than long distance swimmers, in that they utilize more of the body's anaerobic (without oxygen) system to produce energy for muscle contraction. Conditioning for water polo is unique, and is covered in Chapter 5, "Getting in shape to play water polo"

DON'T FORGET TO KICK

Holding the head out of the water causes the lower part of the body (hips and legs) to sink, creating extra drag and slowing the water polo player down. The player needs to have a strong and rapid "flutter kick" to keep the body in a level position in the water and to help him swim at high speeds down the pool. Kicking takes extra energy to perform; but players have to remember that water polo requires bursts of speed for short distances. A strong flutter kick is essential to successfully maintain these bursts. Kicking drills, separate from swimming, should be performed daily in practice.

One of the most difficult parts of swimming up and down the pool is getting a fast start, and then changing directions and starting all over again. Water polo players don't have the luxury of using a wall or bottom of the pool to help get them started. A modified scissor kick is needed in order to get that fast start and sudden burst of speed. In this kick, both knees are bent and the legs are drawn up slightly. One leg is bent forward and one back. They are then squeezed together and back at the same time to produce a surge forward from a "standing start". This is similar to the kick used in the sidestroke, except that the knees are not drawn up towards the waist as far. The scissor kick also helps initiate the momentum needed to help start and maintain the flutter kick and arm stroke necessary for the water polo power freestyle stroke.

DO I HAVE TO JOIN A SWIM TEAM IN ORDER TO PLAY WATER POLO?

In this country we usually learn to swim before we play water polo; but in Europe the exact opposite is true. Water polo players in many of the top European countries start learning how to play water polo at a very young age. They learn to swim as they need to, learning the strokes they need to play the sport. Head up freestyle is the first thing they learn, along with both the eggbeater and sidestroke kicks.

It is not necessary to learn all of the competitive swim strokes in order to be successful in water polo. On the other hand, it can't hurt to learn how to swim in a competitive situation. If swimming on a swim team at the age group and high school level can make you a better and faster swimmer, then by all means go for it. It is also a great way to stay in shape during the water polo off-season.

My advise to players, who want to play water polo in college, is that if they need to improve as a swimmer in order to play at the college level; then they should join a swim team, or go out for their high school team. The pool is longer at the college level, as well as the length of the quarters. Most of the players that you will compete against in college will have excellent end-to-end speed in getting down the pool. The bottom line being, if you need to become a faster swimmer to succeed in the game, then swim in high school.

Other strokes that are important and should be learned are backstroke, breaststroke and butterfly. Backstroke is often used in the game, especially on the counterattack in order to be able to see the ball easier. It is important that the player not lose speed when he turns onto his back. He must take shorter, quicker strokes and keep his head and shoulders high out of the water. The breaststroke is not used much as a stroke in itself, but the "frog kick" is used at times when shooting the ball. Learning the breaststroke kick is important in order to be able to execute the eggbeater kick. The sculling motion of the breaststroke arms is also used by goalkeepers, shooters and vertical defenders as an aid to get up high in the water. The butterfly stroke is not used in water polo games; but it is a stroke that is used in practice as a conditioner for water polo. Sprint butterfly is a great way to train a water polo player to develop power and speed in his freestyle head-up swimming.

THE EGGBEATER IS THE KEY TO BECOMING A SUCCESSFUL WATER POLO PLAYER.

The eggbeater is used in every facet of the game, especially when the player's body is in a vertical position in the water. The eggbeater kick is very unique in that everyone does not have the leg structure to do the kick well. If you have a good breaststroke kick, you will usually have a good eggbeater kick. Essentially, the eggbeater is an alternating breaststroke kick. Genetics are certainly an important factor in a successful eggbeater, just as they are in swimming the breaststroke.

If you look at the 200-meter Individual Medley swimming event, there are swimmers who are strongest in the breaststroke; and then there are swimmers who are strongest in the other three strokes. Free, back and fly all utilize an up and down kicking action, as opposed to the out and back "frog kick" action of the breaststroke. However, I.M. swimmers can be trained to become better breaststroke swimmers, just as the legs can be trained so that any player can have an eggbeater kick that is adequate to compete in water polo. In general, the higher that a player goes in the sport, the more important the eggbeater kick becomes. You will not see a weak eggbeater among the players who represent their countries at the Olympic games.

GOING FROM HORIZONTAL TO VERTICAL AND FROM VERTICAL TO HORIZONTAL.

The game of water polo is played in both vertical and horizontal positions. An essential skill on both defense and offense is to be able to switch from one position to the other, smoothly and quickly. On offense, a player swimming in a horizontal position has to stop quickly and get into a vertical position with his hand up high in order to catch the ball for a shot on goal. He stops by pushing against the water with his hands, and bringing his knees under his body. He then pushes down on the water with his hands and extends his body at the waist into a vertical position, doing a scissor kick to get up into position. To support himself he must continue kicking with an eggbeater kick, sculling with one hand, with his other hand in the air ready to receive the ball on offense, or block the ball on defense

While playing a zone defense, a player will be horizontal when guarding a player who might be receiving the ball on the post, and then go into a vertical position when blocking the shot of a perimeter player with the ball. This "hip-over" maneuver is very important in man-down 5 on 6 defense and will be described in Chapter 11, "Extra-man offense and defense".

EVERY PASS IS IMPORTANT

Turnovers that are created by an incorrectly thrown pass happen in every sport; and many times make the difference in winning or losing a close game. Learn to make a "safe" and correct pass every time you pass the ball. A "safe" pass is one that is thrown to your teammate, and only to your teammate. The ball has to land in a spot that only your teammate can gain possession of the ball, not your opponent. Passes that are thrown incorrectly are ones that can be intercepted by your opponent; and result in a turnover and loss of possession. Have "pride" in making the correct and safe pass every time.

Passes that land on the water (wet passes) are usually the correct passes to make in most offensive situations. Passes to a hand (dry passes) are usually made to a player who is not being guarded closely, and who can shoot the ball when he catches it. Dry passes are used exclusively when playing in a 6 on 5 extra-man situation, or against a zone defense.

ALWAYS KEEP YOUR HIPS UP

Anytime a player is in a horizontal position in the pool, his hips should be near the surface of the water. Having the hips near the surface allows a player to move and change directions with ease, whether playing on defense or offense. If two players, one with hips down and one with hips up, are playing shoulder to shoulder in the water, and a ball is thrown a short distance away from them; the player with hips up will beat the player with hips down to the ball every time. The only time a player would have his hips below the surface of the water is when he is shooting the ball or defending (blocking) a shot from a vertical position.

MOVEMENT ON OFFENSE

Learn to move without the ball when on offense. Movement by an offensive player(s) can create confusion and take a defensive player out of his comfort zone. This will help create more scoring opportunities for the offensive team. A player can free himself to receive the ball against a strong press by moving forward and then releasing for the ball. (See Diagram 7-1, Chapter 7 on "Game strategies and tactics"). Driving past a pressing defender can free the driver to receive a pass for a shot on goal.

DRIVE THRU

Against a zone, driving will take a defender out of his "zone" position and make him follow the driver. This can create a space in front of your 2-meter player and allow a pass to be made to him. It is difficult to gain offensive advantage when "driving thru"; but the driver should remain alert for the possible pass from a teammate, if the defender does not follow or pay attention to him.

What kind of player do you want to be?

Anyone can learn to play water polo; but what is it that separates the great player from the mediocre player? This section will describe the qualities of a good player and the kinds of things you have to do to become a good player. Players should always be motivated to improve themselves every chance they get. You cannot just do the minimum expected of you and expect to become a good player. You have to have the motivation to work out on your own every chance you get, and also to work as hard as you can in practice. You have to listen to your coaches and apply in games what you have learned in practice. A great player is constantly trying to improve and never stops learning. The day that you think that "you know it all", is the day that you become a mediocre player. In the end, it is up to you to decide how good of a player you can be.

PRACTICE HARD, PLAY HARD

There is a saying in sports that states, "You play the way that you practice". You can't take it easy in practices and then suddenly "turn it on" in a game. Learn to practice and play with intensity. Practicing hard will get you ready for any tough situation that you may encounter in a game. The same holds true for swimming. Swimming fast during the entire practice will get you ready to swim fast in the game. Hard swim training will prepare you to swim hard and fast for an entire game. It will also allow you beat your opponent by wearing him out. A creed to live by is that "you will be in better shape than your opponent, because you have worked harder than him; and that you will beat him in the 4th quarter when the game is on the line".

GET THE MOST OUT OF YOUR PHYSICAL TALENTS

Every player has physical abilities to start with. It is the players that do the most with their abilities that succeed in their sport. Learning to work hard, and spending the time to improve and develop your playing skills, will separate you from the rest of the players. This is especially true if players are willing to do extra work outside of the pool and apart from the required practice sessions. Simply doing the minimum that is necessary to play the game will not elevate you above others who play the game. To get the most out of your talents you have to go all out, both in practice and in games.

WORK ON YOUR GAME

The reason that some basketball players are more successful than others is that they carry a ball with them everywhere they go, and practice with the ball every chance they get. If you want to improve as a player, work on your game outside of the practice organized by the coach. This is a little harder to do with water polo, because you need to find some water to play in. Maybe you can use your neighbor's backyard pool or the local lake or beach area. If you can't find a pool, you can ask your coach to open up the practice pool for you and a friend; or you can practice catching and shooting the ball with one hand by throwing it against a wall or a wooden backboard. When practicing together with a teammate, one player is the shooter and the other plays the goalie position. Switching back and forth in the goal helps condition the field player's legs for the eggbeater kick.

Using a basketball to throw against a wall is even better, because it is larger than a water polo ball. If you can handle a basketball well with one hand, you can handle a water polo ball. Throwing a "little" heavier ball will also help strengthen you arm for shooting a lighter water polo ball. It is very much like swinging a heavy bat in baseball.

Be careful that you don't over-do the passing with a ball that is too heavy; or there is a good chance of injury to your shoulder. A 3-4 pound ball is the maximum weight for throwing with one arm. Heavier balls can be used if you use both hands at the same time to throw the ball. Your legs will also benefit from any kind of passing and shooting done in the water; especially two-handed passing with a ball weighing 6-12 pounds.

LEARN TO EXECUTE THE FUNDAMENTALS CORRECTLY

It is the job of the coach to teach the basic fundamentals of the game, and it is up to the players to learn to execute them properly. In water polo, every game situation calls for the execution of a fundamental part of the game. If players learn the proper way to handle these situations in practice, they will be able to execute them in the game, no matter what the opponent does tactically. (See Appendix C at the end of this chapter for basic fundamentals of the game).

Vince Lombardi, the great Hall of Fame football coach of the Green Bay Packers believed strongly in the correct execution of the basic fundamentals of the game. His philosophy was that you didn't need fancy plays to beat the other team. He believed that if you executed the basics of blocking and tackling better then the other team, that you would win the game. He worked on these skills over and over again in practice, until the players could execute them in their sleep.

The same holds true in water polo. Learn to execute the fundamentals in practice and learn to execute them the right way, and the same way every time. You and your teammates will have an excellent chance to win a game when you have learned the fundamentals correctly, and can repeat them in a game without having to think about what you are doing.

GAME CARRY-OVER

Game "carry-over" is the amount of what you learn in practice that you carry over into a game. The purpose of practice is to learn how to play the game correctly and prepare for your opponent. "Learn from your mistakes". Your coach will critique your play during practice as a way of improving your play. Listen to what he says and make the necessary adjustments in your play. If you are not sure what the coach expects of you, then be sure and ask questions so that you are clear of what he wants you to do.

Even more important, be sure that you execute in the game everything that you have learned in practice. If your coach has given you a "game plan" for your opponent, make sure that you and everyone on the team executes the planned strategy. All players have to be on the same page. If one player does not follow the plan, it can affect the outcome of the game in a negative way, resulting in a loss instead of a win.

TEAM PLAY

A lot of ingredients go into making a successful team. A team who has talented players will certainly have success; but even more important than talent is a group of players working together as a team. Many times a team with less talent, that plays together as a team, can beat a team with more talent. An excellent example of this happened at the 2008 Olympic games. There are a lot of talented water polo teams representing their countries in the Olympics; the USA team is one of them. But, over the past 10-15 years the US team has not been among the top six teams in the World. Teams like Spain, Italy, Serbia, Hungary, and Croatia have dominated the world water polo scene ahead of the US team.

Going into the 2008 Olympic games the USA was ranked only ninth in the world. At the Olympics, the USA team reversed this trend and beat many of the top teams, winning the silver medal in the process. What was it that caused this surge ahead of the best teams in the world? According to Terry Schroeder, USA Head Coach, the team played together as a true team, playing for each other instead of playing for themselves. If the best players in our country can sacrifice for the "good of the team", then any team can do it.

WHAT IS TEAM PLAY?

Team play is unselfish play. Unselfish play is a player passing up a chance to score a goal and passing the ball to a teammate who has a better chance to score the goal. Remember that the pass leading to a goal is just as important as the goal itself. True teammates don't care who scores the goal, as long as the goal gets scored. Team play on defense is coming back and covering for a teammate who is shooting the ball, and has been beaten on the counterattack. On defense, simply guarding "your man" is not enough. A defender should also be constantly looking around and being aware of helping out or switching with a teammate when the situation calls for it.

THINK DEFENSE WHEN YOU ARE ON OFFENSE

One of the hardest things for players to comprehend is to start thinking about helping a teammate defensively while their team is still on offense. Players always have to be anticipating that their team will eventually loose the ball, and they must be ready to go back on defense, sometimes even before the ball is turned over. Players must always be on the alert for these kinds of situations and be ready to help the player that has been burned; usually the man passing the ball or the man shooting the ball. Think ahead and anticipate the turnover before it happens. Be thinking about going back on defense while you still are on offense.

BE IN BETTER SHAPE THAN YOUR OPPONENT

There will be games when you come up against a team or player that has more experience and perhaps more physical talent then you. You can overcome these kinds of teams if you and your team are in better shape than your opponent. It takes a well-conditioned player to swim up and down the pool at full speed, over and over again. By working harder than the other team in swimming, drills and practice scrimmages, you will be in shape to take advantage of this situation. A well-conditioned team will win a close game in the 4th quarter, when your opponent is tired and worn out from all the swimming that you made them do throughout the game.

COUNTERATTACK AT EVERY OPPORTUNITY

One way to wear out your opponent and also create more scoring opportunities for your team, is to counterattack every time the ball changes hands. Countering at every single opportunity not only wears out your opponent; but also makes them more tentative to run their offense. They will be worried that you will counter them whenever they take the shot. You can get easy goals from the counter; but if you don't score, it can quickly move up our offense into position in the front-court.

Learn to react to every single turnover (shot, offensive foul, intercepted pass, etc) by immediately taking off towards the other end of the pool. Take advantage of the shot-clock and any situation where you know the other team has to shoot or turnover the ball. If you are in position where your man is not a threat to shoot the ball, and your opponent is running out of time, you can release early on the counterattack and create a one-on-nobody shot for yourself at the other end of the pool.

PLAY YOUR BEST

One of the philosophies of the great UCLA and Hall of Fame basketball coach John Wooden was that no matter what the outcome of the game, a player could feel good about his performance, if he felt that he played the absolute best that he could play. If his team won the game, but the player did not play well, then he needed to work harder and improve his performance for the next game. If his team lost, and he played well; then the player could at least feel that he did everything that he could do to help his team win.

Players need to understand that playing well includes all parts of the game, not just scoring. Players can contribute to a win even if they don't score a goal; if they can help their team win by performing all the other aspects of the game well. Things like making good passes, not creating turnovers, and playing good defense are parts of the game in which a player can contribute to the success of the team without scoring a goal.

MAKE THINGS HAPPEN

A player could overcome deficiencies in his play by playing aggressively. There are two kinds of athletes, those that "make things happen" and those that "let things happen to them". Coaches would rather have a player who is over-aggressive than one who is passive and doesn't do anything. The latter player is just "taking up water". The coach will encourage players to play aggressively; but it is entirely up to the player to do so.

As a player, you have to instill in yourself the desire and will to become an aggressive player. Passive players usually find themselves sitting on the bench. A player cannot be afraid to do something aggressively or be afraid of making a mistake. Everyone makes mistakes; but a mistake made while playing aggressively is much better than doing nothing at all.

AWARENESS OF WHAT IS GOING ON AROUND YOU

Some players always seem to know what is happening in a game situation, while others seem to be playing with horse "blinders" on their head, seeing only what is happening directly in front of them. If you get a chance, watch Steve Nash or Jason Kidd play NBA basketball. They always seem to know where their teammates are and where their opponents are; and are usually one step ahead of everyone in knowing where or when to pass the ball. You can be a player like this by constantly moving your head, and especially your eyes; always observing the situation around you. On offense you should do this even when in possession of the ball; always looking one step ahead and being aware of what you will do with the ball next. A player on defense should be able to guard his man, and the same time look around and be ready to help out in guarding another player, or helping a teammate.

PAY ATTENTION TO TRANSISTION!

The situation that requires the most attention by players is in the transition from offense to defense and from defense to offense. In both situations players need to be aware of the time on the shot clock, time left in the game, score of the game, where the ball is situated, and their relative positions in the pool. A player should always anticipate the situation when the ball is about to change hands, and be ready for what he will do when this situation occurs; depending on the score, time left on the clock and who is in possession of the ball. (See Chapter 7 "Game strategies" for more information).

COMMUNICATION

Verbal communication skills are an important ingredient in team play. Call out switches and defensive help. On offense call out where the ball should be passed or where your teammates should be positioned. Help direct your teammates to the correct defensive positions by both talking and pointing. There is a saying that exclaims "Don't be a sheep and just follow the rest of the flock. Take charge and be the leader of the sheep." This means that you should be a leader in the pool instead of just blindly following everyone else. It is especially important for the goalkeeper to take charge and direct the players in front of him, even when they are on offense.

TEAM UNITY

Team unity means that players can count on each other in every phase of the game. Everyone must understand what his role on the team is, and must do his part for the team to succeed. This also includes little things like putting in and taking out the goals, and putting pool covers on the pool. Everyone helps out in these situations. If you go to the shower room while your teammates are taking the goals out or putting in pool covers, how can they count on you to do your part in a game?

OVERCOMING ADVERSITY-DON'T FEEL SORRY FOR YOUR SELF

Everyone encounters adversity and players must discipline themselves to do the best that they can under the circumstances. Don't whine, don't complain, learn how to except criticism without making excuses. Don't sit back and pout when you miss a shot, while your teammates are covering up for you on defense. Forget the missed shot and get back on defense! Players need to be mentally tough and be able to handle pressure situations. Players need to overcome a bad situation by not feeling sorry for themselves; but by moving on and playing the rest of the game well.

OVERCOMING THE BAD CALL

Players need to understand that no matter how good a referee might be, he is only human, and may make a bad call once in a while. Players have to overcome the bad call by playing better, not by falling apart. I have seen teams lose games that they shouldn't have, because they could not handle a referee's bad calls. Players have to learn not to challenge a call by the referee. It is the coach's job to challenge a call by the referee, not the players. Learn how to handle calls that go against you in practice. A player who cannot handle a bad call in practice, certainly cannot handle one in a game.

RESPECT OTHERS

The way that you and members of your team interact with other people that you come in contact with, reflect on your school and your team. Remember that you represent your team, not only in the pool but outside of the pool as well. Treat people that you come into daily contact with respect, both at the pool and in your everyday life. This includes teachers, parents, coaches, teammates, opponents, referees, and everyone from the pool manager to the waiter at a restaurant. Young players should especially be polite and respectful to their elders and people of authority.

PLAY WITH DIGNITY

Learn how to be a gracious winner and win or lose with dignity. A player should not act any differently whether his team has won or lost a game. Hold your head up high after a loss and don't gloat after a win. Don't make excuses or blame someone else for losing a game, especially one of your own teammates. Never blame one player for a loss, even though he might have made a crucial mistake at the end of a game. The point is that "we are all in this together." We win as a team and we lose as a team. The team, together, puts themselves in a position to win or lose the game. No one individual can win or lose the game without help from his teammates.

GOOD SPORTSMANSHIP

Show good sportsmanship towards your opponents. Fear no opponent, but have respect for him. Players should not taunt other players, and not show excessive celebration after scoring a goal. If you score and want to put your fist or finger in the air, that is fine; but nothing beyond that. You have just scored; you don't need to call more attention to yourself by grandstanding or pointing at your opponent. That is just rubbing it in. Act like you have been there before. Your opponent will not forget your gestures. You will pay for it somewhere down the line. Instead of celebrating a goal, you should acknowledge and thank a teammate for the pass that he gave you, so that you could score the goal. Always shake hands with the opposing team after a game, win or lose.

DISCIPLINE

Discipline your self to play the game correctly. This means doing what you have to do, doing it as well as you can, and doing it the same way all of the time. It is not enough to talk about being disciplined; you need to implement it in the pool and in your daily life. Discipline on offense has to do with proper shot selection, knowing when to shoot or when not to shoot, and making the correct and safe pass every time you pass to a teammate.

Discipline on defense has to do with pressing your man every time, playing in the passing lanes, and taking away part of the goal with your arm while your goalie takes away the other part of the goal. Discipline away from the pool has to do with keeping yourself in shape year around, keeping up on your school studies, and not doing things in your personal life that will keep you from becoming as good a player as you can be, be it diet, sleep, drugs, alcohol, etc.

ARE YOU COACHABLE?

What does being "coachable" mean? Ask your self these questions. Do I accept criticism from the coach without making an excuse; and use the criticism as a way to better myself? Do I listen to my coaches and try to learn and understand the correct way to play the game? Do I accept my role on the team without complaint, and try to do everything that I can to help out the team? Am I always supportive of my teammates? Am I constantly trying to improve myself as a player; even on my own, and without prodding from the coach? Do I always play my best at all times? If you answered "yes" to the above questions, then you are definitely coachable and will be an asset to any team.

Contrast this to the type of "me first" behavior that you see from some of the athletes in professional sports in our country. Believe me, it is better to have a player with less talent and with a good attitude on the team, than a "star" player with a lousy attitude. The latter type of player hurts the team with his bad attitude, rather than helps the team with his talent.

WHAT ARE COACHES LOOKING FOR?

It varies from team to team and the level of play; but basically coaches are all looking for the same thing. They are looking for players who can contribute to the success of their team, help their team improve and move up to the next level. Certain coaches look for different physical characteristics like size and speed and good legs. They feel that if they get a big player who can swim fast and has good legs, they can teach this person how to play the game.

If I had to choose which physical characteristic was most important for my teams at the college level, I would have to choose speed first; because of our emphasis on the counterattack. I have had many smaller type players who have been very successful on my teams, because of their speed, quickness and determination. If you have good legs, good speed, a good attitude, are willing to learn, and you are a hard worker, you can be any size and still succeed in water polo.

Appendix C:

The Commandments of Water Polo

Important parts of playing the game of water polo that are essential to success as a player and as a team:

1. Learn the basic fundamentals of the game and learn to execute them properly.

2. Practice hard and play hard. Learn to practice and play the game with enthusiasm and intensity.

3. Speed and quickness are important physical aspects of the game. Learn how to swim fast in games by swimming fast in practice.

4. A strong eggbeater kick is necessary for success in playing water polo

4. Playing good defense is a key to winning water polo.

5. Take pride in making a good pass every time.

6. Counterattack at every opportunity.

7. Anticipation and reaction are important ingredients for a successful counterattack.

8. The pass leading to the shot is more important than the shot itself.

9. The success of the extra-man offense and man-down defense usually determines which team will win a close game.

10. Avoid turnovers while on offense and create turnovers with a pressure defense.

11. Knowing that you can count on your teammates, and that they can count on you, helps to promote team unity.

12. Team play is unselfish play. Passing up your chance to score to set up a teammate to score, and covering up for a teammate on defense are examples of this.

13. Learn how to overcome adversity and discipline yourself to do the best that you can under the circumstances.

14. Fear no opponent, but have respect for him.

15. Get the most out of your physical talent by playing your best every time you jump into the pool

CHAPTER 4

PLAYING WATER POLO IN COLLEGE

Choosing a college is one of the important decisions that a person will ever make. The education that you receive in college is very important to the success of your future career and life after college. There is more to college, however, than the education that you receive. Playing on an athletic team in college can also be a rewarding and fulfilling experience. There are obvious life lessons that you can learn from being on a team, and playing together with a group of people that are working together towards a common goal. The bonds that you form with the other members of the team will stay with you for the rest of your life. Many teammates will become lifetime friends.

If you want to play on a college water polo team, there are many options open to you. Not only will you have to choose the type of college that you want to attend for academic reasons; but also the kind of team that you want to play on. A college should have the right combination of academics, athletics, and social structure; and provide an atmosphere in which the student/athlete will feel comfortable and have the opportunity to achieve success. One of the main criteria for choosing a college is to determine how your own academic and athletic abilities fit into the college's academic and athletic programs. You have to ask yourself the question, "Does this college meet my needs, and how do I fit into both the academic and athletic programs?"

The purpose of this chapter is to help guide the college bound water polo and his parents in choosing the college that is the right fit for the athlete; and also to help them learn about the college recruiting process.

WHAT'S AVAILABLE FOR THE COLLEGE ATHLETE?
Before we start looking for a college, we have to know what colleges offer water polo programs and what kinds of programs are offered. There are basically two kinds of water polo programs offered at many colleges across the country. "Varsity" programs are under the jurisdiction of the National Collegiate Athletic Association (NCAA) and have a strict set of rules that must be followed.

There are rules regulating everything from how an athlete is to be recruited, to how many years an athlete can participate on a college team. Different rules regulate things like the number of games played for each sport, the length of the sport season, how many hours per week can be spent on practice and games, what an athletic scholarship consists of, and hundreds of other regulations that affect the college athlete. In order to play Varsity Water Polo, an athlete has to abide by the rules of the NCAA, and has to be certified by the school and by the NCAA as being eligible to participate.

Athletic scholarships can also be offered to student/athletes who participate in most sports, depending on which division of the NCAA they are part of. Divisions are classified as Division 1, 2 or 3. They usually are based on the size of the school student-body, whether the schools offer a football program, and whether scholarships can be offered. Larger schools that offer "big time" athletic programs in football and basketball and other sports are usually in Division I. Division 3 schools are usually much smaller and do not offer extensive athletic programs. They also do not offer scholarships at division 3 schools. Division 2 schools fall somewhere in-between, both in population and in athletic offerings. The NCAA also sponsors a National Championship for every varsity sport, and in every Division under its jurisdiction. Ironically, football is one of the only sports that does not have an official NCAA Championship.

Many colleges also offer "Club" water polo teams. There are no eligibility requirements to be on a club team and any student can play. But, at the same time there are also no scholarships offered nor is there a NCAA Championship for club sports. In fact, club sports do not have to follow NCAA rules and regulations; because they are not under the jurisdiction of the NCAA. They are usually sponsored to varying degrees by a college athletic department; but are not fully funded and usually have volunteer or partially paid coaches. Travel, uniforms and other necessities, usually are paid for by the students on the team. Some club sports do offer their own "collegiate" national championships. These are usually funded by the participants in that particular sport.

WHAT IS AVAILABLE FOR WATER POLO?
Varsity water polo is offered at about 45 colleges for men, and at about 80 colleges for women. A complete list of varsity programs can be found on the USA Water Polo and Water Polo Planet web sites, www.usawaterpolo.org and www.waterpoloplanet.com. Even though there are men and women's water polo teams in all three NCAA divisions, only one national championship is offered for each sport. The men's teams are organized into three leagues, with each league champion and one at-large team invited to the four-team national championship. Six different league champions, plus two at-large teams with the best records, give the women a total of eight teams in their national championship. Many Division I schools offer some sort of water polo scholarship, although there is a limit of 4 1/2 full scholarships for each men's team. Because of the Federal Government mandated Title 9 for equality for women, 8 full scholarships can be offered for each women's team.

Water polo is also organized as a club sport at many other colleges and universities. At the time of this book printing, a national collegiate club championship is available for men's club teams; but not yet available for women's club teams.

STARTING THE PROCESS
You should start the process of identifying schools that you are interested in sometime during your sophomore year, junior year at the latest. Some of the factors that you should consider in the college that you are looking for are:

1. Type of school- large, small, private, public, military.
2. Location of the school- urban, rural, east, west, distance from home.
3. Academics-Liberal Arts, Humanities, Science, Engineering, special programs, all-around or general campus. Does it fit your needs?
4. Athletics-Do they have a water polo program, division I, II or III, varsity or club?

5. How do you fit into the water polo program? What are your chances of playing?
6. New or established program? Experienced coach? Past successes of team? Rebuilding?
7. Cost of attending college? Financial aid availability? Athletic scholarships?
8. How do you like the atmosphere of the school? Do you fit in socially?

ASSIGN PRIORITIES

Assign priorities in your identification process. Which of the above factors is most important to you? If you are not sure what you are looking for, identity a variety of different kinds of schools in different locations; but narrow your choice down to a workable number of about six to ten schools. Later on you might want to narrow it down even further to about four or five schools that you will apply to. Filling out applications for more than that is unnecessary, and very time consuming. It is better to do a good job on fewer applications than do a poor job on too many applications. Starting in your freshman year, work hard to achieve the highest grades and test scores that you can, and at the same time become the best water polo player that you can. The better your grades are, and the more water polo ability you have, the more choices you will have.

INTRODUCE YOURSELF

It is up to you to start the recruiting process by sending a letter or e-mail to the coaches of the schools that you are interested in. You should do this during the winter of your junior year, right after your fall semester grades are in. By that time, you will have completed three high school seasons if your sport is played during the fall semester. By then you should also have accumulated enough information about yourself; so that both you and the coaches will have a good idea of where you stand academically and in water polo.

DON'T SIT AT HOME AND WAIT FOR COLLEGE COACHES TO CONTACT YOU

Coaches may not know who you are; or you may have slipped through the cracks. It is up to you to make yourself known to the schools that you are interested in. Don't let your ego keep you from contacting a school you are interested in, just because the coach may not know you. It is up to you to sell yourself to a college, not the other way around.

NCAA RULES

Remember that there are NCAA rules that coaches have to follow in regards to recruiting and in their communications with you. Officially, coaches cannot initiate contact either by letter, e-mail or phone, to a high school prospect, until September 1st at the start of his/her junior year in high school. If you contact the coach prior to that time, he can send you back a generic letter, and also ask you to fill out a questionnaire that you can send back to him. A college coach also cannot call you on the telephone, or have personal off-campus contact with you, until July 1st after you have completed your junior year of high school.

So, if you run into a coach at a summer tournament in your sophomore or junior year, he may greet you; but he is not allowed to talk to you. He is not trying to snub you. He is just not allowed to have personal contact with you other than a short cordial greeting. You and your family, however, can visit any college at any time, and speak to the coach while on campus. You might want to give the coach a courtesy letter or phone call indicating when you will be on campus to visit. That is allowed by the rules as long as you initiate the call or letter.

After July 1st following completion of your junior year in high school, there is a limit to the number of times a coach can see you off campus; and he can only call you on the telephone once per week. There is no limit to the number of times he can correspond by mail or e-mail after July 1st.

ARE YOU BEING RECRUITED?

Once a coach gets past the questionnaire stage with a high school athlete, and starts corresponding and calling; that athlete is considered a "recruited athlete" by NCAA rules. An athlete is subject to different NCAA "recruiting rules" after he has been classified as a "recruited athlete". You may contact the NCAA by e-mail or letter, and request a copy of their recruiting rules pamphlet. The coach should be aware of the rules, and keep you informed; but sometimes mistakes are made that can lead to a loss of eligibility to play at a particular school. Be informed and avoid potential violations that you may not be aware you are committing.

LETTER TO THE COACH

Include in a letter to a college coach some information about yourself:

1. GENERAL INFORMATION- Include name, address, phone, e-mail address, year in school, high school, coach's name, GPA for academic courses, SAT scores, swim times, etc.

2. HIGH SCHOOL GRADES AND SAT SCORES- Some schools accept weighted GPA's and some do not. Weighted means that Honors and AP classes are weighted higher than the grade received. For instance, a "B" grade received in an Honors course is recorded as an B+ on your transcript. Honors classes look great on your transcript, but don't take so many that your grades suffer. You should plan on taking SAT tests several times during your junior and senior years. Some schools require only the three standard SAT I tests, critical reading, writing, and mathematics; while others require both the standard tests and three SAT II advanced placement tests. Get a tutor if you test low in standardized tests. It is well worth the investment. The earlier you take the SAT test the better for you. You should improve each time that you take the test, and only the highest scores will be considered by the college. Some schools also accept ACT test scores. Find out if they are accepted before you take the test.

3. WATER POLO STATISTICS, HONORS AND AWARDS, AND SWIM TIMES- It is strongly recommended that you go out for your high school swim team in order to improve your swimming ability, and also to give the college coach some swim times to look at. It is also a good idea to try out for US Water Polo Cadet, Youth, and Junior National teams. This is great way for coaches to see where you stand in relation to other players from around the country; an important consideration, especially in awarding scholarships.

4. LETTERS OF RECOMMENDATION FROM INFLUENTIAL PEOPLE-These are not absolutely necessary unless the person writing the letter knows you well. More important is a letter from your high school coach about your playing ability, and your attitude (hard worker, loves the game, team player, etc.). Even more important is to include your high school coach's phone number, so that the college coach can call your coach and talk to him directly. A letter from your parents saying what a great person and water polo player you are is also not necessary.

5. IT IS BEST FOR THE COACH TO SEE YOU PLAY- Send a copy of your game schedule so that the coach can come and see you play. Remember that when high school and college seasons are at the same time, a college coach might not be able to attend your games. Attending college water polo camps is a good way to be seen and evaluated by coaches. Plus, you can learn something about the coach, the school, the water polo program and the system that they play, all at the same time.

6. VIDEO/CD- If the coach can't see you play in person, then send a video or CD of one of your games. Make sure the quality is good, and not something put together by a parent standing on the deck with a wobbly camera. A voice-over and hat number that can identify you in the water is also helpful. Water polo is not an easy sport to video; and many times it is difficult to identify the players. Send a video that shows your water polo skills; not just scoring a lot of goals in a blowout game against a weak opponent.

TWO THINGS THAT YOU SHOULD NEVER DO!
1. Never send a generic letter or form letter! Take the time to learn the coach's name and include that along with the school's name and something specific about that school; and why you are interested in that program.

2. Do not immediately ask about athletic scholarships in your first letter to the coach! The time to discuss financial aid is during your campus visit, or during a phone contact; well into the recruiting process. Wait for the coach to bring up the topic of financial aid. If that doesn't happen, then you can inquire about the criteria and the availability of scholarships.

THE CAMPUS VISIT
For boys, the best time to visit college campuses is during spring semester of your junior year, or in January or February following your last water polo season of your senior year. For girls, the best time is prior to November of your senior year, or the spring of your junior year. You may visit as often as you like at your own expense. Let the coach know when you would like to visit, and arrange to meet him on campus. He will probably arrange for someone to show you around; so it is a good idea to visit when classes are in session and the students are on campus. You might also want to see the coach and team in action by attending a practice or game.

The coach may be preoccupied with coaching his own team and might not be able to spend a lot of time with you. If you just want to see a game, then go on your own. Let the coach know that you will be there, and are interested in the program and the school. He might invite you to meet him after the game, especially if his team has won the game. Be careful about approaching a coach immediate after his team has lost a game. On the other hand, this might give you some perspective and insight into how the coach and players handle a tough loss.

WHO PAYS FOR A CAMPUS VISIT?
Recruited athletes are allowed to make expense paid visits, paid for by the school; but a recruited athlete is limited to visits to only five different schools. If you are lucky enough to be invited for a paid visit, the coach will make all the arrangements. It is up to you to make sure that you don't exceed the limit of five visits. Hopefully, by this time you will have narrowed your choice down to five schools. A paid campus visit cannot exceed 48 hours on campus and should be monitored by the coach.

Because of limited finances in water polo, however, not all colleges can pay for your visit to their campus. You may not receive a paid visit to a school that you want to visit. If you don't, pay your own way and visit the schools that you are most interested in. You may visit at your own expense as often as you like, anytime that you want to, and for as long a period as you want. When planning a visit to a school during your own competitive season, be sure and coordinate the visit with your high school coach. He may not want you to visit a college if it takes time away from practice for an important game.

ASK QUESTIONS?

During your visit is the time to find out whether the school and the water polo program is the right fit for you. Attend classes, attend practice sessions, visit or stay in a dormitory, and find out what campus life is like. Don't be afraid to ask questions of the players and the coach about water polo and academic topics. When and how long are team practice sessions, how do you fit into the team, how many players are playing your position, what are your chances of playing right away, what about red-shirting, what is the coach's "style" of coaching?

You may bring your parents on your campus visit; but I would recommend visiting on your own at least one time. It is you that the coach is interested in; and he wants to talk and get to know you, without a lot of parental interference. If you do bring your parents, make sure that they do not dominate the conversation with the coach. There will be plenty of time for the coach to talk to your parents, especially if he decides to visit your home.

HOME VISITS

If you are a "recruited" athlete, the college coach may want to visit your home and meet your parents, family and your high school coach. If he does visit your home, there are certain restrictions about what you can or cannot do during the visit. The coach will know the rules and let you know what to expect. Let the coach initiate the topic of the home visit. Some colleges do not have the budget to pay for the coach's home visits; so don't expect this to happen very often, unless you are a highly recruited athlete to a college that has the finances to pay for the coach's trip.

GETTING ACCEPTED – WHAT IS REQUIRED?

Every university has different criteria for being accepted. The same holds true for student/ athletes. Almost all college coaches can submit names to their admission office for consideration. Where the difference lies is in the criteria that a school will accept for an athlete to be accepted. At some colleges it is very easy to be accepted if you are on the coach's list; even if you don't meet the academic requirements for admission. Other schools are much more difficult to be accepted to; and at some schools you have to meet the same stringent academic requirements as a normal student. The best way to find out what your chances are for admission is to ask the coach. He cannot submit the name of every recruit. In some cases the number he can submit to admissions is very limited.

Some schools have a certain number of slots available to each sport. Those are usually reserved for the top athletes that are being recruited. Most colleges look at several key factors like GPA, SAT scores, and athletic ability. Other schools will also look at your GPA in core courses only, strength of your high school curriculum, status of you high school, number of honors and AP classes taken, outside activities besides athletics, and family history at that particular college. These are things that you should find out early in your high school career, so that can make adjustments in the classes that you are taking if you have to.

EARLY DECISION

Early decision at most colleges is reserved for outstanding students who want to find out early in their senior year if they have been admitted. Some universities have dropped the practice, but there are still many that still have early-decision. This usually requires a commitment on your part that you will attend that school if you are admitted. In most cases, if you are also an outstanding athlete, the coach would rather have you on his athletic track, then on the school's early decision track. You will get the decision at about the same time, and it is usually easier to get in through the athletic track. Talk to the coach about this before you decide to apply for early decision at a particular school.

WHAT ARE COLLGE COACHES LOOKING FOR?

All college coaches are looking for talented players that can help their program. Some coaches recruit for size and speed, some recruit for need at a certain position, some look at the player's intensity and aggressiveness, passion for the game, attitude, coachability, knowledge of the game, and the ability to make things happen. College coaches are looking for players that can contribute to the success of their team. Most coaches look for all of these criteria; with some having more weight than others. Making the All-American or All-League team is important, but is usually not the deciding factor in whether the coach wants you on his team or not. Coaches have to also consider the level of play in your league, and also in your state, when looking at these kinds of honors. All-American honors do not tell the coach what kind of attitude you have, or whether you can pay defense or not.

IT'S A DIFFERENT GAME

Remember that the game is a lot different at the college level. For one thing, the water polo course for men is longer, 30 meters versus 25 yards. For women it is 25 meters. This means that swimming ability and speed become more important. The game is played at a faster pace at the college level than it is in high school. The players that you will compete against for a position on the team were possibly all high school all-stars. If you are looking to receive a scholarship or simply to make the team, know that coaches are looking to recruit "difference makers." Players who can help the team compete at the national level; versus players who are good, but won't help the team get to the next level.

BE REALISTIC

Be realistic about your abilities as a water polo player. Aim for the programs that suit your abilities and for a college that you will feel comfortable with. Success at the high school level does not guarantee success at the college level. There are no guarantees of playing time. You will have to earn your position on the team along with everyone else. There is nothing worse then playing for a college team that is far above your abilities and talents; and then dropping off the team after you don't make the cut. Find a program that fits your talents, and where you can enjoy four years of playing on the water polo team.

FINANCIAL AID

There are many different ways to obtain financial aid to help pay for your college education. Full ride athletic scholarships consist of tuition, room and board, books, and fees. Division I and II colleges can offer a maximum of 4.5 full scholarships for men's water polo, and 8 full scholarships for women's water polo. Division III schools are not allowed to offer athletic scholarships. PLEASE NOTE THAT THERE ARE NOT THAT MANY SCHOLARSHIPS AVAILABLE IN WATER POLO, especially on the men's side. There are probably less than ten colleges in the country that offer the maximum number of scholarships for men.

More schools, as many as twenty-five or more on the women's side offer some scholarships. Most collegiate teams have to offer more for women because of Title 9 requirements, and the need to balance scholarships between men and women. If 50% of a school's student body is composed of women, then 50% of the athletic scholarships offered must go to women. A university that offers 85 scholarships to football must offer the same number to women's programs. Because of football and the need to balance out the high number of football scholarships, many schools offer more women's teams than men's teams.

CLUB WATER POLO

If you don't feel that you have the ability to play NCAA sponsored varsity water polo, then maybe club level water polo is for you. Playing on a club team can be a great way to continue playing water polo while attending college, without all of the pressure and restrictions of being on a varsity-team.

COMMUNITY COLLEGES

In California, two-year Community (Junior) Colleges offer Varsity water polo programs and are a great alternative to four-year colleges. Junior colleges are far less expensive than four-year colleges, they give you a chance to build up your grades, they give you an opportunity to improve your game, you will receive an AA degree, and all of your courses will transfer to any four-year college in the country. Two years of JC water polo will use up two years of your four years of eligibility at a four- year college; leaving you with two years of eligibility remaining. A student may transfer to a four-year college after one year at a JC; but two years is usually recommended.

EQUIVALENCY SPORT

Water polo is an equivalency sport; which means that the sport can offer the equivalent value of 4.5 full scholarships for men and 8 full scholarships for women at any one time. A full scholarship consists of tuition, room and board, books and fees. A full "ride" for one person in water polo is very rare. Most schools will offer partial scholarships of less than full value. In that way, more players on the team can receive some financial aid. These partial scholarships range in value from books, to room and board, to partial or full tuition. The total value of all the scholarships on the team added together, however, cannot be more than the value of 4.5 full scholarships for men and 8 full scholarships for women.

Some schools may have committed most of their scholarships to returning players, and only have a small amount of scholarship money available for incoming freshmen. In that case, the coach may start a player out with a small scholarship in his freshman year; and then increase that amount each year, as more money becomes available when players on scholarship graduate. To obtain a scholarship to a Division I school, you must be one of the top players in the country, and be able to contribute significantly to the team's success.

Contrary to popular opinion, athletic scholarships cannot be promised for four years. They are automatically renewed each year, unless you break rules that cause you to lose the scholarship. They cannot be taken away for lack of ability, or if you are injured and cannot play. Division I Ivy League schools do not offer athletic scholarships in any sport; but do offer academic and need based financial aid that is available to all students. On the other hand, every student at a military school has their education completely paid for, whether they are athletes or not.

RED-SHIRTING

All collegiate athletes have only four years of eligibility; but have five years in order to complete those four years. The process starts once you enroll in college. An athlete may red-shirt, or sit out one year during his college career. He may practice with the team; but cannot play in games during his red-shirt year. By red-shirting one year, he may come back and play in his fifth year. He may also receive financial aid during that fifth year, but at the coach's discretion. If the coach does not want to give financial aid for that 5th year, the athlete has the option of playing without the scholarship, or not play at all.

Red shirting is usually done in the freshman year, so that a player can gain one year of experience and develop physically, without losing any eligibility. If he is not going to play very much in his first year, he might as well red-shirt, rather than sit on the bench and not play. Some schools will red-shirt upperclassmen, so that other less experienced players on the team can catch up to them; thus producing a team full of experienced players, and a better chance for the team to win.

If an athlete has enough units to graduate after four years, he may elect not to graduate and play for the first semester of his 5th year; or he may elect to graduate and play during the first year of graduate school at the same college. Again, an athletic scholarship is not guaranteed for the fifth year on the team. Playing and receiving scholarship money for a fifth year has to be negotiated between coach and player.

MEDICAL RED-SHIRT

Once you play one minute of one game in any year, then that year counts as one of your four allotted years of eligibility. That is, however, unless you happen to get hurt early in the season and cannot play again for the rest of the year. If you have only played in 20 percent of the games in the first part of the season before you get hurt, then you may petition the NCAA to receive an additional year to play. This is called a "medical" red-shirt and is in addition to a one-year "athletic" red shirt.

If you are hurt after you have played more than 20% of the games during one season, then you will lose that year of eligibility. Extra eligibility or red-shirt years can also be granted for military service or religious missions. If a player receives both a "medical" red-shirt year and an "athletic" red-shirt year, it may take him six years of college to complete his four years of water polo. Players with eligibility remaining may also play as graduate students.

OTHER SCHOLARSHIPS

There are many other ways to obtain financial aid besides athletic scholarships. These other scholarships are available to all students at that college and are usually based on academics. They cannot be based on athletic performance if you are part of a varsity athletic team. If athletics are any part of the criteria for awarding the scholarship, it must count toward the team's equivalent number of scholarships.

Some schools offer academic scholarships to outstanding students in order to attract top scholars to the school. In some cases these are worth more than an athletic scholarship that may be offered in water polo. If you are a truly outstanding scholar, you should consider applying for an academic scholarship. An Academic scholarship, or any scholarship that is not based on athletic performance, can be used by an athlete and will not count against the equivalency for his sport.

NEED BASED SCHOLARSHIPS

Many schools, especially the private schools and Ivy League schools, offer financial aid to all students on a need basis. If you are accepted to a school, the amount of aid that you receive is determined by a formula based on your family income and other factors. Because of the high cost of private colleges, many families can qualify for aid in this way. Some states offer State Scholarships to residents of that particular state. Again a formula is used to figure out the amount that you may receive based on both academics and need. Federally financed student loans are also available from financial institutions that are guaranteed by the U.S. government. The advantage of these loans is that the interest rates are low, and you do not have to start paying back the loan until you graduate from college.

LOCAL AND NATIONAL SCHOLARSHIPS

There are also scholarships available for graduating high schools seniors from the community that you live in, or from various national organizations. National Merit scholarships are awarded nationally to students that do well in the National Merit Exam. Check with your high school counselor about National, state and community scholarships. Community scholarships have to be based on other criteria besides athletics, or they will be counted against a school's equivalency amount.

WORK-STUDY

University financial aid awarded to students based on "need", usually consists of a package of 60-80% cash, 15-20% student loan, and about 5-10% work-study. Work-study allows students to get a job on campus, for which the University will pay a salary; up to a certain limit that is specified as part of the financial aid package.

COMBINING SCHOLARSHIPS

Remember, that if any part of a scholarship is based on athletic ability, it will count against the team equivalency at a Division I or II school. Also know that you cannot combine athletic and non-athletic scholarships from the university that you are attending, without the total amount of both scholarships counting against the team equivalency limits of 4.5 for men and 8 full scholarships for women. You can receive one or the other; but not both kinds of scholarships at the same time, without both of them counting. Academic scholarships, by themselves, do not count against the team's equivalency limit.

LETTER OF INTENT

A Letter of Intent is offered ONLY to incoming freshmen that will receive an athletic scholarship. So, unless you are receiving an athletic scholarship, don't except a Letter of Intent. Once you sign a letter that has been offered, you are committed to attend that school for one year. If you decide, after signing the letter, that you want to change schools, you may do so. However, the penalty is harsh. You may not receive athletic aid, and also have to sit out and not play for your first year at the new school. Another alternative is for the original school that you signed with to release you from your obligation; thus freeing you to play and receive aid right away at another school. Once you have signed a Letter of Intent, however, it is very rare that a school will release you from that letter.

SIGNING DATES-DECISION TIME

There are specific signing dates for Letters of Intent; an early signing period in February of a students senior year for men, and November for women, and then again in April for both sports. The early signing period in November for women makes it even more important to have all of your paperwork done before the start of your senior year. You have a two-week period after the letter is issued to decide which school you want to sign with. If you cannot make your decision in two weeks, then another letter may be issued. Sometimes the decision is difficult to make; but if you have done your homework on the various schools, you should be able to decide within the two-week period.

Try not to string schools along for a long period of time. Athletic scholarships are limited and someone else will be waiting for that scholarship if you turn it down. On the other hand, don't let coaches pressure you into signing a letter of intent immediately, especially if you are not sure about your decision. Remember you have two weeks to sign. After that, if you don't sign, the school at their discretion can withdraw the Letter of Intent, or issue you another one.

VALUE OF YOUR EDUCATION

There are a lot of factors to consider in making the decision on which college to attend. Academically, you are going to get a good education at most colleges in the United States. Some colleges are better in some areas than in others; but you are going to get a quality education no matter where you go. Some schools have more prestige than others. But, when it comes to getting a job when you graduate, how you interview and how you did in school are more important than which school you attended. If you want to attend medical, law, business or graduate school, how you do in the standardized graduate tests for those particular professions are important in deciding whether you get in or not. Personal interviews and grades are also important factors. Attending a college as an undergraduate does not necessarily give you an advantage in getting in to a graduate school at the same college. Sometimes it even has the opposite effect. Many graduate schools are looking for diversity of applicants from other colleges around the country, not just from their own university.

MAKING THE DECISION

When you are making a decision, try to take water polo and the coach out of the equation if you can. If water polo doesn't pan out for you, or if you are injured and cannot play again, pick a school that you will be comfortable with; one in which you will enjoy the other aspects of college life. The same holds true for picking the school for the coach. What if he decides to take a job at another college after you arrive there? You can always transfer to another school if it doesn't work out for you; but transferring can be messy and difficult. Do your homework and know what you are getting into. Choose a school that fits your needs and is a comfortable fit for you.

If water polo is one of your main criteria for selecting a college, pick a school that is best suited for your talent and ability; and where you will get a fair chance to play and contribute. Be honest about your capabilities. Not everyone is suited for Division I level water polo. Sometimes it is very difficult for your parents to do; but try taking money out of the equation. There are a lot of ways to finance your education. Once you have exhausted all of the financial-aid possibilities, and you still cannot afford a particular school; then look elsewhere, perhaps a local school or community college that will allow you to live at home and save money. You have to spend four to five years of your life at the college of your choice. The college you choose will effect your future profession, and the friends and contacts that you make will last a lifetime.

MAKE IT A GOOD CHOICE!

CHAPTER 5

GETTING IN SHAPE TO PLAY WATER POLO

Getting in shape to play water polo requires a lot of hard work and sacrifice. Training for water polo is unique to the sport, just as basketball training is unique to basketball, and swim training is unique to swimming. Because swimming and water polo both perform their sport in the water, coaches make the mistake of training water polo players like they train swimmers. That idea is simply not correct. With a background in exercise physiology and 50 years involved in the sport, I have come up with a system of training that applies exercise physiology to the specific needs of water polo. Swim training is included in the system; but it is "water polo swim training" that follows general training principals; but is at the same time unique to water polo.

The training program that is presented in this chapter will allow the water polo player to perform at the maximum level possible. Many of the specific swim sets and exercises described in this chapter can be used by the individual player to train for the sport. I would be remiss if I did not include team drills and exercises that are essential for getting in shape to play a team sport such as water polo. However, I don't feel that they are appropriate for this book. It is up to individual coaches to introduce exercises and drills that involve the entire team. Coaches and other persons interested in coaching can find information of this sort in my coach's manual "A Practical Guide To Coaching Water Polo" published by Lulu Publishing Company, www.lulu.com.

PART ONE OF THIS CHAPTER
Part one of the chapter explains what happens to your body, specifically your muscles, when you swim up and down the pool or throw a ball. Once the player understands the "science" behind water polo, then he can make the right decisions on how to effectively train for the sport.

PART TWO OF THIS CHAPTER
Part two of the chapter deals with specific training methods used in water polo, based on an assessment of the energy requirements of the sport, and the correct application of the principals of exercise physiology. Information on "how to train" for water polo is aimed specifically at the athlete who wants to improve by training in the off-season, or by training outside of the required team practice sessions. Specific information is included on water polo swim sets, drills to get you in shape, leg improvement drills, strength training and dry-land exercises, and information on warm-up, diet and stretching.

Part 1

THE SCIENCE OF WATER POLO

WHERE DO WE GET THE ENERGY TO FUEL OUR MUSCLES?

Your body is perfectly designed to move by a series of coordinated muscle contractions. When your brain tells your body to move, nerve signals trigger a powerful release of muscular energy through a special molecule called adenosine triphosphate (ATP). ATP is a high-energy molecule, that when the chemical bond that holds it together snaps apart, energy is released and used by the muscles to contract and away you go.

ATP is generated in mitochondria, tiny little bodies that are the powerhouses of each body cell, from the energy you eat as food. Each muscle cell contains thousands of mitochondria, and each muscle contains thousands of muscles cells. The process that causes this to happen is simply converting chemical energy from food to mechanical energy for muscle contraction. Three systems in the body create the ATP energy required for physical activity.

ATP-CP SYSTEM

The ATP-CP system provides enough energy for a five to eight-second sprint or other rapid muscle contraction such as lifting weights. Creatine phosphate (CP) is a high- energy molecule that can deliver its energy to manufacture ATP very quickly. CP is readily available and stored in large quantities in the muscle fibers. Immediately upon the start of exercise, CP is the preferred method of supplying energy before other methods can "kick-in". It is short-lived, however, because the CP reserves are depleted very quickly, possibly up to ten-seconds; about the time it takes to swim 20 meters down the pool. If you stop and rest after your 20-meter sprint, stocks of CP are remade during the rest period, to be utilized again at the next sprint.

This is very similar to what happens during weight training, when you do one set of a particular exercise and then take a rest before starting the next set. The CP that you utilize performing the exercise is regenerated during the rest period. This system of short exercise/rest/short exercise/rest can go on indefinitely as long as the rest period is long enough to regenerate enough CP for use by the muscle. No oxygen is required for this system to work; so you don't need to inhale air during a short sprint. Because no oxygen is required, it is call anaerobic (without oxygen) exercise.

Some strength and sprint athletes now take creatine supplements to make sure that they have maximum creatine-phosphate levels in their muscles. It is still a controversial subject because scientists are still not sure that supplements actually help performance, whether extra CP provided by supplements actually gets to the working muscles, and whether there are side effects to the body from long-term use.

GLYCOLYTIC SYSTEM-ANAEROBIC GLYCOLYSIS

If a swimmer continues swimming at a fast pace after the • rst 8-10 seconds, there will be a lag in time when ATP produced from Creatine Phosphate runs out, and the supply of oxygen is still being delivered by the blood. The ATP needed to continue muscular contraction is supplied by anaerobic glycolysis, the breakdown of glycogen, again with little requirement for oxygen. The glycogen used for this process is found in the muscles and in the liver; and is actually the storage form of the simple carbohydrates that you eat in your diet. Before it can be utilized, the glycogen is quickly broken down into glucose, which is then converted into ATP. This system does not produce a large amount of ATP, only about two ATP molecules from each glucose molecule.

It does produce enough ATP to sustain the exercise for a longer period of time, about 40-50 seconds, and up to 2 minutes depending on the level of training of the athlete. This process quickly delivers enough ATP to allow the swimmer to maintain a fast pace, even after the CP levels are low. The drawback to anaerobic-gylcolysis is the production of lactic acid. Even though the athlete can swim at near maximum speed for this time period, the accumulation of lactic acid will eventually cause the muscles to fatigue, and muscular contraction to slow down.

Again, we can use weight lifting as an example of anaerobic glycolysis. Depending on the amount of the weight being lifted, a point is reached where CP is depleted and the muscles are utilizing the anaerobic breakdown of glycogen to provide ATP for muscle contraction. When the muscles reach a point where enough lactic acid has accumulated, the pain and tightness requires the athlete to stop lifting the weight. This threshold is different for each athlete, depending on his conditioning and the amount of weight being lifted. Training helps to increase this "lactic acid threshold". The better trained the athlete is, the longer he can tolerate a heavier workload.

AEROBIC SYSTEM

The body avoids acid fatigue by switching to a third system that requires oxygen, the aerobic system. In order to utilize the oxygen system, however, the pace of the exercise has to be reduced. The intensity of the exercise, and the bodies ability to deliver oxygen to the muscles, are important factors in which system is being utilized. As long as the intensity and pace is high, the body relies more on the glycolytic system fueled by glucose. The cardiovascular system simply cannot deliver oxygen fast enough to supply the demands of the high intensity exercise. When the intensity is lower (e.g. during slow swimming or jogging), the body prefers the aerobic system that uses both fat and glucose for muscle fuel.

This system is most important in any exercise that lasts longer than two minutes. The inhaled oxygen helps the muscles to produce and extra 34 ATP molecules from only one glucose molecule, compared to only two without oxygen. The more efficient and well trained the body is in delivering oxygen, the more the aerobic system plays a role in muscle contraction. Speed and intensity are still important factors; but the better-conditioned athlete is able to swim at a faster pace, and still be able to deliver needed oxygen. This is because the athlete has trained at faster and faster speeds, and developed his cardiovascular system to deliver oxygen more efficiently; and not rely so much on the anaerobic glycolytic system and the resultant build-up of lactic acid.

During exercise, all three systems come into play. The contribution of the three systems depends on the speed and intensity of the performance, and the conditioning of the athlete. Generally, fast pace swims utilize more of the anaerobic systems while slower paced swims utilize more of the aerobic system. There is a small amount of oxygen stored in the muscle fibers and in the blood in the vicinity of the muscle. This can be utilized right away and does contribute to the production of ATP, even for short and fast paced swims. Oxygen contributes about 20% of the ATP for short sprints of 20-25 meters, and about 30% to swims of 30-75 meters. Slower paced swims are almost entirely aerobic.

WHAT HAPPENS WHEN YOU GO TOO FAST, TOO SOON?

To illustrate what happens when the swimmer goes too fast and uses anaerobic glycolysis to produce ATP for energy, imagine a swimmer who is swimming a 500-meter race. If he swims the • rst 75 to100 meters as fast as he can go, the accumulation of lactic acid can become a problem. Because of his fast pace, the athlete performs this part of the swim without utilizing much oxygen. The cardiovascular system simply cannot deliver enough oxygen to the working muscles to meet the energy demands of the muscles. Thus, the body turns to anaerobic-glycolysis to quickly produce enough ATP to meet the demands of the muscles. The result is that the swimmer cannot keep up the fast pace, because of fatigue caused by the accumulation of lactic acid. He consequently must slow down the pace of the swim.

The other swimmers in the race, who have gone out at a slower pace, will eventually pass the fast paced swimmer as he slows down. They can afford to swim the last part of the race at a fast pace, because they did not accumulate lactic acid by going out too fast. A swimmer has to find a slower pace that he can swim at first, so that he doesn't produce too much lactic acid at the beginning of the event. A general conclusion is THAT THE FASTER A PERSON SWIMS, THE MORE LACTIC ACID IS PRODUCED. The better conditioned the swimmer is, however, the faster pace he can swim without producing lactic acid.

Watch an Olympic games one-mile run sometime on TV, and see what happens to the jackrabbit that sprints out ahead of everybody in the first of four laps around the track. He either pulls out of the race, or is passed by the rest of the field. He cannot maintain that fast pace at the beginning because of the accumulation of lactic acid. Many of the runners will sprint the last lap of the race, because lactic acid accumulation does not affect the runners once the race is over. However, the timing of when to start the last sprint is critical to winning the race. Start the sprint too early, and you will also suffer the effects of lactic acid before you finish. Runners who waited before they started to sprint will pass the early sprinter at the finish line.

MAXIMUM FUEL STORES

Glucose is stored in the muscles and liver as long chains that form the giant molecule called glycogen. Hence, we refer to glycogen as the primary muscle fuel. It is specially structured to break down quickly to glucose as required by the muscles to produce ATP. Carbohydrate in food is digested, absorbed into the blood, and transported to the muscles and liver where it is converted to glycogen and stored for later use. The average 160-pound person will have about 40 calories (measure of energy) of glucose in the blood, 260 calories of glycogen in the liver, and 1400 calories of glycogen in the muscles. If you want to train and compete efficiently, you need a full tank of glycogen every time you start your exercise.

During exercise the body will burn a mixture of fat and glycogen; but glycogen is the fuel that will burn out quicker. Unfortunately, burning glycogen is much more efficient in producing ATP than burning fats. As intensity of exercise increases, glucose (glycogen) is the preferred muscle fuel. During high intensity exercise, glycogen is used at a very fast rate and may become depleted after 30 to 45 minutes.

At lower intensity exercise, both body fat and glycogen are used as fuel. At lower intensity exercise, the burning of fat is in effect a "glycogen saving" mechanism; that saves the glycogen for use when the exercise becomes more intense. Even a slim person has more than 60,000 calories of fat stored in the body; so fat fuel never runs out. When the body turns to fat to produce ATP, however, the athlete has to slow down. This is because fat is not very efficient in producing enough ATP for a high intensity and fast pace. This is usually what happens when marathoners or bicyclists "hit the wall" or "bonk out".

THE REASON FOR A HIGH CARBOHYDRATE DIET

It is critical for good performance, both in training and in competition, that an athlete has plenty of glycogen stored in his body. The glycogen that is utilized during training has to be replaced every day, or performance will suffer. This can only be done with a diet that is high in carbohydrates. Another way to insure a good supply of glycogen for a big competition, is to rest for a few days prior to the event, and allow the glycogen to build up. This mechanism is called a "taper" and will be discussed later in this chapter.

When muscle glycogen levels are low and blood glucose levels start to drop, it is called "hitting the wall" as mentioned above. It happens to all athletes at one time or another, but especially to marathon runners and cyclists in events that last for a long period of time. It can also happen to water polo players who train hard every day and fail to restore the glycogen in the body before a game. It can also happen when players have to play several games in one day.

As the glycogen stores run out during the event, the body turns to fat utilization. Because fat cannot produce enough ATP necessary for muscle contraction, the runner has to slow down dramatically as in "hitting a wall". It is usually accompanied by an unsavory feeling of extreme fatigue, dizziness and hunger. This feeling can be partially reversed by consuming some quick to absorb sports drink, candy or gel during the event.

Many athletes do not realize that the body will also utilize proteins in extreme cases to help produce ATP. This means that the body is using (eating up) its own muscles to produce energy, since proteins are the building bocks of muscles. Not a good idea, especially when you need strong muscles to perform you activity.

THE ROLE OF TRAINING

By training correctly, the athlete can condition himself to become more effective in utilizing oxygen, without relying on anaerobic glycolysis and the debilitating effects of lactic acid. The keys to success in swimming and water polo lie in the efficiency of the aerobic system. The most highly trained athletes can swim at a faster speed, without having to resort to the anaerobic systems.

TRAINING THRU "ADAPTATION"

Everything that a water polo player does requires energy to contract the muscles involved. The speed of the water polo player when moving through the water, and the strength of his upper and lower body muscles when performing skills, all requires energy. The ability to maintain these skills throughout an entire game, or practice session, is determined by the capacity of the body to release chemical energy and transform it into mechanical work.

Because energy availability is the factor that governs the speed and pace of the player as he is moving and performing in the water; the purpose of training should be to make more chemical energy available to the muscles at faster rates, and to replace the energy lost from those chemicals as rapidly as possible. Training does this thru "adaptation". This is the essence of training for water polo, or for any sport for that matter. Training places specific demands on the body, and the body's physiological mechanisms "adapt" to these demands; so that more energy is available to perform more work with less fatigue.

SPECIFICITY OF TRAINING

An athlete just can't perform any kind of training, or place any demand on the body, and hope for improvement in their sport. The training has to be specific to the sport. This is called the principal of "specificity of training". It states that "for training to be effective, you must make the same demands on the your body, and in the same way, that they are made in a game." The closer the training routine is to the requirements of competition, the better the outcome. This principal is what we base a lot of the training routines that are described in this chapter.

A simple explanation of "specificity of training" has to do with swimming. The swimming that we do in water polo is completely different than the swimming we do in competitive swimming. Competitive swimming requires that a swimmer swim with his head in the water at a certain pace for long periods of time, while turning and starting from a wall. Water polo requires head-up swimming for shorter distances, at all out bursts of speed, changing direction without using a wall, and playing in both horizontal and vertical positions. It would be a mistake to train a water polo player like a middle distance or long distance swimmer. Training as a sprinter and then adding all the nuances of playing water polo, such as head-up swimming, eggbeater kick, bursts of speed, changing direction, etc, would be much more effective for training the water polo player.

OVERLOADING

The principal of "overloading" is also important for the improvement of the systems that provide energy for muscular contraction. The principal simply states "in order for a body system to improve, it has to be overloaded beyond the normal requirements of the particular system." This is why long distance swimming at slow speeds does nothing to improve the energy systems used in the game of water polo, because it does nothing to "overload" and improve the body at the fast bursts of speed necessary to play the game.

Both the principals of "Specificity of Training" and "Overload" have to correctly be applied in order for the water polo athlete to improve and adapt to the rigors of practice and of a game. Both principals will be applied to water polo specific training, as described in Part 2 of this chapter. Before that we have to look at the body's energy systems that provide energy for muscular contraction.

TRAINING AND GENETICS

The ability to swim fast can be improved with training; but genetic endowment contributes in a major way to the success that an individual can achieve. Speed is a result of training, and also the type of muscle fibers that an individual has. A marathon runner has many red slow-twitch endurance fibers that have the ability to utilize oxygen as their primary function. This gives him the ability to run long distances at a slower speed. Whereas a sprinter has a lot of white fast-twitch muscle fibers that are designed to produce ATP anaerobically. This allows the sprinter to run very fast, but for a short period of time. Most individuals fall somewhere in between, and have different proportions of red and white fibers.

Training can change the characteristics of muscle fibers, but only up to a point. If you want to be a fast water polo player, hope that you were born with a higher percentage of white (sprint) fibers than red (endurance) fibers. Then train the muscles to use the fibers that you are born with in an efficient manner.

TRAINING EFFECTS

Training over a period of time eventually improves all of the energy systems by increasing lung capacity, improving the heart capacity and the circulatory system that delivers oxygen to the working muscles, increasing the muscle's capacity to utilize oxygen by increasing the number of mitochondria in the muscle fibers, increasing the efficiency of the anaerobic systems by increasing the amount of PC and glycogen stored in the muscles, and increasing the bodies tolerance for and ability to dissipate lactic acid. For all of these things to happen, however, the energy systems have to be stressed, or "over-loaded", as described above.

Part 2

TRAINING FOR WATER POLO

WATER POLO ENERGY REQUIREMENTS

Short and long bursts of speed followed by rest periods of different lengths are required to play the game of water polo. In film-analysis studies done in various countries, it was found that 70% of the time in a water polo game is spent in short bursts of speed of 5-25meters. These swims require use of both anaerobic systems, the breakdown of creatine phosphate and the breakdown of glycogen by anaerobic glycolysis. Aerobic glycolysis also contributes to the production of ATP for all activities, regardless of speed. It also contributes to water polo; but water polo remains a predominantly anaerobic sport.

The trick here is to train the aerobic system at faster and faster speeds without the accumulation of lactic acid. Consequently, training for water polo requires training for something that is called "speed endurance." Athletes with poor speed endurance are unable to accelerate and sprint at the same high level repeatedly during competition because of fatigue.

At a certain point after the start of a fast swim (depending on the condition of the athlete), slowing occurs because of lactic acid buildup. The athlete with good "speed endurance" can go on and on at a fast pace without accumulating the fatigue causing lactic acid.

OVERLOAD

An athlete has to train the cardiovascular system to improve its ability to deliver oxygen to the working muscles when he swims at a faster pace. The goal here is to improve the aerobic system so that you can swim at faster paces without the accumulation of lactic acid. Training at faster and faster speeds will "overload" the whole system and cause adaptations to occur; thus improving both the anaerobic and aerobic systems. But, you don't overload the system by swimming slowly.

INTERVAL SWIMMING

The beauty of "interval swimming" is that by alternating rest intervals with work intervals, you can swim at a faster pace during each interval; faster than you can by swimming a long swim without rest intervals. As an example we can look at a 1000-yard straight swim. If you break down the 1000 yards into 10 X 100 yards, and put a rest interval in-between each 100-yard swim, the pace of each 100 is much faster than the pace of the straight 1000 yard swim. Breaking down the 1000 into 20 X 50 yard swims can produce an even faster pace. Interval swimming is great for water polo conditioning because it stimulates game conditions; which is bursts of speed followed by slower paced or no swim rest intervals.

LEARNING TO SWIM FAST

Speed is necessary for improvement; and this can be accomplished in several ways. One way is to decrease the distance that you swim. The shorter the distance, the faster you can swim. 10 X 50 yards with rest intervals can be swum at a much faster pace then a straight 500-yard swim. Another way to swim faster is to lengthen the rest interval between swims. Each 50-yard swim in a 10 X 50 yd set, with 30-second rest intervals can be swum at a much faster pace than a 10 X 50 yd set with only 5-second rest intervals. The shorter rest intervals do not allow the athlete to recover, and so he must slow down the pace. Please note that the longer the swim, and the shorter the rest interval, the more the aerobic system is stressed. Shorter swims with longer rest periods stress more of the anaerobic systems. By combining different length swims with different length rest intervals, we can stress both anaerobic and aerobic systems.

ANAEROBIC SWIM SETS

Examples of swim sets that stimulate the ATP-CP anaerobic system: 10, 20, 25, 30-yard swims with 1:1 or 1: 1/2 work: rest intervals (e.g. 15 sec swim: 15 sec rest, 20 sec swim: 10 sec rest intervals.

Examples of swim sets that stimulate anaerobic glycolysis (lactic acid) system: 50, 75, 100, 200 yard swim repeats with 1:1 or 1: 1/2 work: rest intervals. (E.g. 45 sec swim: 45 sec rest, or 60 sec swim: 30 sec rest).

A set of 50-yard swims that is strictly anaerobic in nature is the following set: Swim an all out 50 yards. Then immediately swim a very easy 25 yards followed by about 30-45 seconds of rest. Repeat 10-12 times. The easy 25 after swimming a hard 50 yard swim will help to dissipate the lactic acid that accumulates and prepare the swimmer for the next hard swim.

Anaerobic swim sets require a lot of energy to perform, and can easily tire out players. These types of set should not total more than 1000-1500 yards. Players should swim the hard and fast anaerobic swims at the beginning of the week, so that they have time to rest for the game at the end of the week. Less and less swimming should be done as the week goes on while at the same time, more water polo related drills and scrimmaging should be preformed as the week progresses.

AEROBIC SWIM SETS

Examples of swim sets that stimulate aerobic systems:

20 X 50 yds with 5-10 second rest intervals

15 X 100 yds with 10-15 second rest intervals

10 X 200 yds with 15-20 second rest intervals

2 X 400 yds with a one-two minute rest interval.

There is not a need to do aerobic sets more than once a week, because they have to be swum at a slower pace. Perhaps early in the season, or during the off-season, the team might perform more aerobic sets than during the competitive season. Anything slower than counterattack speed doesn't necessarily train the muscles for water polo.

SWIM SETS THAT ARE BOTH ANAEROBIC AND AEROBIC AT THE SAME TIME

10 X 200 yds with 1:1/2 work: rest intervals, e.g. 2 min, 30 sec swim: 1 min, 15 sec rests

15 X 100 yds with 1:1/2 work: rest intervals, e.g. 1 min, 10 sec swim:30 sec rest

MIXED ANAEROBIC-AEROBIC SWIM SETS

These sets are designed so that the first few repeat swims are done with very little rest between repeats and are aerobic in nature. As the set goes on, more and more rest time is added until the last few swims become almost completely anaerobic; with lots of recovery time between swims. In designing the repeat times, you should take into account what most of your team can do for the repeat swims at the distance you are swimming. For example, if most of the players swim an average of 1:05 for 100-yard repeats, set the first two intervals on the 1:10. This will give most of the team about 5 seconds rest between the first two swims.

There will be a few players on the team who will not make that interval, and they will get no rest. The next two repeats should be on the 1:20, the next two on the 1:30. Add 10 seconds rest to every two repeat swims until the last two, which will be on the 2:00, almost a 1:1 swim to rest ratio.

If the set is designed correctly the first part of the set will be aerobic, the middle of the set will be a mix of aerobic and anaerobic, and the end of the set will be all anaerobic. The speed of each 100 yard swim should get progressively faster as the players get more rest between repeats.

Other examples of mixed sets:
1. Four sets of 5 x 50 yards- first set with 5 second rest between swims, second set with 10 seconds rest, third set with 20 seconds rest, and the last set with 30 seconds rest. The swimmers should take about a one-minute rest between each of the 4 sets.

2. 10 x 50 yards with 5-10 seconds rest between swims, rest several minutes, then swim 10x 50 yards with 30 seconds rest between swims. On the last set the players swim every other 50 with their heads up. The average time for each swim in the second set should be one-two seconds faster than in the first set, because there is more rest time. The time for each 50-yard swim in a head up position should not be less than 2 seconds slower than swimming 50 yards with the head down.

3. Three sets of 5 x 75 yards. First set with 10 seconds rest between swims, second set of mixed strokes (fly, back, breast; back, breast, free; breast, free, fly, and free, fly, back), or instead of mixed strokes swim the second set freestyle with 15-20 seconds rest; then the last set freestyle with 30-35seconds rest between swims. On the last set the players swim repeat number 2 and 4 heads-up. A 75 yards head-up swim is equivalent to a three-way counterattack in a 30-meter pool. To truly make it a water polo swim, the players should not use walls to start or make turns.

4. Three sets of 5 x 100 yards, two minutes between sets. The first set with 10-15 seconds between repeats is mostly aerobic; the second set with 20-30 seconds rest stimulates the anaerobic glycolysis (lactic acid) system; the last set with 50 seconds to one minute rest utilizes the CP/ATP anaerobic system.

In all of the above sets, the more rest the players have between repeats, the faster they should swim. Every swim should be timed. Every repeat should be done at a fast pace. Some players will loaf the first nine repeats and then go all out on the tenth one. If the swim is monitored; then this should not happen. Consistency is essential on these kinds of repeat swims. It is much better for the players to go hard on every swim, and die on the last one, than go slow for the first nine swims and then go all out in the last repeat.

SWIMMING TO GET IN SHAPE FOR THE SEASON
Players should arrive at the first day of practice, already in shape and ready to go. Don't expect the coach to get you in shape quickly before you start playing games. There just isn't enough time to get in shape, and still spend time preparing to play water polo. Arriving in shape will also make the practices easier to handle, especially if the team does two-a-day sessions prior to the start of school. Plus, the player can concentrate on learning team concepts and basic skills, without being too fatigued from hard training. Players can start training at home about three to four weeks before the season starts.

Training with a teammate or friend can make it easier to do, and also give a player a chance to get his arm in shape by passing with a ball. A minimum of three to four days per week for three weeks should be done, swimming anywhere from 2000-2500 yards per day. The first week should be mostly aerobic in nature, the second week a combination of aerobic and anaerobic glcolysis, and the third week utilizing both the anaerobic (lactic acid) and CP/ATP systems. Passing for 20 minutes a day, and performing shoulder exercises with elastic bands, will insure that you don't injure your shoulder in the first day shooting drills. About 15 minutes of additional leg work with a heavy ball, or teammate pushing down on your shoulders, should prepare your legs for hard practice sessions and scrimmages.

WATER POLO SPECIFIC SWIM SETS

A high percentage of the swim sets of 50-yard repeats should be done with the head- up in order to simulate water polo type swimming. All 25-30 yard swim sprints should be done head-up, and all should be started without pushing off the wall to start the swim, or to make the turn. An excellent water polo swim set is to go all out from the 2-yard line to the opposite two-yard line 20 times, with the head up and not using a wall. Head up sprints are the best water polo related swims that a player can do, and should be done every day in practice.

A strong scissor kick or breaststroke kick should be used to start every swim. In order to simulate water polo starts the players should start out by facing the wall or the goal, opposite the direction in which they will be swimming. On the whistle, they must turn around, and then do a scissor kick to get a fast start. Turning around and changing directions is preformed a lot in a game, especially when the ball changes hands.

CHANGE OF DIRECTION SWIMS

Players can practice changing directions on their own, by starting in the center of the pool with hips up and facing a wall. Immediately turn around and sprint six strokes in the opposite direction, spin around and swim six strokes again. Repeat until you have changed direction 6 to 8 times. Keep the head out of the water, turn quickly, give a big scissor or breaststroke kick to get started again, and swim with all out intensity to get the most out of this drill.

WATER POLO IM's

100-yard water polo Individual medleys should be swum once a week or every other week, so that the same swim muscles used in water polo will be utilized. A water polo IM consists of one length of butterfly, head up, with a breaststroke kick, one length of backstroke with the upper back and head high out of the water and with an eggbeater kick, one length of breaststroke with the chest coming completely out of the water on each stroke, and one length of head-up freestyle.

KICKING DRILLS

A strong flutter kick is important in water polo. As a player swims with his head out of the water, his legs and hips will sink low in the water unless he uses a flutter kick to keep the legs near the surface. Swimming with the legs and hips underwater can cause unnecessary drag that will cause the player to swim slower. Players should always use their legs when swimming with their head up.

Practice the flutter kick by doing kick sprints of 25 yards with or without a kick-board; or use a water polo ball for support. Submerging the ball under water, or sinking a kick-board in a vertical position as you kick, will add extra resistance.

Using the flutter kick while in a vertical position, with the hands out of the water, and holding a heavy ball for added resistance, is also a great leg conditioner. This kicking drill is especially useful when a player has a shoulder injury, and cannot use his arms to swim. Anywhere between 30 seconds and one minute vertical kicking repeated 10-15 times will help get the legs in shape in a short period of time.

DON'T FORGET THE SCISSOR AND BREASTSTROKE KICKS
Scissor kicks and breaststroke kicks are used all of the time in water polo in order to get a quick start; but seldom practiced. Starting from a stopped position, change of direction, going from horizontal to a vertical position, defending a driver and shooting the ball, all require the use of these kicks. A scissor kick is usually used when the player is on his side in the water, while a quick breaststroke (frog) kick is used when the player is more horizontal and on his stomach.

Practice these kicks the same as you would the flutter kick, using a ball or kickboard for arm support. Players should switch from one side to the other when performing 25-yd scissor kick sprints. A good sequence is 25-yard scissor on the right side, 25-yard scissor on the left side, and 25-yard breaststroke kick. Repeat seven times. Quick change of direction drills like the "six whistle" drill, are also good for practicing the scissor kick.

SPEED SWIMS
Since 70% of a water polo game is swum under anaerobic conditions, 70% of your swim training should also be workouts that stress the anaerobic ATP-CP and the anaerobic glycolysis (lactic acid) systems. Take caution that quality fast swims that stress the anaerobic ATP-CP system should not be done for more than a total of 500-1500 yards per day, and only for two days maximum per week. Speed swims like these can take a lot out of the players. It is best to alternate anaerobic ATP-CP days with aerobic/anaerobic glycolysis days.

Distances over 200 yards are not really necessary for water polo players; because the pace is too slow to stimulate the anaerobic systems used in a game. A 200-yard set is fine to do once in a while; but only if the players get a lot of rest between repeats. This is so they can swim each repeat at a faster pace. I have observed water polo coaches that have their players do a set of 20 x 200 yds, with only 5-10 seconds between repeats; or a set of 10 x 500 yards with 15 seconds rest. Sets like this are very aerobic in nature, and are almost like swimming a straight 4,000 or 5,000-yard swim. How many times have you seen water polo players swim 2,000-5,000 yards in a game at a slow pace? Players should swim distances in which they can swim faster than, or the same as game counter-attack pace. Anything slower than that is not productive.

HOW FAR AND HOW FAST SHOULD I SWIM?
To see how you are progressing and how hard you are working, you should use a pace clock to time all swims. A player who loafs swim sets is doing himself and the team a disservice. Swimming everything at a fast pace also means that you don't have to go as much mileage in practice. It is better to train hard and do less mileage than to swim slow and do a lot of mileage.

Your daily workouts will be shorter than our opponents, but everything that you do will be preformed with intensity. Workouts longer than 2 to 2 1/2 hours can create boredom and can be a waste of time in accomplishing the goals of the team. Players tend to pace themselves during long workouts, instead of performing at the intensity required in games.

IF YOU WANT TO SWIM FAST IN GAMES, YOU MUST SWIM FAST IN PRACTICE

If you want to play with intensity, you must practice with intensity. Shorter workouts allow the players to play with greater intensity. They have to be in great shape to do this. Conditioning can help win a game in the 4th quarter for a team; when the other team tires out from fatigue. Long swim sets and long swims don't have a place in water polo training. If the athletes know the training will be for a long period of time, they will pace themselves and not go all out. This is exactly the opposite of what you are trying to achieve. It is better to make the swim sets shorter and go all out, then make the sets too long and swim at a slower pace.

FITNESS IS HARD TO GAIN, BUT EASY TO LOSE

A timed 400-yard swim on the first day of practice tells you what kind of shape you are in. It also tells the coach which players have been consistent with their training. Consistency in training is one the most important factors in conditioning for any sport. There is an old saying that "Fitness is hard to gain but easy to lose." It seems that It takes several months to get in shape and about two weeks to get out of shape. Players should get in shape and stay in shape all year around.

The worst thing that players can do is to get into the vicious cycle of getting in shape, and then getting out of shape. That is why most successful programs have some kind of year around training for the players that are closely monitored by the coach. Players left on their own during the off- season usually will do very little in the way of conditioning. Have the discipline that it takes to condition on your own, if necessary during the off-season, or prior to the start of the season. The player who can train on his own, without coach supervision, will be way ahead of the game. This will show the coach that the player is willing to work hard to improve.

WATER POLO SKILL SWIM DRILLS

Following are some specific water polo skills that can be practiced during sprint swims of 20 yards to 30meters:

>Head-up "look-swim" swims. Look-swim means that the player should look back on every other stroke. This is useful on the counterattack when looking back for the ball. As your hand pulls back underwater, turn the head to that side and look behind you.

>Start all swims without using the wall; so players must use a scissor kick to start. Start facing the wall with the hips up, and then turn to swim as you kick back to get you started.

>Stop and start swims on the whistle, with and without the ball. Or, throw the ball ahead about 5-6 feet, and then sprint to the ball. Stop and repeat all the way across the pool.

>Going from vertical to horizontal and from horizontal to vertical, with and without the ball. Alternate swim bursts with vertical leg jumps. With the ball, go up into a shooting position and eggbeater forward. Without the ball, go up into a blocking position or do several jumps. Jumps can be straight up or lateral, one to the right and one to the left.

>Bursts of speed. Face each other, one player blasts around the other. Turn and catch the player who has just gone around you and pass him. One player starts first. The trailing player must catch him and get around him and into a defensive facing position. Or, simply start one player first, and have the second player try to catch and/or pass the first player.

>Working in pairs, passing the ball while swimming. This drill teaches the players how to pass while on the move. The players pass with either hand and pass to their teammate both wet and dry, to inside and outside arms, and in front of the face.

>Change of direction angle swims- Fast start with a scissor kick, swim straight ahead for four strokes. Quickly change directions and swim at a 45-degree angle to the right for four strokes; change direction and swim at 45-degree angle to the left for four strokes. Repeat again by swimming straight ahead. Always make a deliberate 45-degree turn. Perform this drill with and without the ball.

DRILLS FOR POWER
Increasing your power helps to accelerate and perform bursts of speed.
>Use power racks that have weights and a pulley system that allows a swimmer to swim away from the wall and lift a set weight on the rack. This same system can be simulated by using surgical tubing instead of a power rack. The tubing is tied around the swimmers waist. As he swims away from the wall, the tubing tightens and creates more resistance. More power is needed to overcome the increasing resistance as the swimmer moves away from the wall.

>Drag Partner- One player holds the legs while the other player drags him down the pool. Switch roles every 25 yards. The player being dragged should not try to help the swimmer by kicking his legs. He must remain motionless so that the swimmer has to pull his full weight down the pool.

>Explosive start and stop swims- It takes more power to start an explosive swim from a stopped position in the water. From a hips up position in the water, use a scissor or breaststroke kick to start, and then explode for 4 strokes, stop and repeat. Use the ball and toss it ahead as described above

TRAINING THE LEGS
Leg strength in the water is probably the single most important physical attribute that a player can possess for success in water polo. Almost every aspect of the game requires strong legs to perform at your best. Shooting, driving, shot blocking, pressure defense, extra-man 6 on 5 offense and defense, 2-meter offense, 2-meter defense and the goalie position are just some of the parts of the game that requires good legs.

CHOOSE YOUR PARENTS CAREFULLY

Genetics is an important factor involved in leg strength in the water. Legs that are built to perform the breaststroke and eggbeater kicks depend on different bone, ligament and joint configurations in the ankle, knee and hip joints, than legs that are built for the flutter kick. Another factor is that in breaststroke type legs, there are probably a higher percentage of white, fast-twitch muscle fibers than red slow-twitch fibers. This probably accounts for the explosive nature of a good breaststroke/egg-beater kick. Most people are born with these qualities and it is probably the reason why some players have better kicks than others.

If you are not born with the correct joint structure that will produce a good eggbeater kick, there is not a lot that you can do about it. Training the legs will certainly improve the qualities of your red and white muscle fibers, allowing you to improve your kick up to the point that your joint structure will allow. If you are going to play the goalie position in water polo, hope that you were born with the leg structure that will allow you to have an explosive eggbeater kick.

FLUTTER KICK OR EGGBEATER?

The ideal water polo player is good at both the eggbeater kick and the flutter kick. If you had to choose one over the other for success in the sport, it would have to be the eggbeater kick. A player can "get by" with a weaker flutter kick by using his arms to propel himself through the water when swimming. It is difficult, however to get by with a weak eggbeater kick. As a younger player you can play a decent game of water polo by using your swimming skills, your athletic skills, and your water polo skills to excel. However, as you grow older and move up to higher levels of play, and against better and better players, your legs will be the physical factor that most determines your success and failure in the game.

FOR BEST RESULTS, WORK YOUR LEGS IN THE WATER

You can improve your legs with training, up to a point; but if you want to be a successful water polo player, hope that you were born with good legs. Be specific and do most of your leg training in the water. Water polo drills that involve the legs, like shooting the ball, blocking shots, playing defense, etc are ways that a player can use the legs the same way they are used in a game. Adding resistance of some kind will overload the legs and also help to improve them. A player can put a weight belt around his waist while shooting to help improve his legs. Caution: Use heavy weights in the water sparingly so as to not cause injury to the legs.

WALKING IN THE WATER

Walking with both hands out of the water is one way to condition the legs. The player's elbows should remain out of the water when walking. Changing body position while walking, so that the player goes forward, backwards, and sideways, insures that the legs are fully conditioned. Start out in forward position and rotate a quarter turn to the right on each whistle or every few yards. On the next lap rotate to the left instead of the right. 20 yards is about the maximum distance to cover doing this type of drill.

SHOOTING AND BLOCKING LEG CONDITIONING

Using the legs and moving forward in a vertical position, with the hand in a shooting or blocking position, more closely resembles the way that the legs will be used in the game. If shooting with the right hand, the left shoulder should be pointed forward, the left hand in the water and using a sculling motion, and the right hand in the air and held above the right shoulder and the head. The body position for blocking is more "square" to a shooter, with one hand straight up and slightly in front of the shoulder and the other hand in the water for support. These skills must be practiced in shooting and blocking situations; and also preformed while walking the length of the pool.

PUSH DOWN FOR RESISTANCE

Pairing up players, and having one partner push down on the other partners shoulders while doing eggbeater repeats is a great way to increase resistance on the legs. Players can alternate between having the hands in or out of the water. The time that the player is being pushed down can vary from 5 to 15 seconds. Less time means more pressure from the player doing the pushing, while more time means less pressure. An example of this sort of exercise would be 10 reps of 5 seconds each, 8 reps of 10 seconds each, and 5 reps of 15 seconds each. The coach should also vary the rest period between each repeat, usually 5 or 10 seconds. Alternate the player who is pushing, and the player doing the eggbeater, back and forth after each set.

JUMPS

Explosive jumps are an important part of the game and should be practiced every few days. On the whistle, players jump up as high as they can. Players do this while walking, while in a stationary position, or even while swimming. Half of the jumps can be done by pushing off with the hands, and half without using the hands. Another great conditioner is to start at one goal post, touching the top bar with both hands, and then moving across to the other post without losing contact with the top bar.

In order to test the players on their ability to get high out of the water, find a device that is used to measure vertical jumps on land. This device is a vertical pole with swivels sticking out to the side at one-inch intervals. The player starts with his armpit at the surface of the water. He then reaches up and touches one of the swivels in order to measure his arm length. The player then jumps up out of the water and hits the highest swivel that he can. The difference between the lowest and highest swivels that he can hit is a measure of his water leaping ability.

PAIR RESISTANCE TRAINING

Two players face each other, with their bodies in a horizontal position in the water, hips up, and with their hands on each others shoulders. On the whistle, both players do an eggbeater kick, trying to push the other player backwards. This is great resistance training for the eggbeater kick, especially if both players are evenly matched.

LEAP FROG

This is an excellent leg training drill for all players, especially for the hole-forward and defender positions. This drill can be done in pairs or with three players. The players line up facing in the same direction, with one player behind the other. The player in the back position puts his hands on the shoulders of the player in front of him and "leap frogs" over his head and shoulders. They alternate leaping over each other until they have gone a set distance of 75-100 yards. The player that is being leaped over must keep his head above the water by using both his legs and hands for support. In the three-player drill, the players line up in a row and the last player must leap over two players before he stops. (See Pictures 5-A and 5-B below)

Picture 5-A: Start of the leapfrog   Picture 5-B: Leaping over the top

VERTICAL/HORIZONTAL

Going from a vertical position to a horizontal position and visa-versa are skills that are used in the game all of the time, both on offense and defense. The players should practice these skills until they become comfortable changing quickly from one position to another. Any combination of bursts of speed interspersed with vertical jumps, changes of direction, walking with arms out, etc are great vertical /horizontal drills and great leg conditioners.

A good drill to practice this is to position one player between two other players spaced about 8 feet apart. The player in the middle starts on the shoulder of one player, in a horizontal position, and with his feet pointed towards the other player. He then pivots over his hips and up into a vertical blocking position, eggbeater forward until he reaches the other player. Once he reaches the second player, he immediately turns around and swims quickly back to the first player. Repeat ten times and then switch the player in the middle.

HEAVY BALLS

Weighted balls are great for leg training in the water. See the next section on "Resistance Training" for details.

RESISTANCE TRAINING

Training with weights can help a player succeed in water polo, up to a point. The weight training should target specific muscles that are used in water polo, and trained as close as possible to the way that they are used in the water. Heavy weight training during the season can add unnecessary bulk that a player has to drag up and down the pool, especially to the legs and lower body. During the off-season, heavier weights with lower number of repetitions (6-8) are recommended at least three days a week.

During the competitive season use lighter weights with higher number of repetitions (8-12) and/or resistance tubing and bodyweight exercises, so that players do not unnecessarily bulk up. Twice a week during the competitive season is sufficient for strength maintenance without tiring the muscles. A minimum of one day off between weight training sessions, and one day off prior to competition is necessary to rest the muscles before a game.

LEVERAGE-LEGS AND CORE

Strength in the water has more to do with leverage than anything else. Long arms, leg support, and a strong core help to achieve leverage and strength in the water, much more so than huge bulky muscles. Athletes who perform on land have the advantage of a stable ground base on which to push off to gain leverage. In the water, strong legs give the player a platform from which he can push off of to gain leverage, and a strong core helps transfer power from the legs to the upper body.

LAND EXERCISES FOR THE LEGS

It is questionable whether weight training will improve a player's leg strength in the water, mainly because that kind of training is not specific enough to simulate the eggbeater kick. General leg exercises to strengthen the leg muscles around the knee and hip areas, such as leg extension, leg-flexion, leg-press and squats are good, as long as they are not overdone. If strength in the legs from squats are that important to a good eggbeater, then a person who can squat 500 lbs should have a better eggbeater kick than someone who can only squat 250 lbs. This has not shown to be true.

BUILT LIKE A FISH

Big and bulky legs are one attribute of heavy weight lifting that can be detrimental to water polo players, as well as swimmers. A typical swimmer's body is streamlined for speed, big in the front for strength, but slim in the legs like a fish. Neither a strong flutter kick nor breaststroke kick require big legs. A big bulky rear end and big legs only serve to slow the swimmer down, especially in water polo, where swimming is preformed with the head out of the water. This causes the legs to sink even more, and creates more resistance and drag in the rear end. The more a water polo player uses a strong flutter kick when swimming, the less the legs will sink in the water and cause drag.

BODY WEIGHT EXERCISES FOR THE LEGS

Exercises utilizing a person's body weight can be more beneficial and can more closely simulate the eggbeater motion. Slide boards where the players wear socks and slide back and forth in a skating motion are excellent, as well as plyometric jumps up and onto different height platforms. Players should not jump down from a great height, but step down to prevent injuries to the knee.

Another land exercise for strengthening eggbeater muscles starts with a player straddling a bench, with a leg on either side of the bench. He then jumps up and lands with both feet on top of the bench. Step down rather than jump down from the bench. This can be repeated in 3 sets of 10-20 repetitions with different height benches. This exercise is the dry land exercise that most closely simulates the eggbeater kick in the water. (See Pictures 5-C and 5-D on the next page). Roller-skating and ice-skating also closely resemble the motion in the eggbeater kick, and are excellent off-season conditioning for the legs.

Picture 5-C: Straddle bench-starting position   Picture 5-D Jump up on bench with
both legs. Then step down.

ALTERNATIVE STRENGTH TRAINING-WITHOUT WEIGHTS

There are many other ways to perform strength training during the season without using heavy weights. Stretch cords are a great alternate to training with weights. They can be incorporated into a circuit that also includes body weight exercises such as pull-ups, push-ups and dips. The advantage of stretch cords over other types of resistance training is that you can train the muscles in the same way that they are used in water polo. (See circuit at end of chapter)

STRETCH-CORD EXERCISES

Arm exercises that mimic the shooting motion, and exercises that mimic the swimming motion are examples of specific stretch cord exercises for water polo. In most of these exercises the cord is tied to a stationary object, unless otherwise specified:

1.Straight-arm pull down- Cord is attached above and in front of the player's face. Reach up and grab the cord handles with both hands, slight bend in arms, and pull down to below the waist. This duplicates the pull down and "catch" at the beginning of the water polo freestyle stroke, especially if the hands are kept wide of the shoulders. (See picture sequence 5-E below)

Pictures 5-E: Pull down

2.Swimming motion. Same as exercise # 1 above except that when pulling with both arms, bend them at the elbow so that both hands go down the center of the body. This motion duplicates the swimming motion of the hands and arms in the underwater part of the pull.

3.Triceps extension. Bent over as #2 above, but start with the elbows tucked into the waist, and the hands up by the chest. Keep the elbows tucked in and extend the hands down to the legs. (See Picture sequence 5-F below)

4.Shooting triceps extension. Player stands with his back to where the cord is attached. Hold the right arm out in front of the shoulder with the left hand cupping the elbow. Bend the elbow and hand back and grab the cord. Keeping the elbow up and in front, extend thehand forward, similar to the last part of the shooting motion. (See Picture sequence 5-G below).

Pictures 5-F: Triceps extension

Pictures 5-G: Shooting triceps extension

5. Shooting from the shoulder. Again with the back to the cord attachment, hold the elbow out to the side of the shoulder with the hand in an upright position. Grab the cord and move the elbow and hand forward, together, a few inches and then back to the starting position in rapid movement. Repeat ten times at three different positions, in front of shoulder, side of shoulder and behind shoulder. (See picture sequence 5-K on the next page)

| a) start | b) forward | c) back to start | d) forward |

Picture sequence 5-H: Short rapid movements in front of shoulder. Elbow and hand move together, both forward and backward.

6. Rowing. In a seated position, pull back on the cord, similar to a rowing motion.

7. Upright row. Standing on cord, grab cord at waist level and pull up under the chin.

8. Shoulder. Standing on cord, start with hands at the side of he body below the hips. Bend the arms slightly and pull up and to a side position, at or slightly above shoulder level. Do another set with the hands starting in front of legs and below the waist. Bend arms slightly and pull up to position in front of the shoulders. This same exercise can also be done with dumbbells, as shown below in Picture sequence 5-Q and 5-R.

9. Rotator cuff exercises. See Below

STRETCH CORDS AND POWER RACKS IN THE WATER
In the water you can do leg work, and also swim against resistance provided by stretch cords or power racks. The power rack is situated on the deck and the cords are tied to pool railings, while the cord from each is attached around the player's waist. The player starts in a position close to the wall and then gradually swims or eggbeaters away from the wall. You can change the resistance by increasing the weight on the power racks. With stretch cords, the further the player moves away from the side of the pool, the more resistance is created.

WEIGHTED BALLS
Weighted balls are also great to use for legwork in the water, but should be used only every other day. Older players can handle heavier balls than younger players can. Be careful when passing with heavy balls so that you do not injure the shoulder. Use lighter balls of 2-5 pounds for passing with one hand. The weight used with one hand is too heavy if the player has to "shot put" the ball rather than throw it.

Basketballs, or Mikasa weighted balls that are a little heavier than a normal weight ball, use the same principal as a baseball player who swings a weighted bat in the on deck circle. Two hands should be used to pass the heavier 6-12 pound balls. You can pass between two players in the water and/or pass back and forth between a player in the water and a player standing on the pool deck. Remember that heavy balls are used to condition the legs, not the arms.

SHOOTING MUSCLES

Before coming up with ways to increase shooting speed, an analysis must be made of the muscles used in shooting a water polo ball. The muscles used in the overhand shooting motion are similar to the muscles used in throwing a baseball. There are differences in the two actions that change the relative contribution of different muscles to the throwing motion. (See Chart 5-A on next page)

Since baseball players can push off a solid piece of ground rather than water, they can generate more power for shoulder and trunk rotation from pushing off the ground. Because a player is pushing off the soft water, only about a third of the speed in throwing a water polo ball is generated from the rotation of the shoulder. Whereas, throwing a baseball gets about two-thirds of the speed from shoulder rotation. This underscores the importance of a strong egg-beater kick to generate more power to throw the water polo ball hard and fast.

A water polo player has to rely on other muscles to generate ball speed. Another one-third of speed comes from the muscles of the shoulder that cause internal rotation and horizontal adduction of the arm. Internal rotation contributes more to the standard overhand throw in both baseball and water polo, whereas horizontal adduction contributes more to a side arm sweep throw.

Internal rotation can be described by holding the arm out to the side, parallel to the ground, with the elbow bent at a 90 degree angle. Rotate the forearm forward and hand down by rotating the upper arm along the axis. Horizontal adduction can be described by extending the arm out to the side, keeping the arm straight. Bringing the straight arm to the front of the body is horizontal adduction.

Elbow extension where the arm is extended in front of the body also contributes to ball speed in water polo, about 20-22 % of the total. The primary muscle used in this movement is the triceps muscle located in the back of the upper arm. Wrist flexion also contributes to ball speed in both sports, about 8-10 % in water polo and more in baseball, perhaps over 20 %. This is because throwing the smaller baseball gets more speed from a wrist snap than the larger water polo ball does.

In summary, the baseball player relies more on shoulder rotation and wrist snap to throw the ball, while water polo players rely more on the combined effects of all four muscle actions, with more speed coming from internal rotation/horizontal adduction and elbow extension than in baseball. (See Chart 5-A on next page)

CONTRIBUTION OF DIFFERENT MUSCLES TO THROWING A WATER POLO BALL VERSUS THROWING A BASEBALL.

	BASEBALL	WATER POLO
SIZE OF BALL	Small	Large
VELOCITY OF BALL (MPH)	80-90	40-50
TRUNK ROTATION	60%	30%
ELBOW EXTENSION	10%	20%
WRIST FLEXION	20%	10%
INTERNAL ROTATION (HORIZONTAL ADDUCTION)	10%	20%

Chart 5-A Comparison of throwing a ball in baseball and water polo.

EXERCISES TO IMPROVE YOUR SHOOTING

If you want to improve your shooting, one of the things that you can do is to improve your legs, so that you can generate more power when you push down on the water. A strong eggbeater kick is one of the most important factors in shooting the ball. The next thing you can do is to improve your shooting technique, rotating your shoulders to add the torque of your body to the power of the shot. Then follow thru by extending your arm in front of you and snapping your wrist.

You can also strengthen the shooting muscles to help improve the velocity of the shot. The triceps muscle is one of the primary muscles utilized in shooting the ball, as well as forearm and shoulder muscles. Triceps extension exercises using stretch cords and weight machines can both be used. In both cases the elbow should be held directly in front of the shoulder, the hand must start back by the face, and then pull the resistance forward to full extension in front of the shoulder. (See Picture sequence 5-G above)

Exercises for internal rotation include holding the arm parallel to the ground, hand in a vertical position, and pulling down on an overhead pulley weight. An exercise for horizontal adduction involves holding the elbow out to the side and parallel to the ground with the hand up in the air. Pull a stretch cord or pulley forward while utilizing small movements back and forth of both the hand and elbow together. This can be done in several positions with the elbow and hand behind, in front of, and directly out to the side of the shoulder. Forearm curls with dumbbells can also be added for forearm strength. (See picture sequence 5-H above)

TRAINING TO PREVENT SHOULDER INJURIES

Injury to the shoulder is the most common water polo related injury. Because of the shallow socket of the shoulder joint, it is difficult for the ball of the humerus bone of the arm to stay in place when the arm is rotated; especially when the arm is in an overhead shooting position. Ligaments, tendons and muscles surrounding the joint are required to provide stabilization of the joint when movement occurs. However, when the muscles of the shoulder (rotator cuff and scapular stabilizers) are weak, overuse of the shoulder joint from swimming and throwing the ball can cause injury to the joint.

Because most strength training programs do not focus on the shoulder muscles that provide stability to the shoulder, overuse can exaggerate the injury even more. Strengthening the muscles surrounding the shoulder before injuries occur, can help prevent many of the injuries that are common in water polo. Since many of the muscles used in shooting the ball are the same muscles in the rotator cuff of the shoulder, strengthening those muscles will also help improve shooting velocity.

WORK THE BACK, SAVE THE SHOULDERS

Overdoing chest exercises like the bench press, without strengthening the other muscles surrounding the shoulder, causes an imbalance between the front and the back of the shoulder that can lead to shoulder injuries. It is recommended by exercise physiologists that there be a 2:1 ratio of back to front exercises for the shoulder area. Players should add back and shoulder exercises to their routine, such as front narrow and wide-grip lat pull downs, lat pullovers, upright rows, seated rows, and back, side, and front deltoid exercises.

Exercises for the chest and arms, such as the bench press, should be done with a narrow grip rather than a wide grip on the bar in order to put less stress on the shoulder. Chest fly exercises done while on the back and using dumbbells, or sitting on a fly machine while bringing the elbows together, are excellent for strengthening the muscles that bring the arm forward while taking a shot.

ROTATOR CUFF AND SCAPULAR (SHOULDER BLADE) STABILIZER EXERCISES

Specific exercises that strengthen the rotator cuff and scapular stabilizer muscles in the shoulder can be done every day as an injury preventative. Many can be done at home by using stretch cords, exercise balls and body-weight exercises. To insure that water polo athletes perform the needed exercises, coaches should require the team to perform them 10-15 minutes a day for three days a week. Taking the time to do them each week will pay off with less shoulder injuries in the future.

The most common rotator cuff exercises with stretch cords are internal and external rotation of both arms, empty coke can exercise, straight-arm pull away from midline of body at below waist, above the waist, and at the shoulder level. In addition, the internal rotation and horizontal adduction exercises as described in the above section on shooting, can also be used to strengthen the shoulder muscles. (See picture sequences 5-I and 5-J, and 5-K and 5-L on next page.

Pictures 5-I: External rotation   Pictures 5-J: Internal rotation

Pictures 5-K:Pouring coke can, thumb down. Pictures 5-L:Waist mid-line to side,   straight-arm. Also done below waist and at shoulder levels.

Other exercises that can be performed in the weight room include push-ups performed on a ball, one arm stabilizing on a ball, dribbling a slightly heavier ball against a wall with the arm out to the side of the body, shoulder shrugs with dumbbells, seated rows, bent over rows, and horizontal rows laying on an incline bench. Utilizing different exercises each day will help insure that all the correct muscles are being strengthened. A player can choose five different rotator cuff and shoulder exercises for two days a week, and then alternate with five different exercises for two other days.

HOW MUCH RESISTANCE SHOULD YOU USE WITH STETCH CORDS?
As mentioned above, stretch cords come in different color-coded sizes. Generally the bigger the diameter of the cord, the harder it is to pull. You can also change the resistance by shortening the cord at the point of attachment or by starting with the cord in a stretched position. As the distance between the cord attachment and the handles is shortened, the resistance increases, and the cord is more difficult to pull.

The more the cord is stretched prior to starting the exercise, the more resistance there will be. In order to judge the proper length and cord to use, do the exercise that is called for. If 25 repetitions are required, then perform 25 repetitions. If you can perform 25 reps easily, then get a more difficult cord, shorten the cord by changing the point of attachment, or stretch the cord before you start.

As you are pulling the cord, you should feel some resistance. The 25th repetition should be very difficult to perform, and you should feel a burning sensation in the muscles involved in the exercise. If you can only do 10 repetitions, then you should get a little easier cord. In general, the less repetitions you perform (10-15), the more you are working on strength; while higher reps (15-30) means you are working less on strength and more on endurance. According to the overload principal, the muscle will only improve if you overload it. You can overload by either increasing the resistance or increasing the number of repetitions.

CORE EXERCISES

Core muscles help transfer muscle power from the legs to your upper body. The core muscles of the stomach and back can be strengthened while in the water, especially with drills that require going from horizontal to vertical positions and motions that require twisting the trunk. Dry land exercises for the stomach can be as simple as doing sets of crunches. The stomach oblique muscles on the side can also be strengthened by lying on your back, bringing the knees and elbows together at the same time, and alternating touching the left elbow to the right knee and the right elbow to the left knee.

Add resistance to stomach exercises by throwing a heavy ball to another person as you go from a horizontal position on your back and up into sit-up position. Start with your arms extended over your head and the ball in both hands. Exercises to strengthen the muscles in the lower back are also critical to core strength. The most common being trunk extension on an upside-down V-board, with a weight held across the chest for added resistance. Start with the head near the floor and then extend up into a horizontal position.

BASIC STRENGTH TRAINING USING WEIGHTS

Weight training is a great way to increase muscular strength. Try to utilize the muscles that are used in water polo, and try to use them in the same way that they are used in performing water polo skills. 1 to 3 sets of 8-12 repetitions will add strength without adding unnecessary bulk. Increase the weight and lower the repetitions from the first to the last set.

To determine the correct weight to use, first choose a weight that you think you can lift about ten times. If you can easily lift it more than 12 times, increase the weight. If you can only lift it less than 8 times, decrease the weight. When lifting the weight, do so in a two-second period. When lowering the weight, do it more slowly, about 3- 4 seconds; so that you will be working the muscles in both directions. Use both free weights and machine weights for variety; although free weights require more balance to use.

Studies have shown that once strength is established at a desired level by doing two or three sets of each exercise, it can be maintained by doing only one set of each exercise with 8-12 repetitions. This saves time during the competitive season that can be utilized by doing more water polo related drills and exercises.

BASIC STRENGTH EXERCISES WITH WEIGHTS
Divide the body into sections, and do one or two exercises for each body part, as follows:

1. Chest – Wide hand bench press, fly exercise on back with dumbbells.

2. Mid-back – Rowing exercises, lat exercises (wide grip lat pull-downs; one knee on bench, bent over one-arm lat-pulls) (See Pictures 5-M and 5-N below)

Pictures 5-M: Seated row

Pictures 5-N: Bent over one-arm lat pull

3. Upper back – Up-right rows, shoulder shrugs, straight-arm pull down

(See Pictures 5-O and 5-P on next page)

Picture 5-O: Up-right rows

Picture 5-P Straight-arm pull-down

4. Shoulders –Deltoid arm raises (side, front, and bent over) (See pictures 5-Q and 5-R below and 5-S on next page)

Picture 5-Q: Deltoid (shoulder) side raise.

Picture 5-R: Deltoid (shoulder) front raise.

Picture 5-S: Deltoid (shoulder) bent over side raise

5. Arm triceps – Arm extension, dips, triceps pull downs

6. Arm biceps – Curls

7. Lower back – Back extension

8. Stomach – Crunches, obliques

9. Legs – Leg extension, leg flexion, squats with legs wide and toes pointed out at an angle, step up on bench with weights in hand, one legged squats

Consult a weight training manual, coach, or fitness trainer for the correct way to perform the above exercises.

CIRCUIT TRAINING

Circuit training consists of a series of stations, with a different exercise at each station. The circuit can be set up with as many stations as necessary to accomplish the goals of he team. Stations can be situated around the pool deck or in a weight-room, with two players assigned to each station. Twelve stations can accommodate 24 players at the same time. When a whistle or horn blows, everyone starts together by performing the particular exercise at that station. After the first player performs the exercise, then the second player also does the exercise. Upon completion of each exercise, a horn or whistle indicates that each pair must rotate to the next station, in a clockwise direction. Once they arrive at the next station, another horn will indicate the start of the next exercise.

The beauty of circuit training is that everyone on the team can work out at the same time, and it doesn't take a lot of tie to complete. A circuit can be set up around the pool deck, utilizing only stretch cords and body weight exercises. This is particularly helpful during the competitive season, because it will allow players to maintain strength without utilizing heavy weights. A circuit requires little time to complete, allowing the team to spend more time in the pool and preparing for games. During the off-season a circuit can be set up in a weight room, utilizing weight machines and free weights instead of stretch cords. The off-season circuit can also be performed twice in one session, so that each player performs two sets of each exercise.

Following is a circuit that can be set up around a pool deck. The team can do this circuit twice a week, just prior to jumping into the pool for water polo practice:

Station 1- Push-ups: 1 set x 12-15 reps (body weight)

Station 2- Dips (triceps): 1 set x 12 reps (body weight)

Station 3- Crunches: 1 set x 40 reps (body weight)

Station 4- Bent over straight-arm pull: 1 set x 30 reps (stretch cord)

Station 5- Bent over triceps extension: 1 set x 30 reps (stretch cord)

Station 6- Bench leg straddle jump: 1 set x 15 reps (body weight)

Station 7- Rotator cuff exercise: Right arm X 15 reps, int. and ext. rotation (stretch cord)

Station 8- Rotator cuff exercise: Left arm x 15 reps, int. and ext. rotation (stretch cord)

Station 9- Rowing exercise (seated): 1 set x 25 reps (stretch cord)

Station 10-Upright row (standing): 1 set x 25 reps (stretch cord)

Station 11- Pull-ups (pull-up bar) as many as possible; or one arm lat exercise

      (dumb bells): 1 set (each arm) x 15 reps

Station 12- Triceps extension (shooting motion) front of face: 1 set each arm x 20 reps (stretch cord).

More stations can be added utilizing other muscles or other rotator cuff exercises. If there are more stations than players available, leave the extra stations at the end of the circuit, so each pair of players will always have an open station to rotate to.

CHAPTER 6

EXPOSING DIET AND EXERCISE MYTHS

There are a lot of misconceptions in the world of diet and exercise that people just blindly follow without questioning. Part of the problem is that for many years these myths have been perpetuated by persons who have a lot to gain by spreading them, or know nothing about what they are talking about. Either they purposely do this because they are trying to sell you a product like an exercise machine, or a pill that will magically give you abs of steal; or they have an agenda that promotes whatever they believe to be true. Quite often they are just spreading the word about something that has always been done that way, without questioning whether it is right or wrong, or whether it is true or not. As long as there is money to be made and gullible people who are willing to try anything, these kinds of products will flood the infomercial channels on TV.

I was educated as an engineer and a scientist; and I was taught to question everything that I did not understand. I was also taught that when someone made a statement about something, that they had to back it up with proof. Not just proof as in " I took this pill and it made me stronger". That is not proof! That is only one persons opinion and really doesn't mean anything. For all we know, that person could have taken a sugar pill and it was six months of weight training that made him stronger. I am talking about proof that is based upon documented research and science, is a proper "blind" study, and involves several groups of people who may or may not be taking a "placebo". Properly conducted research is the only way to find out if something works or doesn't work.

I was also taught that "if something sounds too good to be true, it usually is". Nothing ever comes easy; you usually have to work for it. Be suspicious of anyone who tells you that something is easy, and you don't have to work hard for it. All you have to do is take this pill and your worries are over. "There are no magic pills" that can do the work for you. Don't believe that something works or that everything is true, even if a coach tells you so.

COACHES DON'T ALWAYS KNOW EVERYTHING
I like to think that we know everything; but we don't. Players should not just blindly accept everything that people tell them, even if it comes from their water polo coach. It is amazing how many coaches do not have any understanding of how to properly train for the sport. That is because they have never been trained in, or tried to learn anything about the science of exercise (exercise physiology). They might have an excellent understanding of how the game is played, probably because they played the game themselves; but they don't know a lot about things like diet and exercise, food supplements, training, warm-ups and cool-downs, stretching, etc. Many just accept what they have been told by their coaches before them, who learned from their coaches before them.

I listened to my coaches and utilized many things that they taught me when I became a coach. However, I constantly analyzed what I was doing and why I was doing it. If I couldn't answer questions about why we were doing something; or didn't understand something myself, I would find out the answer or change to something different. If you as a player do not understand what you are doing, and why you are doing it, then ask the coach and make sure that you both understand.

FALLACIES IN SPORT

Many fallacies about training for sports have been handed down from generation to generation, without questioning whether it was right or not. An example of this is the idea of withholding water from athletes when they are training in hot weather, because it makes the athlete mentally tougher. How many football players have died, or have been severely injured, by not drinking water during a two to three hour training session in high heat and humidity; simply because the coach didn't know any better? It seems absurd now that we know about it; but it is amazing that for years a lot of football coaches really believed that withholding water made the player tougher. Who did they learn this from? The coaches before them who did this to them when they were players.

Stretching is one of the same kind of myths that have been passed down over the years from coach to coach, and exercise teacher to exercise teacher; without ever questioning whether it really works or not. I hope that this chapter will help to dispel the "stretching myth" and some of the other misconceptions associated with sports; or at least cause you to think or question something that you have been told to do. The primary questions that both coaches and athletes have to be constantly asking is "Does it work" and "Why or why not"? All the information that we will discuss in this chapter, as fact, has been scientifically proven. If something has not been proven, I will state that it has not.

FOOD FOR ATHLETES

Food comprises protein, carbohydrates, fats, fiber, vitamins, minerals, and many bio-active compounds such as anti-oxidants. There are no "magic" foods that will improve your performance, just as there are no magic pills. There is one big difference, however. Between food and pills. Food, including water, is essential for survival. Everything contained in food is utilized by the athlete, and is necessary if the athlete is to perform at his best. Certain ingredients in food, however, are more necessary for the athlete than for the normal person.

Carbohydrates, in the form of glucose and glycogen, are the single most important element in food that is necessary to provide crucial energy for muscle contraction and brain function. Any athlete that utilizes both the anaerobic and aerobic systems that produces ATP for muscular contraction need a constant supply of glycogen (the storage form of carbohydrates) in the body. The likely cause of poor performance and fatigue in practice, or in games, is because of low levels of glycogen in the muscles.

ATP can also be produced from fats and proteins; but the amount is much smaller and the process is slow and inefficient. Glycogen stored in the liver and muscles comes from a diet high in complex carbohydrate; and under normal circumstances is readily available for glycolysis and the production of ATP. However, frequent long and hard training sessions and games can reduce the amount of glycogen available. Studies have shown that the glycogen stored in the body will start depleting after only one hour of continuous exercise. It can be depleted completely if not restored through diet and rest.

MYTH- CARBOHYDRATES ARE BAD!

TRUTH- High-protein, low-carbohydrate diets cannot support optimal health very long, especially for the young, active athletic person. There is one reason why some people lose weight on this type of diet. Do you know how hard it is to find any kind of food that doesn't contain carbohydrates? Because of the very limited foods that they can eat, people will eat less. By eating less they take in less calories, and thus lose weight. This weight loss cannot be sustained however; because people lose interest in the few boring foods that they are allowed to eat that do not contain carbohydrates. They usually gain all of the weight back that they lost. Besides, the no-carbohydrate diet doesn't do your body any good at all!

First, the quality of the diet suffers when carbohydrates are restricted. Without fruits, vegetables, and whole grains there is a lack of fiber, vitamins, minerals and anti-oxidants; all dietary factors that protect against disease. Low carbohydrate diets include extreme amounts of saturated fats that usually accompany high-protein foods, the leading cause of heart disease caused by clogging of the arteries. Excluding carbohydrates can lead to nausea, fatigue, constipation and low blood pressure; and that is for the average sedentary person. An active and fit person such as a competitive athlete cannot survive without carbohydrates. Both your health and your performance will suffer.

HOW MUCH CARBOHYDRATE SHOULD YOU EAT?

Most athletes that perform strenuous physical activity for several hours daily require a diet that is high in carbohydrates, a minimum of 55-65 % of the total food intake. (Player's diets should also include about 20-30 % protein for muscle and enzyme build up, and about 20 % of the good mono and poly-unsaturated fats. How much carbohydrate should you eat? Plenty, if you are a water polo player who trains several hours a day of high intensity exercise. Most adults eat only 150-250 grams of carbohydrate a day. That might be OK if you are sedentary. That is certainly not enough to fuel an athlete's body.

Most elite athletes need a lot more than the normal person, probably anywhere from 400-600 grams a day, depending on your training level, intensity and amount of training, gender, size, etc. Most water polo players, performing at a high level of training for ten-plus hours per week, will need about 3-4 grams of carbohydrate per pound of body weight. So, if you weigh 150 pounds, you will need between 450 to 600 grams per day of carbohydrate

WHAT SHOULD I EAT AND WHEN?

Just to give you an idea of what a gram of carbohydrate is, consider that a banana has about 20 grams, a large potato has 30 grams, a cup of fruit flavored non-fat yogurt has 24 grams, a sandwich with a lot of bread and some lean meat has 50 grams, while a plate of pasta has about 80 grams. Other good sources of carbohydrates include whole wheat breads and cereals, rice, beans, corn, fruits, and fruit bars.

It seems that it might take a lot of eating to get to 450-600 grams. There are several ways to accomplish this feat! One trick is to cut back on fatty foods to make room for more carbohydrates. Fats have a tendency to fill you up, and should be used sparingly. Instead of piling on tons of cheese and meat sauce on top of your pasta, eat the pasta with tomato sauce and sprinkled with a little parmesan cheese on top. Instead of eating french-fries that are loaded with saturated fats, eat baked potatoes or sweet potatoes and go light on the sour cream and butter. Milk is a great source of calcium and fairly good source of carbohydrates, but drink 2% fat milk instead of whole milk.

Try eating within two hours after training. This is the time when the body is more acceptable to carbohydrates and has the ability to store more glycogen in your muscles and liver. Eating after training is not always easy to do, especially if your team has an early morning training session, and you have to go to class right after training. Bring some food with you to morning practices for eating after training; something that you can carry and is easy to digest.

Fruits like bananas and apples, and food-bars are easy to carry; or if you can stop at a fruit bar and get a fruit smoothie. Smoothies are a great source of carbohydrates, they go down quickly, and they digest quickly. Watch the ones that are high fat though. Many fruit bars will list the ingredients in their smoothies, and will also list the percentages of fat, carbohydrates and proteins. Pick the ones with the most fruit and the least amount of fat.

Food bars (sport/energy bars) are a great way of meeting some of your carbohydrate needs and are easy to carry with you in your backpack. Make sure that you get high carbohydrate/low fat bars. Read the label and apply the 4 and 20 rule. Any bar that provides more than 20 grams of carbohydrate and less than 4 grams of fat is a good choice. Also, make sure that you drink water with your food bar to aid in digestion. If you can't meet your carbohydrate needs with three meals a day, try snacking between meals with food bars, fruit, fruit muffins, half a sandwich, anything that you can think of that provides some carbohydrates.

HOW DO I KNOW IF I AM NOT GETTING ENOUGH?
There are several ways of determining if you are getting enough carbohydrates. Probably the best way is how you feel. Everyone gets fatigued during a hard practice or game; but if you are still fatigued at night or the next day, if your performance in practice and games is lacking, if you aren't mentally alert, if you are tired all of the time and you can't seem to keep your weight at a normal level, then you probably need more carbohydrates in your diet.

If eating more and adding snacks doesn't work, then you might consider carbohydrate supplements. Supplements are available as gels and in liquid form. Marathon runners or tri-athletes that train many hours a day, and who start losing a lot of body weight usually use them. When the body runs out of glycogen, it turns to fats and proteins as a source for producing ATP. Burning fats is not much of a problem; but burning protein can be. Utilizing body protein means that a person is essentially using muscle tissue for energy. Not what an athlete would want if he wants to perform well.

During a ten-hour triathlon race, the body cannot store enough glycogen to get through the entire distance. So, many tri-athletes ingest high-glucose gels, or other high carbohydrate sources, during the actual race. Water polo players probably would not need this kind of supplement during a game or practice; but it might be a way to replenish your carbohydrates between games, when you have several games in one day.

TAPERING FOR GOOD PERFORMANCE

During a two-hour water polo practice you will probably use up many of your glycogen stores. So, if you don't replace the glycogen every day through ingesting carbohydrates, you will probably start the next days practice with a little less glycogen than you had the previous day. By the end of the week, it is possible that your glycogen stores will be at a very low level. That's OK if you are going to take the weekend off. But if you have an important game to play that will decide your league championship, or will decide whether you make it to post season competition; you may need to rest to help you restore your glycogen levels and give you the energy necessary to help win the game. The only way to accomplish this is to take in more carbohydrates in your diet, and burn off less carbohydrates by training less.

The best way to do this, and still get in the necessary training during the week, is to do a gradual taper. You can still have long and strenuous training sessions at the beginning of the week; but the practice sessions at the end of the week should be much shorter and much less strenuous. In other words, the practice sessions have to be "tapered down" in terms of intensity and length. If winning the weekly game is not that important to your team, and you don't need wins to take you to the post season, then you don't need to rest until the very end of the season. Many swim teams will not taper until the end of the season. That is when the swimmers have to do their best times. In swimming, taper means faster.

RESTING BETWEEN GAMES

Tournaments that require 4 or 5 games in a two or three-day period can be very demanding and require special rest and dietary requirements. Immediately after a game the players must do an easy loosen down swim in order to help dissipate the lactic acid that has built up during the game. They should then immediately eat foods that are easy to digest and high in complex carbohydrates, in order to help replenish the carbohydrate stores in the body. Fruits such as bananas not only add complex carbohydrates, and are easy to digest, but also add potassium; which helps keep a player from cramping up.

Pasta, potatoes cereals, whole-wheat breads, etc are also great carbohydrate sources, but don't load up too much on fats and proteins. Not only will they slow down the absorption of carbohydrates from the stomach, but will not help in producing energy stores for the next game. High energy glucose snacks like carbohydrate gels, or even jelly beans, can provide 25-30 grams of glucose to the body, as long as water is included to wash down the food and insure good absorption from the stomach.

It takes several hours for your stomach to empty so that you will feel comfortable playing in a game. That is why something that digests quickly, and still provides high carbohydrates, is the best food source for a between game snack. Fruit (mostly fruit) smoothies are probably the best food that meets these criteria; because they are high in carbohydrates and easy to digest.

HOW MUCH WATER SHOULD I DRINK?

Yes, even if you are playing in a pool full of water, you can still sweat and loose body fluids. Do you need to drink 8 glasses of water a day as some nutritionists recommend? It depends on several factors: How hot is the air and water temperature, how hard and how long you practice, and how much food you eat that contain large amounts of water. Thirst is usually a good indicator of your fluid needs; but when you are participating in physical activity in warm weather, you might not feel thirsty.

Athletes should start drinking before they start feeling thirsty, and continue drinking small amounts of water during training in warm conditions. The color of your urine is a good indicator of body fluid needs. Yellow or yellow-orange color indicates water stress, while nearly clear or light-yellow means that you are well hydrated. Foods also can provide certain amounts of fluid in your diet. If you keep track of your water needs and hydrate ahead of time in hot weather, you should be fine. If you start to feel light headed or nauseous, then you are possibly suffering from dehydration.

SPORTS DRINKS

Sports drinks are not only a great source of carbohydrate to help fuel your muscles; but also a great source of fluid for your body. Be careful that the sports drink that you drink does not contain too much sugar. Drinks that are have more than 8% sugar interfere with water absorption from your stomach. You may end up with a full and bloated stomach and very little fluid in your body where it is needed. Check the label. If it has more than 8 grams of sugar in 100 ml of volume, then it is too high in sugar. Also, make sure that you are getting a sports-drink and not an energy-drink. The energy from an energy-drink comes from huge amounts of caffeine, and not a lot of sugar. Caffeine will not help you perform better if you need more sugar to fuel your muscles.

NUTRITIONAL SUPPLEMENTS

Athletes are always looking for something that will give them an edge over their opponents. Be for-warned that there are all kinds of claims for this supplement, or that supplement, providing you with benefits that no other one can. Since nutritional supplements are technically classified as food, companies who manufacture these supplements can make any claim that they want, without doing any kind of research to support their claims. Most supplements are the same thing that you can probably get from the food that you ingest, and are not really needed.

THE FICTIONAL COMPOUND X

This is the way that these companies work: Let's say that your body needs a certain chemical (Compound X) to help you wiggle your big toe. Compound X is commonly found in tropical fruits like the Malay rose apple. You eat rose apples because you will be entering the toe wiggling Olympics next year, and you feel that you need Compound X to perform at your best. A company will come along and manufacture a pill that contains one thousand times the amount of compound X than your body needs to wiggle your toe, and then claim that their pill will make you a champion toe wiggler.

Since you want to be the best toe wiggler in the world, you will do just about anything to become the champion. Of course, the Compound X company has not done any research proving that their product improves your performance; doesn't have any proof that the huge amounts that they are giving you are any better than the amount you already have in your body, and have not been around long enough to determine if there are any long term side effects that could be detrimental to your health. But, after taking Compound X for a year, lo and behold, you just happen to win the Toe Wiggling Olympics! Of course, the reason for this was the Compound X pills, wasn't it?

It doesn't matter that you trained four hours a day wiggling your toe, or that you did hundreds of toe lifts with 5-lb weights, or that you did hundreds of toe stretches every day; or that you are just genetically endowed with the perfect toe that you inherited from your great-great grandmother. You won the Olympics! The company then approaches you with large amounts of money, and asks you to do ads for them promoting their product. Because you are the world champion, every toe wiggler in the world will buy the product that you endorse. The company will make money, you will make money, and every body is happy except for the poor sucker that does not improve his toe wiggling one little bit by taking Compound X pills.

Does this hypothetical situation sound a little preposterous to you? Actually this is a very common practice, especially when it comes to the sale of vitamin pills and other supplements in this country. This multi-million dollar industry will sell you vitamin pills that you do not need, will not improve your performance, can be toxic in large doses, and which are commonly found in most of the foods that you eat. There is a saying that Americans have the most expensive urine in the world; because that is where most of these vitamins end up. Save yourself a lot of money and eat a well balanced diet instead of buying expensive vitamins and supplements that you don't need.

DO YOU NEED ERGOGENIC (PERFORMANCE ENHANCING) AIDS?
Think twice before you consider taking any kind of supplements or ergogenic aid. Is it worth it to you to ingest a questionable product into your body, without really knowing the effects of the product? Is there enough proof, besides the word of the company selling the product, that it can help you to improve your performance? Has the product been around long enough to show long-term benefits, or long-term side effects?

Some products have proven ergogenic properties in some athletes, under certain conditions. They are creatine, sports drinks, carbohydrate supplements, caffeine and bicarbonate. But even those products cannot guarantee good performance. Long term effects of creatine are still not known and not recommended for athletes under 18 years of age. Creatine may help a 100-meter runner by providing a little more creatine phosphate for a 10-second sprint; but has not been shown to be beneficial in events that take longer to perform.

Are the benefits any better than a regimen of avoiding excess body fat, drinking plenty of fluids to avoid dehydration, eating enough carbohydrates to fuel your training program and resting to build up energy supplies. The bottom line is that "most nutritional supplements will not enhance sports performance in well nourished and well trained athletes". Train hard and eat well, instead of relying on a magic pill. There is no "easy road" to success.

Supplements are often better at making profits for their manufactures than they are at enhancing sports performance. The current climate in the world of supplements is that manufacturers can make any claim they want for their product, especially if it is labeled "natural", leaving it up to scientists to spend years of research to determine if they work, whether they are safe, and what is the best dose if they do appear to work. Caveat emptor (let the buyer beware).

MYTH- IF I EAT A LOT OF PROTEIN, I CAN BUILD BIG MUSCLES
TRUTH- In some sports there has been an over-use of protein supplements in order to help

grow bigger muscles. There is no scientific evidence supporting the popular belief that developing muscle mass requires massive amounts of protein. Gee, I wonder where that came from? Somebody trying to sell protein powder supplements perhaps? (remember Compond X) Please note that most people in our country have no problem in getting all the protein they need in their diet. In fact, we probably get more from our food than we will ever use, and that includes athletes and body-builders.

As in the ingestion of vitamin pills, most of the excess protein taken in by your body is often flushed out. In fact, too much protein has been implicated in chronic diseases such as osteoporosis, kidney stones and kidney disease, some cancers, heart disease and obesity. Bottom line: To gain muscle, follow a well-designed weight-training program and eat a healthy diet.

PLACEBO EFFECT- IT'S ALL IN YOUR MIND
Some athletes who take supplements will see an improvement of some kind and swear that they work. Performance improvement is not proof that a supplement worked. It may just be a convenient coincidence. Proof only comes when the same results can be repeated time and time again, under controlled scientific research. It is well known and documented that giving an athlete a pill can improve his performance, even though the pill was just simple sugar.

The question remains: what caused the change? The supplement itself, the fact that the athlete thought it would improve his performance, or the fact that the athlete would have improved for some other reason, without taking a supplement. (see Compound X).

MYTHS STARTED BY SWIMMING COACHES
First of all let me explain that swim coaches are involved in a sport that is completely different from water polo. The only thing the two sports have in common is that the athletes have to swim in the water to perform both of them. However, many of the training techniques that are used in swimming simply do not apply to water polo. Secondly, you have to understand that most swim coaches do not like water polo. The main reason being that they do not want to lose their swimmers to another sport, especially one that involves a ball, and scoring goals, and having fun. Let's see, what would you rather do? Put your face in the water and follow a little black line up and down the pool for hours; or play water polo? No brainer on this one!

Don't get me wrong. I am all for letting my water polo players join the swim team during the off-season. I think that it helps them to become better water polo players. What bothers me is the swim coaches that will not allow their swimmers to play water polo at all; not even for a few months. It would probably help the swimmers mentally to play a team sport for a few months out of the year, and get away from staring at the bottom of the pool. Some of the myths that swim coaches perpetuate are simply to keep their swimmers on the swim team, and off the water polo team.

WATER POLO MESSES UP YOUR SWIM STROKE
This is the first myth that swimming coaches try to spread about water polo. While it may be true that the freestyle swimming stroke is different than the water polo freestyle stroke, you are still using similar muscles and using the same muscles and cardiovascular systems. It would seem that it would be rather simple to change from one to the other. What is the difference between switching from water polo freestyle stroke to swimming freestyle stroke, and switching from butterfly, backstroke and breaststroke to freestyle stroke? Those four swimming strokes are completely different; yet swimmers make that switch all of the time,

sometimes during the same event, the individual medley. Actually, the water polo stroke is closer to the freestyle stroke than any of the other three competitive strokes. This argument does not hold water! (Pardon the pun)

WATER POLO GETS YOU OUT OF SHAPE FOR SWIMMING

Water polo is definitely different than swimming a 1500-meter swim race, so I would have to agree with swim coaches there. But, the simple fact is that swimmers probably do a lot of unnecessary swimming as it is. This statement is coming from the same swim coaches who have their swimmers train for a short 50-yard two lap race by swimming 10,000 yards a day. Most swim races are 100-200 yards long and swum at a very fast pace. Granted, water polo will not get you in shape to swim your fastest 200-yard swim race; but it certainly can't hurt you.

Water polo is essentially "speed" work for several hours a day. It is certainly more speed work than some swimmers will get in their swim workouts. I have always believed that swimmers swim more yardage than necessary for the length of the actual race. Maybe they should try a little water polo so they can learn to swim fast? Just kidding, swim coaches!

One of the fastest swimmers in the world played water polo for me at Stanford, Olympic gold medalist Pablo Morales. At the end of the fall water polo season, Pablo would join the swim team and swim in an early season meet. His early-season swim times, coming just off the water polo season, were still the best on the swim team for that time of the year. Of course he would do even faster times at the end of a long swim training season of 4-5 months. After playing water polo in the fall of one year, Pablo broke the world-record in the 100-meter butterfly that next summer. He seems to have recovered pretty well from that "terrible" water polo season that got him out of shape and ruined his stroke.

WARM-UP

The right warm up should do three things: Loosen muscles and tendons to increase the range of motion of various joints, literally warm-up the body by increasing body temperature, and prepare the body for the intensity of the practice or a game. When you are at rest, there's less blood flow to muscles and tendons, and they stiffen. A well-designed warm-up starts by increasing body heat and blood flow. One of the by-products of muscle contraction is the production of heat. So, if you want to increase the temperature of your body, you have to use your muscles.

To raise the body's temperature, a warm-up must begin with aerobic activity, usually light to medium speed swimming of about 400 yards. Gradually increase the speed and change strokes as you go along, utilizing as many muscles as possible. The warm-up also includes some breaststroke, which will help get the legs ready to perform the eggbeater kick. The next 100 yards can be broken down into 25-yard "build" swims that start out slowly at the beginning of each length, and then ending with a little burst of speed at the end. These actions by them self should warm up the swimming muscles and help increase range of motion.

Next the legs should be warmed up with easy eggbeater, and the arms with easy passing. The legs and arms can be warmed-up the same time by gradually increasing the distance between two passers, passing the ball while using the eggbeater kick. After warming up the legs and arms the players should take some shots on the goal, gradually increasing the intensity of the shot. And then finally, about 5-10 minutes before the game is to begin, the team should do about four sprints at full speed. This should get the players ready to go at game speed right at the start of the game, and still give them time to recover from the sprints.

If the team has to get out of the pool for introductions after they have warmed up, they should all get in the pool after the introductions and swim across the pool and back, with a few quick arm strokes at the end; so they will be ready to go once the game starts. The same hold true for a substitute who has been sitting on the bench for a while. When he gets into the game, he should swim from the corner of the pool to the centerline, again with a few quick strokes to get the blood circulating and to get him ready to go hard when the game starts.

MYTH- COOLING DOWN IS NECESSARY AFTER YOU EXERCISE

TRUTH- The primary reason for cooling down (i.e. swimming easy at the end of the workout or game) is to help dissipate any lactic acid that has built-up from anaerobic-glycolytic work. Swimming slowly will help your circulatory system move the lactic acid around the body, so that it is not concentrated in the working muscles. This is NOT necessary unless the lactic acid build up might have an effect on your very next performance. This can only happen in a swim meet when you have two events close together, or a water polo tournament where you have two games very close together. Other than that, there is no need to cool down after you swim, especially if your next time in the pool is the next day, or much later on the same day. Lactic acid will dissipate completely by itself over a period of time. Most certainly, it will be gone after a period of several hours.

Some water polo teams will have their players do a several-minute easy swim at the beginning of the long ten-minute half time of a game. This serves two purposes. For the starters, or players who have played an intense first half, it will help dissipate lactic acid accumulation and prepare them for the start of the second-half. For the players who have not seen much action in the first half, it will serve as a second warm-up to get them ready to play in the second half, if they are needed.

STRETCHING, IS IT NECESSARY?

When challenged, many stretching teachers and enthusiasts have a hard time explaining why they are stretching. The value of stretching has been elevated to dogma without justification. Everyone just "knows" that it's a good thing. Stretching is a part of conditioning programs in many sports that has been passed down for years, without any evidence that it works, and no reasons for why it is necessary. It is absurd to think that you can actually stretch a muscle, that it will improve you performance, and that it will prevent injuries to that muscle. It is a fact that muscles do not stretch!!

A muscle that is connected to two bones by tendons and ligaments can be contracted to produce power, or elongated when you move the bones away from each other. A muscle will always return to it's original length after is contracted or elongated. What actually stretches in a muscle are the series elastic components of the muscle (mostly connective tissue) and the ligaments and tendons. Stretching of the ligaments that surround a muscle joint and hold it in place actually lessens the structural integrity of the joint capsule, especially of the shoulder joint. The last thing that you want to do to a water polo player is to make the shoulder joint less structurally sound.

When pressed for reasons, people will come up a few predictable "reasons" for stretching. Here are the four "hopeful" reasons that I hear all of the time.

1. Warming up

2. Prevention of muscle soreness

3. Prevention of injury

4. Flexibility

None of these can be supported with evidence, or even has a persuasive rationale. Stretching for these reasons is probably a waste of your time.

DOES STRETCHING WARM UP THE MUSCLES?

Some coaches use stretching for a warm up at the beginning of the workout or game. Stretching does not warm up a muscle. As mentioned above in the section on warming-up, in order to warm up a cold muscle a person needs to contract the muscle to produce heat. Stretching does not contract the muscle, and thus does not produce the heat required to warm up. Stretching a cold muscle can, in fact, injure the muscle and joint and is not recommended by trainers and exercise physiologists. You simply cannot warm up your muscles by stretching them. That's like trying to cook a steak by pulling on it.

STRETCHING DOES NOT PREVENT SORENESS

Another popular idea about stretching is that it prevents that insidious deep tenderness that follows a hard workout. That soreness is called "delayed onset muscle soreness, or DOMS for short. Many people stretch after exercise in hopes of eliminating these sore muscles. People believe this like it's a religion. Unfortunately, the evidence suggests that they are kidding themselves. Many studies have shown that nothing short of amputation can prevent DOMS, and certainly not stretching.

STRETCHING TO PREVENT INJURIES?

The most common reason that you hear about the benefits of stretching have to do with preventing injuries. The most common water polo injuries are shoulder related, usually from a traumatic event that pulls the arm back when it is extended, or from overuse of the shoulder from too much shooting and swimming. Stretching the muscle does nothing to help prevent or overcome this kind of injury.

In land sports like football and baseball, pulled hamstrings are a common injury that occur frequently, even though players stretch the hamstrings constantly. Usually these kinds of injuries are caused by a sudden contraction of a cold muscle. Players sit around for long periods of time, let their muscles cool down, and then suddenly run an all out sprint. Stretching can do nothing to prevent this type of reaction by the muscle. A good warm-up before they use the cold muscle will help a lot more than anything else.

DOES STRETCHING MAKE YOU MORE FLEXIBILE?

There are not any studies in exercise physiology that show that stretching can aid athletic performance by making you more flexible. It is a fact that stretching does not make you more flexible. Flexibility or lack of flexibility is limited by the structure of the bones and the muscles that are connected to the bones. You can only extend your arm so far before it is stopped by the bony structure of the elbow joint. Flex your arm and you will see that you can only go so far before the muscle mass of the forearm and bicep muscle coming together prevent you from going any farther. If flexibility is important in your sport, hope that you were born with a joint structure that allows you go beyond the range for a normal person.

CHAPTER 7
STRATEGIES IN GAME SITUATIONS

Water polo is a game of situations. The strategies that a player uses in those situations can be critical to the success or failure of a team. A player should go over all the possible situations that can occur in the game, and be sure that he understands them and understands what to do in those situations. Most game situations involve clock management, be it the shot clock or the game clock. Managing the game and shot clocks is an important part of the game for all teams, and can make a difference of a several goal swing in either direction.

Team offense and team defense is usually decided on by the coach, and is part of his overall philosophy of the game, and how he wants the game played. Both will be covered in this chapter as part of learning how and why the game is played, and to understand why coaches choose one offense or defense over another. The actual strategies and tactics used will ultimately be up to the coach to decide.

The introduction of the 30-second shot clock makes it even more important for players to know what to do when the shot clock is winding down. Going over game situations and using a shot clock in practice will give players an idea of what they are supposed to do. It is up to the player to go over these situations in his mind, and have a clear picture of what to do. It is up to the coach to practice these situations, and make sure that every player understands what to do. It only takes one player, who doesn't know what is going on, to mess up and cost his team the game.

BASIC TEAM DEFENSE

When a team is prepared and committed to playing defense every time they jump into the pool; that team has an opportunity to win any game. Defense is a constant. It can help you win games even when your team is having an off night offensively. Your opponents may be more physically talented; but if you can limit their ability to score, and take away the things they want to do, you should be in position to win just about every game. Not everyone is skilled at scoring goals, but anyone can play defense. All you need is the desire to stop the other team from scoring

To play good defense it is extremely important to be disciplined and play together as a team. The players all must be working together and playing the same defense. If one player is not doing his job, or not playing within the system, the defense breaks down. Every player must contribute and play within the defensive scheme in order for the team to succeed.

DEFENSIVE GOALS
Defense can change the tempo of the game and be disruptive. It can be used to force opponents into playing offensive schemes that they are uncomfortable playing against. The aim of every great defensive team is to take something away from their opponents. Your goal as a team is to never make it easy for the opposition to execute their offense. By putting constant pressure on your opponents you are able to force them to run out the shot clock, get off an ill advised shot, or force them to throw bad passes.

STRENGTHS AND WEAKNESSES

No defense is perfect. A defense that is designed to take something away from the other team, usually means that the defense is giving up something else. For instance a zone defense helps take away the other teams offense by denying the ball to the center forward; but gives up the outside shot, and also limits a team's counterattack opportunities. If you have a goalie that is good at blocking outside shots and the other team has a good 2-meter player, you might want to play a zone.

A press defense can put pressure on your opponents, and perhaps create turnovers that can lead to counterattack goals. One weakness of the press is that it leaves the area in front of the center-forward open. Players pressing all around the pool are not in position to "crash" back or "slough" back and take or deny the ball to the center forward. This can be overcome; but it requires playing in front of center forward and denying him the ball.

THE ALMOST PERFECT DEFENSE-PRESS TO A ZONE

A defense that combines the two styles of defense as described above, the press and the zone, would seem to be an almost perfect defense; especially if they are both used during the same 30-second possession. The "press to a zone" defense is used by many European club and National teams, and by a few high school and college teams in this country. It starts with a pressing, passing lane, and hole-fronting style of defense designed to delay the ball getting down the pool, and into the center forward. The defensive team stays in the press as long as they can, taking as much time off of the clock as they can, until the hole-defender loses his position in front of the center forward.

It is at this time that the press is most vulnerable to the ball going into 2-meters. To overcome this apparent weakness, the goalie or hole-defender will call the team back into some type of a zone defense that is designed to keep the ball out of 2-meters. Ideally, the offense will have to utilize all of their allotted time and will be forced into a situation where the have to take a low percentage shot or dump the ball into the corner. This style of defense gives the defensive team the best opportunity to do this, and in my opinion is the best utilization of both the press and zone defenses. It is described in the "press to a zone" section later in this chapter.

WHAT DEFENSE TO PLAY?

A coach has to constantly weigh all the factors when he is designing a defense to play. By knowing the strengths and weaknesses of the other team, he can design his defense to take away what the other team does well, and at the same time try to neutralize key players. He can only do this if he also knows the strengths and weaknesses of the different kinds of zone and press defenses, what they take away, and what they allow your opponents and your own team to do.

A coach has to consider many other factors as well when deciding the defense he will play. The game situation, the score of the game, who is in the lead, the time left in the game, the time left on the shot clock, and the kind of calls the referees are making, are all factors that the coach has to consider when making defensive decisions.

Sometimes a coach may want to change the team's defense to surprise the other team when they are expecting something else. After a team's opponents have time to prepare for the defense a team is playing, after a time out, starting or ending a game and/or quarter, and post season competition, are all opportunities to surprise the other team with a different defense.

PRESSURE DEFENSE-DELAY THE BALL

Good defense starts with putting pressure on your opponents. A team should never make it easy for their opponent to swim down the pool and set up their frontcourt offense. Now with the new 30-second shot clock, it makes it even more important to press the man with the ball; because teams will have less time to get the ball into the front-court and get a shot off. The longer it takes to get the ball down the pool and the longer a defense can keep the ball out of the hole position, the less time the opponents will have to run their offense.

CREATE TURNOVERS

By putting good pressure on the ball while the rest of the team plays in passing lanes, including playing in front of the wings and the hole, you can force bad passes and create turnovers. This leads to easy counterattack goals. If you force your opponent into a situation where they have to shoot because they are running out of time, you can counterattack from positions away from the ball and create more counterattack situations for your team. The main thing that a press does for you is that it makes it harder for the other team to score, by limiting the shots that they take. Every turnover results in one less shot on goal for your opponent, and one more counterattack opportunity for your team.

EVERYONE DOES HIS PART

Press defense does require disciplined play from everyone on the team. Every part of the defense is critical. If one player doesn't do his part, the defense fails. You have to put trust in your teammates that they will do their part of the defense. This is where coaching comes into play. Players are well aware of how to shoot the ball and play offense. Coaches have to teach them how to play team defense. Players also have to "commit" to defense and buy into the fact that it can help you win games.

SUCCESS WITH THE PRESS

There are a number of critical elements to a successful press defense. First of all, the ball must be pressed immediately on the counterattack, especially the first pass from the goalie. Every pass must be contested; press hard, but try not to commit a foul. Not fouling the man with the ball is a key element of the press. Fouling stops the clock and defeats the purpose of the press. Try to avoid the foul by not reaching over the right shoulder, use your legs, and always have one hand up; two hands if you can, especially if the player lets go of the ball. Try to disrupt and cause a bad pass by hitting the elbow as the player is throwing the ball.

PASSING LANES

While the ball is being pressed, the rest of the defenders must play in the passing lanes between the ball and the persons they are defending. A poor pass caused by pressure on the ball can be intercepted in the passing lane and lead to a counterattack by the defenders. (See next Chapter 8, Diagram 8-1 and Pictures 8-F and 8-G for details on passing lane defense)

PRESSURE ON THE BALL

Keeping pressure on the ball is a key element in allowing the hole-guard to play in front of the hole man. As the other team is bringing the ball down the pool, the hole guard allows the hole man to swim into the 2-meter position, and then slips in front of him. He cannot do this if the ball is not under pressure, and the passer is allowed to make an easy uncontested pass into the hole as the guard is fronting.

Any overpass to the hole man has to be intercepted by the goalkeeper. The goalie has to anticipate the overpass to the center. He must come out of the goal quickly and arrive as the same time as the ball arrives. This strategy denies the ball into the hole and thus keeps the opponent from running an offensive set.

DENY THE WING

Another critical part of the press is that the ball cannot be allowed to be passed into the fronted hole man from the wing position. Playing in front of the wing player should deny the wing the ball. If the ball does arrive at the wing position, he should be fouled, so that the goalie can come out of the goal to cover the possible pass into the hole man.

COORDINATION

All of the above defensive tactics must happen together in a coordinated manner in order for the press defense to be effective. If one player does not play his role, the defense falls apart. Pressure on the ball is required at all times. If any one player does not press the ball, the defense breaks down and the opposition has an easier chance to score. Pressure allows the other defensive players to play the passing lanes, front the wings, and also front the 2-meter player.

ZONE DEFENSE

There will occur a time during the possession when the hole-guard will lose front position. He may be forced behind by a stronger hole man; or he may choose to go behind when the holeman's position is 4 or 5 meters away from the goal. This is the most logical time to go into a zone defense. The zone will allow a team to be in better position to crash back on the hole man, much more than a press defense would.

PRESS TO A ZONE

Going from a press defense to a zone defense within a single 30 second shot period depends entirely on whether the 2-meter defender can hold front position on the 2- meter center forward. Once the defender has lost front position, the outside defenders must come back into a zone to be in position to double back and help on the center forward. The type of zone that the team will drop into depends on what pre-planed zone the coach wants to implement.

Going from a press to a zone is not difficult at any level. It does take awareness and communication, however. Awareness comes from your outside players knowing that the hole guard is loosing, or has lost front position; and communication from the hole-guard or goalie calling for players to drop back. The easiest way to start the zone defense is to simply have the closest player not guarding the man with the ball drop back in front of the hole man and deny the pass into him. From that initial defensive drop, the rest of the team then ladders back into the zone called for by the coach.

PARTIAL VERSUS FULL ZONES

The obvious reason for running a zone is to put the defense in a better position to double team and crash on to a strong center forward. It does have its drawbacks, however. It allows an uncontested outside shot, and also doesn't put defenders in the best position for a counterattack. Zone defenders have to take several strokes just to get even with the player they are countering, whereas defenders who are pressing only have to take one stroke to get past their man.

A defense can overcome these disadvantages by employing partial zones, where defenders drop off selected players or selected weaker positions, and press everywhere else. The defense can drop off the weakest shooter from the other team and give him the shot; or they can drop off right- handed shooters that are on the left-handers side of the pool. The defenders who are not dropping back into a zone are pressing, and in a better position to counterattack.

THE 2-4 ZONE

Diagram 7-1, below, shows a 2-4 zone defense with the ball at the O2 (right hander flat) position and the hole defender X6 plays on the right shoulder of the hole man O6 inviting the pass to the left shoulder. In this type of defense the X3 (point) defender plays in the passing lane between the O2 and O4 attackers, putting him in position to intercept the pass between them and also in position to counterattack. In this situation the crash (drop) on the hole man will come from the defender at the X4 position. This zone is one of the easiest for a defense to go into when going from a press to a zone, because only two defenders have to drop back, X2 and X4.

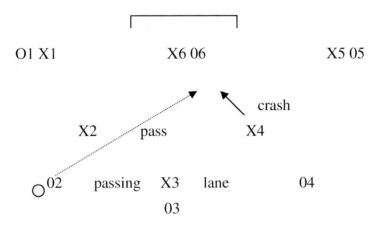

Diagram 7-1   2-4 Zone. X2 and X4 drop back while X3 plays in the passing lane.

THE 4-5 ZONE

A popular partial zone against an all right-handed opponent is to drop off the left wing O5 and left flat O4 positions. If a team has one left-hander, you drop off whatever position, 4 or 5, the left-hander is not occupying. The other defenders on your team are still pressing, thus putting them in better position to counterattack. Right-handers shooting from 4 or 5 are not very effective from that side of the pool and with that angle of a shot.

The biggest advantage gained from this defense is that the X4 and X5 defenders are in good position to crash on the hole man without giving up a high percentage shot from a right-hander playing at O4 or O5. Another advantage of this defense is that both X2 and X3 are in a good position for the counterattack. The goalkeeper can expect the shot from only one side of the goal (from 04 and 05), and he doesn't have to switch sides or worry about shots from the other side of the goal. (See Diagram 7-2 below)

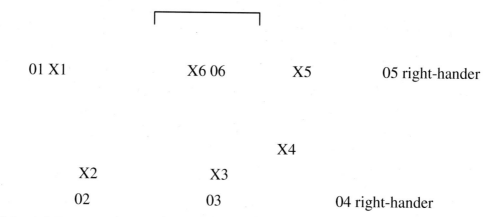

Diagram 7-2: 4-5 Zone. X5 and X4 drop back while everyone else presses.

STANDARD ZONE

A standard zone defense is commonly called a 2-3-4 drop. The advantage of this zone is that it effectively prevents the ball getting to the 2-meter player. If the ball does get in the hole-man all three outside defenders X2, X3 and X4 are in position to crash on the hole man. The disadvantage of this zone is that the top three defenders are not in good position for a counterattack. The counter must come from the wing defenders X1 and X5 and from the 2-meter defender X6. (See Diagram 7-3 below)

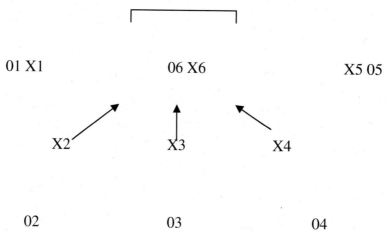

Diagram 7-3: Standard 2-3-4 Zone. X2, X3 and X4 drop back into zone.

GAP DEFENSE

Zone defenses that put a team in the best position for a counterattack are gap defenses, where defenders play in the spaces (gaps) between outside players. The most common gap defense used around the world is called the M-Zone defense (so called because of the letter created when drawing a line between defenders) shown in figure. Besides the advantage that it gives a team on the counterattack, it also keeps the ball away from the hole man by placing a defender both in front and behind him. Disadvantages of the "M" are that it does give up the outside shot, and it can only be run for a short period of time.

Because of the position of the defenders when a shot is taken, they have a good chance of getting a man free on the counterattack. The gap defense is a great surprise defense that a team can spring on an unsuspecting opponent at the right moment. Perhaps a team is behind and needs a goal at the end of a game; or the other team has just called a time out. A team can come out into the "M" zone. As the team on offense takes the shot, the gap defenders take off down the pool, gaining a free man on the counterattack with a good chance to score a goal. At the very least it takes the offense out of what they had planned to do. (See Diagram 7-4 below)

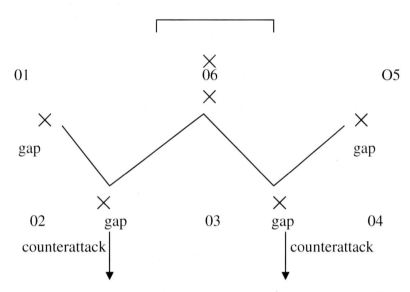

Diagram 7-4: M-zone gap defense. The defenders form an "M" formation.

The basic details of the "M" are that the defense double-teams the hole man by having players in front and behind him. The remaining defenders play in the spaces (gaps) between the five perimeter players, harassing the ball, looking for the steal or the shot, and ready for the counterattack.

SHOT CLOCK SITUATIONS-DEFENSE

LEAVING EARLY

As a defensive player, you are expected to counterattack the other team when there is a turnover, shot on goal, or when the shot clock runs out. A smart defensive player can also create easy goal scoring opportunities for him self by leaving his defensive position before the shot clock expires, and as the team on offense is running out of time. When a defender is guarding an offensive player who is out of position to be a scoring threat, or a player with the ball who also happens to be in a weak scoring position, and there are only a few seconds left on the shot clock; the defender can take advantage of the situation and take off early on the counterattack towards the other end of the pool.

THE PSYCHOLOGY OF LEAVING EARLY

The idea here is that the defender hopes to take advantage of the offensive player with or without the ball who has to stay on offense, won't be in a good shooting position to take a high percentage shot, and will not be able to follow the defender down the pool. The person that you leave has to make a decision on whether to stay on offense, pass the ball, shoot or dump the ball; or follow you down the pool. If the defender does this correctly, the offensive player will not be in a good position to shoot, and he will not be in a good position to follow down the pool. In other words, "He is caught between a rock and a hard place".

Taking off early may not work every time you try it; but once a player learns the correct time and situation to leave early, it can work several times a game and give your team a few goals that you would not have had otherwise. If you can score several goals a game with this strategy, it will be worth it. In addition, it will make the other team be more hesitant on offense for fear of you taking off down the pool every time.

WHO DO YOU LEAVE?

This can be accomplished if the person that the defender is guarding is holding the ball: or even a player without the ball, as long as he is not a threat to score. An example of this would be a wing player, or someone far enough away from the goal that he is not a threat to score or receive the ball and score. Timing is critical in this situation; so the defender has to really be aware of the shot clock and how much time is left. There cannot be enough time remaining on the clock that would allow the player that is left alone to become a threat to score. You have to try this in practice every day, so that you start getting a feel for when to leave and who to leave.

Examples of which player to leave from: 1) Foul the wing player with the ball with less than five seconds on the clock, and then immediately take off down the pool. Fouling takes away his opportunity to shoot the ball. He cannot chase you until he does something with the ball; either pass it or dump it in the corner. 2) Take off on a wing player with the ball without fouling him, so that the clock doesn't stop. The wing has a very bad angle shot and doesn't have enough time to move in for a better shot. 3) Foul the player with the ball at 8-10-yards away from the goal, and then take-off down the pool. He has to take a long distance shot or pass the ball to someone else. He will not have time to do anything else. If you want to avoid stopping the clock, then take off without fouling.

4) Foul the shooter as he is taking the shot, especially if your goalie has a chance to make the block, or you need a goal at the end of the game when your team is loosing. 5) Take off on an offensive player who does not have the ball, and is far from the goal or on the wing. Even if he receives the ball he will not have time to move closer for a shot. 6) You can try and take off on a player with the ball inside the five-meter line; but this is a risky move unless there is little time left on the clock. If you foul him, he cannot shoot because he is inside the five. He also will not have enough time to pass the ball outside and then get it back again near the front of the goal. I would not try this unless it is at the end of the game and you are desperate to get a goal. (See Diagram 7-5 on the next page)

COUNTER THE SHOOTER

Always counter the player who shoots the ball, because he will have to turn around and chase you after he takes the shot. You should be able to beat the shooter every time down the pool. Especially take off on any player who takes a bad angle shot from the wing, or a player who forces an 8-10-yard desperation shot at the end of the 30-second shot clock. The proper technique in this situation is to take off as the shot is being taken. The defender can take off on the shooter even if there is a lot of time left on the clock. Your goalie should be able to make an easy block on these kinds of low percentage shots, and you will be swimming free at the other end. (See Diagram 7-5 below)

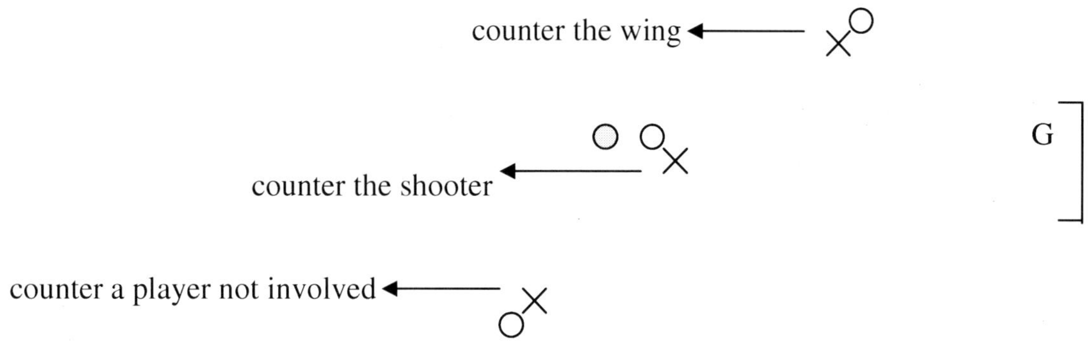

counter the wing

counter the shooter

G

counter a player not involved

Diagram 7-5: Situations for beating your man on the counterattack.

BASIC TEAM OFFENSE

The offense that a team will run will depend on many factors, the most important being the rules of the game and how they are being interpreted at the time. Coaches around the world will try to take advantage of the rules in designing their team offense. For many years in this country the rules that we played by were different from international rules. As a result we played a different game than they did overseas, as well as at the Olympic games. Players on our National team had to make big adjustments in the way they played the game whenever they traveled outside the USA.

In present day water polo the rules and the game that we play in this country are very similar, if not the same, as that played around the world. However there are still differences in the way the game is being called and the style of play internationally and in the United States.

DEFENSE DICTATES THE OFFENSE
Most of the rules of the game are written to control what you can or cannot do on defense. How a player fouls another player, and the consequence of those fouls, are really what the rules are all about. All the offense is doing is reacting to what the rules say the defense can do or can't do. So, in essence, the defense that is allowed by the rules usually dictates what a team will do on offense.

FOCUS ON THE CENTER
Even though the rules are basically the same around the world, the style of offense is different, but the same in one respect. The center forward has always been the focus of the offense. He is usually the biggest and strongest player and also the closest to the goal, and consequently the biggest threat to score. Most offenses in the past 60-70 years have tried to get the ball to the center forward /hole man/2-meter man. In the early years it was because the

center forward was the biggest threat to score from his position just in front of the goal. In recent years it has been to draw an exclusion foul on the 2-meter defender so the team could play an extra-man offense.

THE FOCUS OF THE OFFENSE

Because it is difficult to score from the 2-meter position, most teams focus on drawing exclusions at that position, so they can gain an extra-man situation. The main focus of the offensive game is still to get the ball into the 2-meter position. Because of more sophisticated defenses that drop in on the center-forward from the outside defenders, and just plain outright heavy fouls, it is very difficult for the center forward to score. His main job is to get position in front of the goal, and then draw the exclusion foul. Any natural goals scored usually come from outside shots against a drop (zone) defense designed to keep the ball from the 2-meter player.

WHAT SKILLS DO YOU NEED TO PLAY TODAY"S GAME?

Shooting against a zone is now one of the primary skills that an offensive player must possess in order to be successful. Both the frontcourt offense and the 6 on 5 extra-man offense rely on players who can score by shooting over and around the defender's arm. Zone shooting must be practiced daily with defenders in front of the shooters and from all angles. 6 on 5 shooting must also be practiced with defenders indifferent positions in front of the goal.

THE PRIMARY PASSER HAS BECOME A PERIMETER PLAYER

What has happened in water polo today is that instead of the hole-man being the passer in the offense, a perimeter player who has the ball has become the primary passer. On a team that has mostly right-handed players, the perimeter player at the 04 position becomes the primary passer. Depending on whether the defense is playing a press or a zone defense, the 04 player has different options.

OPTIONS AGAINST A PRESS

Against a team that presses on defense, the first priority is that the primary passer at 04 has a free pass. Without the free pass it is difficult to pass the ball to an open man. Some defenses will foul the 04 player and drop in to cover the center forward, especially if 04 is a right-hander. The thinking here is that a right-handed 05 player is less of a threat than right-handers at 02 and 03, so the defense will foul him. If 04 is not fouled, then he must draw the foul and get a free pass. Once 04 is awarded the free pass, his teammates at 01, 02, and 03, upon hearing the whistle, must create some kind of movement to free themselves to receive the pass. (See Diagram 7-6 on the next page)

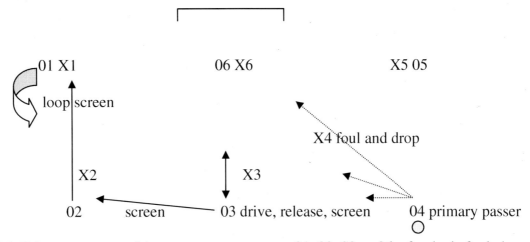

Diagram 7-6: Primary passer at 04 passes to open man at 01, 02, 03 or 06, after he is fouled. Players at 02 and 03 are the primary targets for a pass from 04. Their options include the following:

Drive past the defender for an inside position in front of the goal.

Drive forward and release back to receive the cross-pass for an outside shot.

02 and 03 run a pick or screen to free one of them for the pass and shot.

02 drives and screens off the X1 guard, while 01 loops around and receives the cross pass.

If a team has a player who is excellent at driving for inside water, put him at 02 and let him drive towards the post. Many teams will drop the X1 defender to "help in" on the 02 driver. To open up the space in front of the goal, and to eliminate the help from X1, the wing player 01 must drive all the way across the goal to the 05 wing area, taking the defender X1 with him. 02 then drives to "open water" and receives pass from 04 (See Diagram 7-7 below).

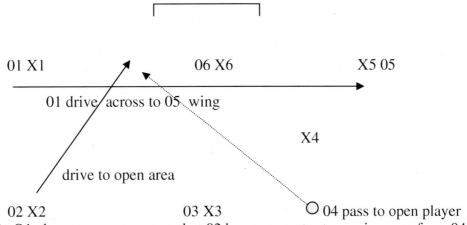

Diagram 7-7: O1 clears out post area so that 02 has open water to receive pass from 04.

OPTIONS AGAINST A ZONE
The primary passer 04 who is playing against a drop defense has several options on what he can do with the ball. He can shoot the ball directly at the goal, he can pass into the hole man (wet or dry), he can pass to the hole man going back door to the post, he can make a pass to a teammate on the other side of the pool, or he can pass inside to a driver who has beaten his man to the post area. It is essential that players who play the 04 position are good passers, and make good decisions on distributing the ball. Aside from the center forward, the primary passer at 04 has become the key player in the offense. (See Diagram 7-8 below).

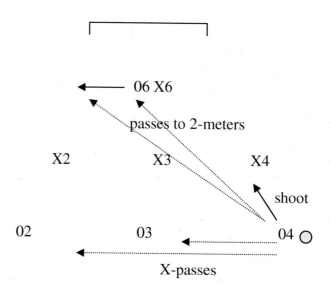

Diagram 7-8: Zone options

GETTING BALL INTO TWO-METERS AGAINST THE PRESS
Before you can even think about getting the ball in two-meters, the hole-man has to get himself set to receive the ball. He should set in one direction and hold that position by keeping the hole-defender behind him by any means possible. If he is being fronted, then he has to make a move like a spin to the outside in order to get to one side. Then he can muscle himself to a front position with his back to the defender and then hold the defender so that he cannot get back around him.

Once the perimeter players can see in the direction that he is set on, they can work the ball around to that side. In order to insure a successful pass, the ball should come into 2-meters from a position that is in front of where the center forward is facing. The two-meter player must turn his back to the defender so that he can face the passer and present a target for him.

RELEASING WITH MOVEMENT
The most effective way to get the ball around to the side the hole man is set to, is for the perimeter player who will receive the ball, to release from the defender who is pressing him. Movement is the key to releasing against the press. A good release move should give that player the space and time he needs to pass the ball into 2 meters. The player who is directly in

front of the hole man can release by moving forward as if to drive, and then release back for the ball. He can also run a little pick or screen to help release the man next to him, or he can drive towards the wing and screen the wing guard; and then have the wing release back out for the ball. (See Diagram 7-14 below for release details).

GETTING THE BALL INTO 2-METERS AGAINST A ZONE

Since there are zone defenders playing directly in front of the center-forward, the first thing the offense must do is clear at least one of the defenders out of the area. It is preferable to clear out the defender X3 who is playing directly in front in front. This can be done by driving the 03 player thru to the wing, or driving 02 to the wing and sliding 03 to the left to take the 02 position. Having players at only the 02 and 04 positions creates a space in front of the hole man, making it easier to get the ball into him.

It also creates a longer cross pass between 02 and 04, moving the goalie and defenders and creating an easier shot off the cross pass. The player with the ball must first move forward in a shooting position in order to commit the defender to him. If the defender stays back, he has the option to shoot the ball. If the defender commits to him, he can either pass the ball into 2-meters, or throw the X-pass to his teammate. One or two cross passes between 2 and 4 will open up that space in front of the center-forward even more, with both outside players having the same options of passing or shooting.

BEATING THE ZONE WITH A DOUBLE POST

Sometimes adding a second forward to the mix at a post-position opposite the center-forward can create confusion among the zone defenders; because there are two centers playing behind them instead of one. Start the team's second center forward, or the best driver, at the 01 wing position. Since the wing player will not draw the opposition's top defender, a mismatch can be created with a smaller person, or non-2-meter defender, guarding that position. The wing then drives ball-side to the post, while the center forward moves to the other post. The ball should go to first post because of the possible mismatch at that position. Once he receives the ball at the post, he can draw an exclusion, or step out and take a shot against the less experienced defender guarding him.

BEATING THE "M" ZONE DEFENSE

The "M" Zone defense can be beat with time and movement of outside players. Because the defenders are playing in-between offensive players and not in front of them, it is easier to drive. Shots can be created for the offense by moving or driving. If the offense is running out of time on the shot clock, then the easiest method of beating the M, that doesn't require a lot of time, is to drive the right-hander at O2. First, the ball must be in the hands of 03 or 04, preferably 04. If 04 is right-handed, he won't be blind-sided by X4. When X2 turns to look at the ball, O2 must take 2-3 strokes to the open area behind X2, and stop quickly and get into a shooting position before X1 can pick him up. On the pass to 02, the players at 03 and 04 must immediately turn around and swim towards the other end of he pool in order to prevent X2 and X4 from getting open on the subsequent counterattack. (See Diagram 7-9 on next page).

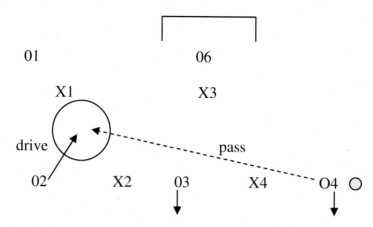

Diagram 7-9: A quick way to beat the M-Zone. Drive 02 behind the gap defender.

DRIVE ACROSS

Have the player at 01 drive completely across the goal to the opposite wing. This really opens up the shot for 02 after the drive, because 01 and X1 are not in the way of the shot. This play takes a little longer to execute so you may not want to try it unless you have the time. Should 01 drive in front or behind the center forward 06? It depends on the position of the 2-meter player and what works best for your team. There might not be enough room to maneuver behind the 2-meter forward and guard. (See Diagrams 7-10a below and 7-10b on next page)

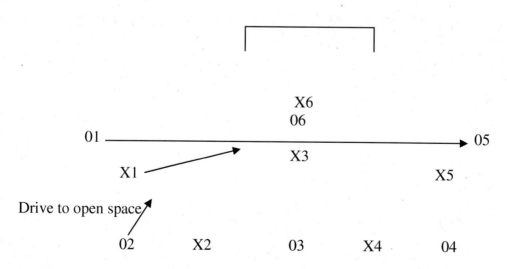

Diagram 7-10a: Drive 01 across the goal to open up space for driver 02

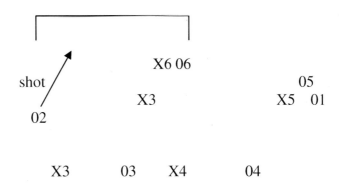

Diagram 7-10b: After drive across goal, area opens up for driver 02 to receive ball and shoot.

OFFENSE AGAINST A 4-5 Zone

Some defenses play a zone by dropping off right-handers at the 04 and 05 offensive positions. Most teams do not put their best shooters in these positions because of the bad angles for a shot. The best way to beat this defense is to drive the player at 05 with the worst angle shot, across the goal to the other side of the pool. This isolates the 04 player with the ball. O4 should then move toward the X4 defender with the ball. If X4 stays back in front of the center, 04 has a good shot and angle on the goal. If X4 moves towards the ball, 04 can then pass the ball into the center forward. An alternate method to beat the 4-5 drop is to drive the 04 player across to the opposite wing and rotate the 05 wing out into the vacated pocket area for a better shot. (See Diagram 7-11 below).

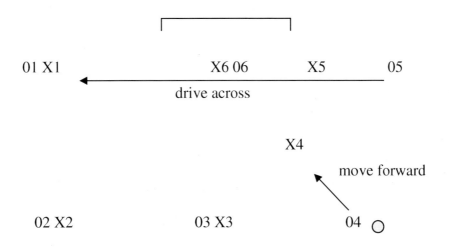

Diagram 7-11: Offense against the 4-5 Zone, drive 05 across, isolate 04.

SHOT CLOCK MANAGEMENT-OFFENSE

END OF THE SHOT CLOCK

The team on offense also has to know what to do in the situation where there is less than ten seconds left on the shot clock. The offense must keep the ball in a scoring position, preferably in front of the goal. The ball should certainly not be passed to the wing. The wing player has only a bad-angle shot on the goal that can easily be blocked by the goalie, and there is more of a chance that the defender can leave the wingman early.

His teammates must always "cover up" for the man who is stuck with the ball. If the man with the ball is in good position to shoot, he should shoot high and hard; so that he might get a new 30-second shot clock when the goalie blocks it out of bounds. If he can't take a good high percentage shot, then he should dump the ball in the corner of the pool. He should never shoot a lob shot in this situation, unless the goalie is way out of the goal.

The shooter is not necessarily trying to score in this situation; so he doesn't need to force a bad angle shot, or shot from way outside, that will put him in jeopardy of getting countered. A good shooter knows when to shoot, and more importantly, when not to shoot. Never take the kind of low percentage shot that will allow a team to counterattack off the shot, unless you are in desperate need of a goal at the end of the game.

COVER BACK AND HELP

Knowing when to start peeling back on defense, when you are on offense, is one of the most difficult situations to learn as a player. If your team is about to shoot the ball, or you are getting to the end of the shot clock, and you are not directly involved in the offense, than you should start releasing back to defense before the ball is turned over. Try to anticipate when your team is about to loose the ball and start thinking about helping back on defense. Usually the person shooting the ball is not in good position to come back on defense. At the very least, you should think about covering for him.

You have some control over these situations, so you should be in position to help your teammates. Situations that you cannot control such as offensive fouls, or bad passes that are intercepted by your opponent, are more difficult to help out your teammate. If you are in position to take the possible free man in this situation, do so. If not, try to press the ball and keep it from getting to the free man.

DUMPING THE BALL

As the shot- clock winds down and the person with the ball doesn't have a good shot opportunity, he has to "dump" the ball. You want to place the ball in a position that will make the defender who has left you recover the ball; or put it somewhere in the corner of the pool, so that the goalie has a long way to swim to get to the ball. A good strategy for a player with the ball, whose defender has left him, is to dump the ball along the side of the pool; so that the defender has to stop and retrieve the ball and lose the advantage he has gained by leaving early. If he has to detour to the side of the pool, you will be able to chase and catch up to him.

When it is obvious that the man with the ball has to shoot or dump the ball, his teammates who are not involved, have to start "peeling" back or releasing back to cover up on defense. In a situation where a player must shoot the ball at the end of the shot clock, every player but the center forward and the shooter should be swimming back on defense. As the goalie recovers the dumped ball in the corner of the pool, the players covering back should have enough time to catch anyone who has released and gotten free. (See figure 7-12 below)

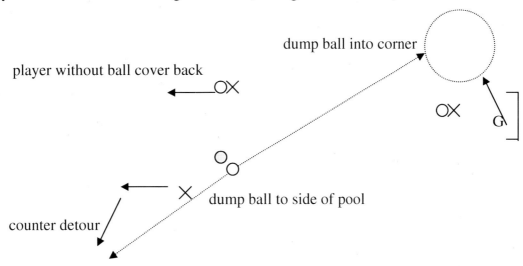

Diagram 7-12: End of shot-clock. Dump the ball-two options

STOP THE COUNTERATTACK BEFORE IT HAPPENS

Once a good counterattack team gets a free man on the counterattack, there is not a lot that the defense can do to stop it. The best way to stop the counterattack is to keep it from happening in the first place. To stop the counter before it happens, the team with the ball must become very conservative on offense, especially as the shot clock winds down; and not put themselves in situations that feed the other team's counterattack. They must control the ball without turning it over by a bad pass or offensive foul, and they must take only high percentage shots on the goal.

Turnovers give the other team an excellent counterattack opportunity. Even a poorly taken or low percentage shot can be considered a turnover. I would rather have my team dump the ball, than force a bad angle or weak outside shot that the other team can counter on. In addition, players on offense that are not directly involved in the offense have to be alert, and cover back to help a teammate who has been burned or is taking the shot.

STOPPING THE COUNTERATTACK AFTER IT HAPPENS

As stated above, the best way of stopping the counterattack is to prevent it from happening while your team is still on offense. There are only a few things that a team can do once the opposition gets a free man. The best thing to do is to simply attack the man with the ball, especially the first pass from the goalie. Press him hard, and without fouling, so that he cannot feed the free man. If you have to foul, then push the ball away a little as you are committing the foul, so that he has to take time to recover it. At the very least make it difficult for him to make the perfect pass to a moving free man on the other side of the pool. If you can keep him from passing for a few seconds, your teammates will have a chance to catch and cover the free man.

Attacking the ball removes all doubt from the defenders mind on whether he should press or drop back and help. The objective here is to stop the ball; or delay the ball from getting down the pool. The worse thing that the defender can do is play in between two players on the counterattack. He is not really stopping anyone; he is simply "guarding water."

WHEN NOT TO PRESS ON THE COUNTERATTACK

The only time that a defender would not press the ball on the counterattack, is in the situation where the defender knows that he can catch the free man himself. Once the free man is past him or on the other side of the pool away from him, he has no chance to catch up and should press the ball without hesitation.

HOW TO PLAY A TEAM THAT IS FASTER THAN YOURS

If the person that you are guarding is faster then you, then you have to react before he does, and get a head start on him. You have to anticipate the ball changing hands and get a head start on the faster player. If he gets the jump on you, even if you start even up with him, then you will not be able to catch him because of his speed. Once you get ahead of him, you have to maneuver and keep your body in front of his; so he can't use his speed to get around you. If your teammates use the methods as described above, then your team has a better chance of stopping a fast team's counterattack. Always attacking and pressing the ball, even if the other team is beating you down the pool, will also help a lot.

END OF GAME SITUATION-PLAYING FROM BEHIND

TAKE A CHANCE

Some of the techniques as described above can also be tried when you are behind by a goal or two at the end of a game. You don't have to wait until the end of the shoot clock to take off early. You may be taking a chance by taking off; but if your team is desperate for a goal at the end of the game, you have to try it. In an end of game situation, the best place to leave early from is the man with the ball, because he will not be in position to follow you down the pool. He has to do something with the ball before he can chase you, either shoot, pass or dump it somewhere. The player taking off down the pool is hoping that the player with the ball panics and takes a shot that he doesn't have to.

It is best to leave someone who is not in good position for a good shot on the goal; but sometimes it can't be helped. The worst-case scenario occurs when you have to leave a player who is right in front of the goal. What you are hoping for is that your goalie can make the block and get you the ball. This should not be done unless you have no other recourse. If you are going to lose the game anyway, then take the chance. You might get lucky; or the player with the ball might do something dumb, like take the quick shot and miss.

IF YOUR TEAM IS LOSING, PRESS AND STEAL

If your team is losing by several goals late in the game, you need to do everything that you can to get the ball back in your possession. You should play a pressure defense, steal and or foul the ball at every opportunity to stop the clock. I would rather have the players try to steal the ball in these situations, rather than foul every time. They have to take a chance and go for the steal. If the player doesn't get the steal, then he commits the foul to stop the clock. Players have to be careful and not commit an over-aggressive foul that results in an exclusion from the game.

HOW SOON DO YOU START?

When do you start the press and steal defense? It depends on the score and how far behind you are. The further behind that you are, then the earlier you start the press and steal. As the game nears the end, the team that is behind has to take more and more chances in order to get the ball back. Practice these situations until your team knows what to do, without the coach having to call a time out.

YOU NEED A GOAL-DRAW AN EXCLUSION

It is a close one goal or tie game and your team needs a goal. Under present day rules, it is best to get the ball into 2-meters and try to draw an exclusion foul. With little time left on the clock you cannot afford to have your 2-meter player fronted by the defender, and have to fight his way into front position. You can assure front position by starting your 2-meter player 06 at the 01 wing position, and then have 02 drive forward to block defender X6. The resulting "loop around" screen will get O6 front position on defender X2, who switches on to him. (See Diagram 7-13 below).

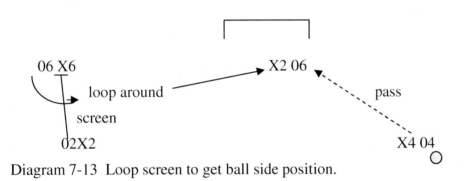

Diagram 7-13 Loop screen to get ball side position.

This same technique can be used to "post-up" a second player on the near post while moving the hole-man over to the other post for a "double post" offensive set up. Start with your best driver at the 01 wing position and have 02 run a screen as described above. When he gets ball-side position on the post, the ball should be passed to him.

Once the ball arrives at the 2-meter position the chances of getting an exclusion foul and trying to score on the resulting extra man situation are a lot higher than a player trying to score on a shot from outside. After the exclusion, a time out can be called to set up a special extra-man play that you have practiced. If the defense does not commit an exclusion foul, then the 2-meter player or post player has to take the shot. The odds are in the offenses favor in this situation. It is either going to be an exclusion, or a shot on goal from 2-meters.

YOU NEED A GOAL-DRAW THE 5-METER DIRECT SHOT FOUL

If you don't have a lot of time to run a play in the above situation in which your team needs a goal, simply put your best shooter at the 03 point position just outside 5-meters. If he cannot get a shot off, he can draw a foul and take the direct shot on goal that he is entitled to under the rules. This may be the best shot you will get with little time left on the clock. The defender either has to let him shoot or foul him in this position 5-meters in front of the goal.

END OF GAME STUATION-YOUR TEAM HAS THE LEAD

PROTECT THE BALL

With little time left in the game and your team in possession of the ball, the other team is in a desperate situation; and will try to do anything to get the ball back. They become very aggressive and will be trying to steal the ball from you, or foul you to stop the clock. Many times the referee in this situation will subconsciously help the team that is behind by letting them foul aggressively, or by allowing them to steal the ball. You can prevent this from happening with movement.

The person with the ball must keep moving towards the goal to avoid stalling, and the rest of the team must be moving to help the ball. Once you stop moving, you give the other team an opportunity to steal the ball or commit a foul. If you are fouled in this situation, do not risk a pass to a teammate. It is better to put the ball in play and keep swimming towards the offensive end. Everyone should spread out around the pool in order to avoid the double team. The closer you are to each other the easier it is for the other team to "double" on you and steal the ball. Protect the ball at all costs and cover up cherry pickers.

CHERRY PICKING

If the other team sends players down to the other end of the pool, you must send players back to cover them. A smart team that is behind by a goal, with little time left, will have a player stay in the back-court while the other team goes down on offense. This is called "cherry picking." Instead of playing defense, the player is at one end of the pool "picking cherries" while everybody else is at the other end of the pool. You have to be aware of this situation and keep someone back with him. If nobody notices the "cherry picker", your goalie certainly should see this, and call someone back immediately to cover up. This situation has to be communicated to the person with the ball so that he doesn't take the shot until the cherry picker is covered.

DON'T GIVE UP THE EASY COUNTER

When you have the lead at the end of the game, you also have to be careful that you don't put yourself in position to give the other team an easy counterattack. You should keep the ball on the outside positions of your frontcourt offense, and keep it away from the wings. This keeps your opponent from countering your wingman, who is usually not a threat to score. Most teams who are behind will try to press and steal the ball.

Movement and helping the ball is the key to not giving up the ball. Since the other team is pressing, they will usually leave the 2-meter player open. Keep the ball on the outside and avoid the temptation to pass the ball into him until there are less then 10 seconds left on the shot clock. The defense will be reluctant to foul him for fear of being excluded, so he may get a good shot on goal, draw an exclusion, or turn his man and try to draw a 5-meter penalty. Hopefully the referees will make the correct call in this situation. However, they may be reluctant to reward the team that has the lead with an exclusion foul, or 5-meter penalty shot, especially at the end of the game. Sometimes referees are a little hesitant to make the call that decides or ties the game.

SITTING ON THE LEAD

In a situation where you have a several goal lead and still a few minutes left in the game, you have to be careful and not sit on your lead; or you will let the other team back into the game. It is human nature to let up when you have a lead and the game is almost over. This can be disastrous to your team! You have to keep playing with the same intensity that got you the lead in the first place, and you must keep trying to score, although you do not need to force a bad shot.

A shot on goal is good, but not at the expense of giving the other team a goal at the other end. A bad-angle wing shot, for instance, is not recommended because it gives the other team an opportunity to counterattack. All of the tactics, as described above, still apply in this situation. Try to score if you are able to take a high percentage shot; but be sure to protect the ball, keep moving to avoid the steal, do not give any easy counterattack opportunity, and cover up on defense. A team that sits and tries to passively protect their lead, will usually lose their lead. If the other team scores and it becomes a one-goal game, then anything can happen.

SUMMARY-END OF GAME SITUATION

How you handle end of game situations depends a lot on whether you have a lead or not, how big or small your lead is, and how much time is left on the clock. If your team has the lead and you are on offense with less than a minute left in the game, then you should try and take as much time off the clock as possible, giving the other team as little time as possible to run their offense at the other end.

Try to get off a good shot at the end of the 30-second shot clock, or dump the ball in the corner and cover up on defense. There is no need to force a bad shot that will give your opponent a counterattack opportunity. If you get a shot opportunity that has a very good chance of scoring a goal, then take the shot and cover back on defense if it doesn't go in. The rest of your teammates should also be covering back on defense when it is obvious that you are going to shoot. If there is less than 30 seconds on both clocks and you have a lead, then it is obvious that you shouldn't shoot at all in this situation. Remember that you don't need a goal! Control the ball and run the clock out.

END OF QUARTER SITUATION

End of the quarter situations depend on how much time there is left on the shot clock. You often hear coaches directing their team to "get out of the quarter." This means that with about 30 seconds left on both the shot clock and the game clock, and your team in control of the ball; you want to protect the ball, get off the last shot of the quarter, and not give the other team an opportunity to score. If you don't have a good shot opportunity with 1-2 seconds left in the quarter, you can probably take a bad shot or lob and hope that it goes in; or try to draw a foul outside five-meters and get a shot off, as long as the other team doesn't have enough time to get off a shot at the other end. The safest thing to do is to simply sit on the ball until the clock runs out. With a few seconds left you can afford to take a chance on a bad angle shot or lob shot.

OFFENSIVE TACTICS

HOW TO BREAK A HARD PRESS AND PASSING LANE DEFENSE

The best way to break a hard press is with movement, especially from the player who is to receive the ball. The player who has the ball and is being pressed, must • rst try to draw a foul and gain a free pass. When the whistle blows, the player receiving the pass must then make a release move to get away from the pressing guard by moving forward, and then back at an angle towards the man with the ball. If the defender does not "honor" his movement toward the goal, then the player simply drives past him towards the goal. The drive should free him for a pass and shot near the front of the goal.

Two players working together can also run a pick or screen in order to release one of them to get free to receive the ball. This is called "helping the ball". It is not only effective during the counterattack, but also against a press in the frontcourt. A team that sits against a hard press and passing lane defense will usually get the ball stolen from them, and then get beaten on the subsequent counterattack by the other team. Players must be taught how to release for the ball with movement or by running screens.

Diagram 7-14 below shows two different release moves. If the ball is on one side of the pool at 01, the center forward 06 is set to the opposite side of the pool, and the defense is pressing, the offense has to move the ball around to the other side by using movement releases or screens. In this diagram, O2 releases for the pass from O1 by first going forward, and then hooking back on the same side of the ball. 02 then passes the ball to 03, who passes to 05 who has released after a screen by 04. 05 then passes into the center forward 06.

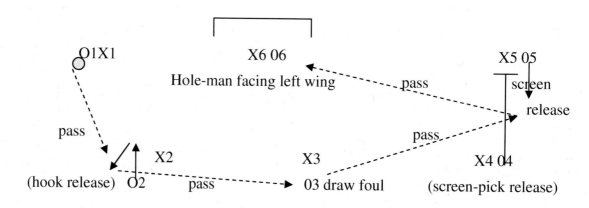

Diagram 7-14: Release moves to get the ball around from 01 to 05, who passes into 06.

HOW TO BREAK A 2-METER FRONT

There are several ways to beat a team that plays in front at the 2-meter position. First, the 2-meter player must move out to the 4 or 5-yard line and then turn and face the goal, leaving a space between him and the goalie. As he does so the ball must go to a wing player, who in turn passes the ball inside to the 2-meter player. Never try to pass the ball inside to a fronted hole-man from an outside position. That is a difficult pass to make. By the time the hole-man and defender untangle, the goalie will intercept the ball.

If the team on defense is fronting the wingman or if they foul and drop from the wing man and bring the goalie out, this plan will not work. The only thing a team can do then is to bring in a new hole-man, or move the hole- man to one post; and then bring in another hole man on the other post; for a double post offense. With the amount of wrestling that is allowed at 2-meters these days, the 2-meter player might be able to fight his way back into a side or front position. The hole-forward should at the very least, turn to a side position, and have the team get the ball around to that side for the entry pass.

OTHER TACTICS

CREATE MISMATCHES
Offensively you should try to create mismatches, especially at 2-meters. Anytime that you have a smaller player guarding a big one, then the bigger player should take the smaller player into the set position. This is called "posting up". If that position is already occupied, then you can either set up a double post, or have the original set move out of the way by moving towards a wing.

Your hole-man can create a mismatch situation before he moves into 2-meters. While he is in a perimeter position, he can run a screen with a teammate who is being guarded by a smaller player. If the defensive players switch positions, you will have your mismatch.

STOPPING THE DOMINATING PLAYER AT 2-METERS
Before you have to guard the 2-meter player, tire him out by making him play defense at the other end of the pool. You can drive him all the way down to the 2-yard line, or take him to 2-meters and try to get him kicked out. Then you have to make him work for position, as he has to swim all the way back down the pool. Once he gets down to the 2-meter area you have several choices on defense. You can front him and press the ball on the outside, and hope that his team cannot get the ball to him; or play behind and double down on him from an outside defensive position. If all else fails, it is better to get kicked out than to allow the 2-meter man to score. Your team has a better chance of stopping the other teams 6 on 5 than stopping a good hole-man from scoring out of the 2-meter position.

QUESTIONABLE TACTICS IN TODAYS GAME

Since my retirement from coaching seven years ago, I have watched many water polo games, both at home and abroad. The game has changed a lot since I first became involved in the sport fifty-two years ago, mainly because of rules changes over the years. Some of the basic fundamentals of the game, by and large, have remained the same. The changes in the game, however, have led to an erosion of the fundamentals and the necessity of teaching these fundamentals. We used to teach defensive positioning and guarding a player with the ball; now we teach fouling. We used to teach driving towards the goal and shooting after receiving the ball. Now we teach holding the ball in one place for a period of time and then taking the shot.

Some of the tactics used by many of today's teams are questionable at best. I constantly scratch my head and question "why did that player do that?" or "why is this team doing this?" In the following paragraphs are examples of questionable execution of basic fundamentals and tactics that I have observed during the past few years.

THE DELIBERATE FOUL

This probably annoys and perplexes me more than any other aspect of the game. Players who don't have to foul, but purposely commit the foul anyway. I don't understand? Why are you fouling when you don't have to? Did you forget that there is a shot clock in the game, and every time you foul you stop the clock? Not only are you giving the team on offense extra time to move the ball into the scoring area, but you are giving them more of an opportunity to score a goal. You are actually awarding a free pass to the player with the ball, instead of forcing the player to pass the ball under pressure. Don't blame the referee for calling this foul. If you have a hand underwater and the player with the ball struggles a little, the referee has to make the call. Learn how to press and avoid the foul by showing both hands, and using your legs in order to maintain pressure on the player with the ball. The referee should not call the foul when you do that.

I have seen games in which every player who has possession of the ball is deliberately fouled. What an ugly game to watch! Whistle after whistle! The only time you should deliberately foul is to prevent a goal from inside 5-meters; or foul the wing player so that you can drop back and help on the center forward.

In a game that I recently observed, a team in possession of the ball was running out of time; and the player with the ball was in trouble, pinned against the lane line at the side of the pool. Instead of letting the clock run out, the defender deliberately fouled the player with the ball, stopping the clock. The awarded free pass went directly into 2-meters; resulting in an exclusion and goal by the team that only a few moments before was in danger of losing the ball.

POSITION DEFENSE AT 2-METERS-PLAY ON THE SIDE

This leads me to another questionable move on defense. A defender guarding the 2-meter player, playing directly behind him, and with one or both arms draped over the shoulder(s); rather than position himself correctly on the side of the shoulder. When the ball arrives in front of the 2-meter player, and the defender is playing directly behind him; it can't help but be called an exclusion. If the defender plays around to the side of the 2-meter player, the same side that the ball is on; he has a chance of making the steal instead of committing the exclusion foul. Reach around the side instead of over the shoulder.

Playing on the side of the ball may also discourage the passer from passing the ball to that side, or from making the pass at all. Getting a "piece of the ball" may even help to avoid the exclusion foul. It is easier to switch from side to side when behind the defender, if the player is playing low in the water, and not up on top of the center-forward. The defender cannot possible move if he is on top of the hole-man's shoulders. Stay low and use your hands to pull yourself back and forth behind the center forward. (See Pictures 7-A and 7-B on next page)

Picture 7-A: Playing behind the center, a certain exclusion foul.

Picture 7-B: Playing on left shoulder, ready to intercept pass.

NOT PUTTING BOTH HANDS UP

When the outside defender is about to steal the ball from the 2-meter player, the 2-meter defender has to immediately put both hands in the air so that he is not called for the exclusion. How many times have you seen the "sure" steal taken away because the 2-meter defender fails to put his hands up? Actually "hands-up" is a misnomer. For the foul not to be called, the whole arm (including elbow) has to be out of the water and not resting on the players back. (See Pictures 7-C below and 7-D on next page)

Picture 7-C Crasher coming in to steal the ball. Defender has hands down. Foul is called.

Picture 7-D   Crasher coming in to steal ball. Defender has hands up.
No foul is called. Successful steal is made.

GIVING UP THE 5-METER PENALTY SHOT

I have observed this situation over and over again, and I don't understand why it happens? A player receives the ball inside the 5-meter line and facing the goal. The defender behind the player with the ball reaches over the shoulder and is called for a 5-meter penalty shot. Why is it necessary to commit the 5-meter penalty, when you have the shooter covered and in a very poor shooting position? Think about it! You are playing directly behind the shooter; so he can't pick the ball up. He has to shoot the ball off of the water with the goalie directly in front and towering above him. He is trapped into taking the lowest percentage shot in water polo!

Why commit the deliberate foul and give up the "for sure" much higher percentage penalty shot? Let's see now? You deliberately foul a player who has less than a 25% chance of scoring the "off-the-water" shot; and give up a penalty shot, which has a 90% chance of scoring. Makes perfect sense to me! (See Picture 7-E below)

Picture 7-E: Why is the defender doing this?

NOT TAKING THE SHOT AFTER BEING FOULED AT 5-METERS

At a recent tournament, I watched about twelve water polo games between many of the best college teams in the country. In 48 quarters of water polo, I saw only a total of six shots attempted after a player was fouled at 5-meters. In some games I didn't see any attempts at all. Why not? You are not going to get a better shot than a free shot on goal from five meters from the goal. You only have to beat one arm up and the goalie. I can understand not attempting the shot if you don't have good body position to take the shot; or if the opportunity occurs very early in the 30-second possession, when you are still trying to work the ball into 2-meters.

But, not attempting the shot at all! I don't understand the reason for this? I recently saw a player fouled at 5-meters and directly in front of the goal, with three seconds left on the shot clock; pick up the ball and dump it in the corner rather than attempt the free shot on goal. Why not attempt that shot? You might score a goal or get a new shot clock to retain possession of the ball. It is sure better than dumping the ball into the corner.

I have several times observed another situation that is even more questionable. The player with the ball is fouled just outside 5-meters and doesn't even look at the goal; but instead looks at his teammate, asking his teammate to release and pass the ball back to him so he can get "live". He passes the ball to his teammate and receives the pass back. Only then does he turn towards the goal and look for his shot.

Why go to all the trouble to get "live", when he had a better chance to score right after he was fouled. Players should always take a shot when a good opportunity presents itself during the game. It shouldn't matter whether it is early or late in the shot clock, unless it is at the end of the game and your team is protecting a lead. Then you might want to take a little time off the clock before you take the shot.

HOLDING THE BALL AND THEN SHOOTING

What ever happened to "shooting off the pass"? With a preponderance of frontcourt and extra-man zone defenses being played, the opportunities to take an outside shot are many. However, it is difficult enough to score against a zone without decreasing your chances even more by holding the ball. I constantly see players catch the ball, wave it for about five seconds, allow the goalie and defenders to position themselves in front of the shooter, and then attempt the shot right into the defender and goalie arms. Result? A blocked shot!

The chances of scoring against a zone are greatly increased if the player shoots immediately upon receiving the ball, before the defender and goalie can set themselves; rather than holding the ball, and holding the ball, and then shooting. The longer you hold the ball, the less chance you have of scoring a goal and the greater chance of someone blocking the shot.

DOES ANYONE PRESS ANYMORE?

We invented the press defense in this country. We probably got it from basketball. Now I see the Europeans press and teams in the USA playing nothing but zone defenses. Don't get me wrong, a zone defense is fine at the appropriate time; and I understand why teams are playing a zone. Most teams are trying to avoid the 5-meter foul and shoot rule, and they want to be in position to crash back on the 2-meter player; so they play a zone.

What kills me is that most teams don't attempt a press at all. They just turn around and swim down the pool, stop in front of their own goal, turn around and put their arms up. Come on! You are allowing the attacking team to easily move the ball down the pool, and giving them all kinds of time to run their frontcourt offense. At least make it a little more difficult for the attacking team to move the ball down the pool, by initially pressing the ball on the counterattack. Then, after you press, you can turn around and go into a zone if you want to.

It is not that hard to accomplish. Press the ball during the counterattack, and then once the ball gets into the frontcourt, come back into your zone. It may be a little more difficult in a 30-meter pool, because you have to cover a greater distance to come back into a zone. But in a 25-yard or 25-meter pool, there is no excuse for not pressing initially, and then falling back. When you are pressing, get you hands up and don't foul! You are just helping the ball get down the pool. When you foul, you are defeating the purpose of the press; namely, to delay the ball down the pool and to create turnovers.

WHAT DO YOU DO WHEN YOU ARE LOSING BY SEVERAL GOALS LATE IN THE GAME?

Teams seem to have no clue on what to do at the end of the game, when they are losing by a few goals. Don't teams ever work on this situation in practice? I will give you a few hints. First you need to get the ball back in your possession, because you need to have the ball if you want to score. You cannot allow the team that is leading to retain possession of the ball and just run the clock out.

Secondly, you need to stop the clock? I have seen teams who are losing simply come back into their zone; or play a very soft press. All this does is to allow the clock to just keep running down; which is exactly what the team that is leading wants to accomplish.
This is the one time in the game where you need to press hard and deliberately commit the foul to stop the clock! A player guarding the ball should go for the steal every time by going for the ball. I don't mean once in a while; I mean EVERYTIME! Then if you don't make the steal, you have to foul, EVERYTIME!

The rest of the defense should be playing in the passing lanes and fronting the hole-man in hopes of intercepting the pass. If you allow the ball to go into 2-meters while your team is pressing and spread out around the pool; you will not be in position to help back at two-meters. An exclusion is likely to happen if the ball is allowed into 2-meters. Not what you need in that situation. Learn to front the hole-man; or at the very least overplay the shoulder on the side that the ball is coming in from. Teams with the lead are not likely to force the pass into the hole-man when the defender is overplaying the ball-side. If they do force that pass, the defender will be in position to make the steal.

WHY IS THIS HAPPENING?

These are some of the situations that I have observed numerous times in games; and that have really bothered me. What I don't understand is why players are doing these things? Are coaches not teaching the fundamentals of the game, letting players get away with playing incorrectly; or are players just not listening to the coaches, and playing the way that they want to? Perhaps it is laziness on the player's part? It is easier to foul rather than have to work hard not to commit a foul. It is also a lot easier to play a zone, rather than press all over the pool.

If laziness is the reason for players playing this way, then ultimately is it up to the coaches to insure that their players are not taking the "easy way" out; but are playing the game correctly and fundamentally sound. Players should also take it upon themselves to perform the fundamentals of the game the right way every time. Taking the "easy way out" will only result in missed opportunities and losing the game.

CHAPTER 8

ESSENTIAL DEFENSIVE SKILLS

Defense is the key to winning water polo games. When a team is prepared and committed to playing defense every time they jump into the pool, that team has the opportunity to win any game. Defense is a constant. It can help you win games even if your team is having an off night offensively. A defensive oriented player can contribute greatly to the success of the team, even if he does not score a goal. Learn to play good defense, as well as offense, and you will have a lot of success in the sport of water polo.

Anyone can play defense. All it takes is the three D's of defense. The DESIRE to stop the other team from scoring, the DISCIPLINE to play defense all of the time and to follow the defensive game plan, and the DEDICATION to the defensive part of the game. Players have to understand that stopping the other team from scoring, and keeping the score low, gives their team a better chance to win. A low scoring game can be won by anybody. You don't have to be better than the other team.

This chapter will cover all of the essential skills that a player must learn in order to play good defense. It is also important that everyone on the team play together in a coordinated manner in order for the team defense be successful. It is the coach's responsibility to put together a defensive game plan that takes away what the other team is trying to do. It is the player's responsibility to execute the defensive fundamentals and the defensive plan correctly.

PRESS DEFENSE SKILLS

The first defensive team concept that players must learn is how to put pressure on the other team. This is done with a press defense. The goals of the press are to delay the ball from getting down the pool and into the 2-meter position. By doing this, the defense can put the offensive team in a position where they don't have enough time left, and have to take the shot or dump the ball. A good press will also put the defense in a position where they can create bad passes and turnovers that lead to easy counterattack goals. Following are skills that a player needs to play a good press defense:

PRESS WITHOUT THE FOUL

A player has to learn how to put pressure on a perimeter player, or counterattack player who has the ball, without fouling him. This is especially important when playing a pressing defense, because you don't want to give up a free pass by committing a foul, and you don't want to stop the clock. Reaching over the right shoulder of a right-handed player will almost certainly cause the referee to call a foul. The key is to be patient and not reach. Position your chest on the left shoulder, and wait until the passer turns to his left to pass the ball. As he is turning, the defender must push down on the arm and shoulder with the right hand and at the same time reach for the elbow of the passing arm with his left hand. The defender should not go for the ball in this situation, but try to disrupt the pass by hitting the arm somewhere near the elbow. The opposite holds true for a left-handed passer. (See Picture 8-C below)

If the player with the ball fakes and tries to draw a foul, the defender must immediately show the referee both hands; so he will not call the foul. With both hands up in this kind of defense, the defender must constantly be kicking with the eggbeater or breaststroke kicks to maintain the pressure on the passer. The proper use of hands when the player has possession of the ball is critical to the success of this defense. The sequence goes like this: Player holding the ball, defense with one hand down on shoulder and one hand up in passers face; player drops ball, defender immediately puts two hands up to show referee. Repeat this sequence every time the player picks up or drops the ball. (See pictures 8-A and 8-B below)

Picture 8-A: No hand on ball, defender has both hands up for "no-foul"

Picture 8-B: Hand on ball, defender has one hand on shoulder

Picture 8-C: Lunge block-left hand going for elbow

FRONTING THE HOLE MAN

In a pressing defense, it is mandatory that the 2-meter defender plays in front of the hole-man. Defenders do not have to be physically large in order to play in a front position. This defense can be useful when a smaller defender does not match up with a larger 2-meter player. Getting in front of the hole-man requires that the ball must be under pressure, and cannot be thrown easily in to the 2-meter position. The defender simply allows the hole-man to swim into position, and then slides in front of him.

If he is caught behind, and with the ball under pressure, he simply swims around in front without making contact with the 2-meter player. He must keep his hips up and his hands free so that the hole-man cannot grab him to get back in front. He must constantly be taking short strokes and moving to stay in front, or to the side that the ball is on. It is very difficult to move with the ball, if the defenders arm is draped over the hole-man's shoulder or neck. Keep the hands moving and in front of the hole man, rather than holding the shoulder.

A defender does not need to control the hole man by grabbing or holding him. It is easier to control him by moving in front and cutting off the direct pass to him. Any overpass into the hole-man must be intercepted by the goalie. As the goalie is intercepting the ball, the defender must put up both hands and not commit a 5-meter penalty. (See Pictures 8-D and 8-E on next page).

Picture 8-D: White hat fronting dark hat center forward. It is difficult for defender to move.

Picture 8-E: Playing in front with hands "free" for easier movement

PLAYING THE PASSING LANES

While the ball is being pressed without the foul, the rest of the defenders must play in the passing lanes, between the ball and the person they are defending. A poor pass caused by pressure on the ball, can be intercepted in the passing lane and lead to a counterattack by the defender. As long as the ball is under pressure, it will be difficult for the passer to complete a safe pass. He may elect not to pass the ball at all, rather than throw a risky pass. Either way, the defense is keeping the ball from advancing into the frontcourt. (See Diagram 8-1 on next page).

A defender can also bait the passing lane by playing on the side of the offensive player receiving the ball, instead of in front. When the player passing the ball looks to see where to pass, he will see an open area to put the ball. As the ball is in the air, the defender uses a slight tug and arm stroke and pulls by the player receiving the ball; jumping in front of him to make the steal. (See Diagram 8-1 on next page and Pictures 8-F and 8-G below).

Picture 8-F: Baiting the passing lane

Picture 8-G: Jumping into passing lane

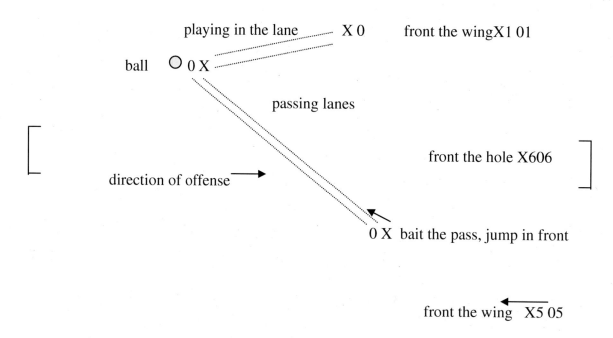

Diagram 8-1: Playing or baiting the passing lanes

DEFENDING THE WING

Another critical part of the press is that you cannot allow the ball to be passed into the fronted hole-man from the wing position. This puts both the 2-meter defender and goalie in a difficult 5- meter penalty situation. You can prevent this by playing in front of the wing and not allowing him to receive the ball. If the wing does receive the ball, the defender must deliberately foul him so he can't take a shot. This then allows the defender to drop back on the hole-man after he commits the foul; or allows the goalie to come out of the goal and double-team the hole man.

Since the wingman is generally not an offensive threat, why not play in front of him? Even if he drives to the goal he will have a difficult time scoring. Especially since he has a bad angle to the goal, the 2-meter line in front of him, and the defender positioned right on his shooting arm. Another advantage gained from fronting the wing player is that it puts the defensive player in great position to beat the wingman on the counterattack. (See Diagram 8-1 above).

POSITION DEFENSE AGAINST THE DRIVER

One weakness in the press defense is that playing tight on a perimeter player makes the defender more susceptible to a drive from that player. In order to prevent the drive, the defensive player must position himself close, but to one side of the driver he is guarding. The basic defensive position against the driver is with the hips on the surface of the water, facing the driver, playing him on the inside shoulder, and with the defender's legs and feet pointed towards the 2-meter player. This defensive position allows the defender to press out if he has to, or to pivot and turn and go with the driver as he moves toward the goal.

Playing on the inside shoulder, closest to the center of the pool, will force the driver to swim to the outside, and away from the goal to a worse angle shot. O2 should be forced to go left and O4 should be forced to go right, away from the center of the goal. The defender should never drop his hips and should never allow the driver to swim across in front of the goal. The drivers at the 2 and 4 positions should be defended this way, while the driver at 3 must be forced to swim to his right if he is right-handed, or to his left if he is left-handed.

Playing to the side of the driver gives the defender an added advantage of a clear path to the goal at the other end of the pool. When the ball changes hands, the driver will have to turn around first, before he can start swimming to the other end of the pool; while the defender has a straight path to the other end. (See Diagram 8-2 below).

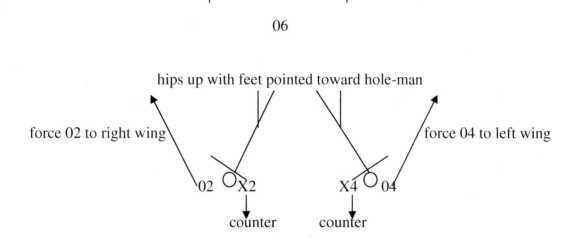

Diagram 8-2: Defensive positions on perimeter drivers. Play on the inside and be ready for counter.

ZONE DEFENSE SKILLS

GUARDING THE HOLE MAN FROM BEHIND
The 2-meter defender must be in a low position in the water with his hips up near the surface. He must play to one side of the hole man, depending on the kind of defense the team is playing. Generally speaking, in a zone defense, the defender usually plays on the shoulder that is on the same side as the ball. The defender must be far enough around the side of the shoulder, and the arm extended in front of the hole-man, so that any ball thrown to that side can be intercepted. In figure 8-3 below, the ball is with the 04 offensive player; so the 2-meter defender must play around the left shoulder of the hole-man. Putting his arm around the hole-man's left side should discourage the pass from being made to that side. If the pass is made, the defender will likely get a steal. (See Pictures 8-H and 8-I on next page).

The goal of playing side position, and taking away the near side pass, is to force the pass to the opposite side of the hole man; where it can be intercepted by the outside defender X2 dropping back on that side. The defender should change sides as the ball moves, so that he can always be on the shoulder as same side the ball is on. He does this by staying low and using his hands to pull himself across the back of the hole-man. He should never play in a position that is high up on the hole-man's back or play directly behind the hole man. It is difficult to move from side to side if the guard is lying on top of the 2-meter player. He should foul by reaching around the side for the ball, and not by reaching over the shoulder. (See Diagram 8-3 below).

Picture 8-H: Playing on right shoulder   Picture 8-I: Playing on left shoulder

CRASHING ON THE HOLE
Crashing in and stealing the ball from the hole man, not only can take away the other team's best offensive weapon; but it also can take away the threat of an exclusion on your center defender, and can effectively stop your opponents offense. The keys to "crashing" are awareness, anticipation, and timing. With the ball at 05, the defender on the opposite side of the ball (X2) has to be aware of the situation behind him and know where the ball is. He must then anticipate the pass into the hole-man; and when the ball is in the air, must immediately and without hesitation crash hard towards the hole-position. He should try to arrive as the ball is landing in front of the hole-man or shortly thereafter. The hole- defender must be careful and not foul the hole-man by putting both arms straight up as the "crasher" is stealing the ball. (See Diagram 8-3 below).

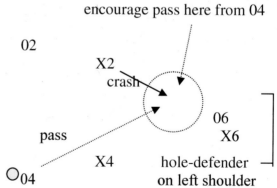

Diagram 8-3: Hole defender on left shoulder, crash from X2 on opposite side.

COORDINATE THE DEFENSE

To play an effective drop on the center forward, both the center-defender and the perimeter defenders must play together in a coordinated fashion. When the ball is at the 02-perimeter position (right side of the center-forward), then the center-defender must play around the side of the center forward and discourage the pass to his right hand. At the same time, the X4 defender must be anticipating the pass and crash in from the left side of the center forward. The same coordination must happen when the ball is at the 04-perimeter position, as shown in Diagram 8-3 above. When the ball is coming in from the 03-point position, then the center-defender should play on one side of the center forward and the crash should come from the other side. In this scenario, both X2 and X4 should be ready to crash, depending on where the ball lands.

ZONE BLOCKING

Blocking a shot is an essential skill in playing a zone defense, whether it is in a frontcourt zone or a man-down zone. The defender should get up as high as he can in the water using the eggbeater kick. He should "match arms" by holding up the arm that is on the same side as the shooter's arm. I.e., defenders right to shooters left or defenders left to shooters right. His shoulders should be parallel to the shooter and his arm should be held straight up and directly above the shoulder. The defender should take away the near side of the goal while the goalie takes away the cross-cage shot.

As the shooter moves forward and towards the goal, the defender should hold his position. If the shooter gets too close, he can eggbeater towards the shooter and go for the shooters arm as he brings his arm forward to shoot. The defender should also move left or right as the shooter moves, always keeping his arm in front of the shooters arm. (See Diagram 8-4 below and Pictures 8-J and 8-K on next page).

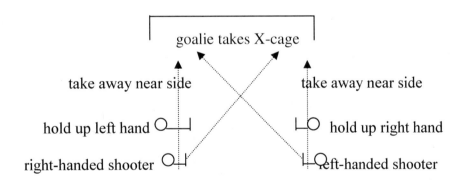

Figure 8-4: Zone blocking

Picture 8-J: Left-handed shooter, right-hand block. Picture 8-K: right-handed shooter, left-hand block.

HORIZONTAL TO VERTICAL-THE HIP PIVOT

A necessary skill when playing a zone defense, especially on the man-down zone, is the ability to go from a horizontal position guarding the post-man, to a vertical shot blocking position on the shooter. When guarding the post player, the defenders hips must be up on the surface of the water, the feet pointed outside towards the shooter, and the hands resting on the post player's shoulder. As the ball is passed to the possible outside shooter, the defender must pivot over his hips so that his feet are now under him and he has moved towards the shooter. He then must give a big scissor kick, push off with his hand, and get the arm into a vertical position in order to block the shot.

If he has time, the defender can take a few strokes to get him closer to the shooter, before getting his arm up. If not, he must eggbeater out towards the shooter. Never swim towards a player who already is holding the ball. The hip-pivot move can also be used in the frontcourt zone, when the defender has crashed back on the center forward, and then has to go back out and block a shot from a perimeter player.

FOUL AND DROP DEFENSE

OUTSIDE FIVE-METERS

The defensive strategy of fouling the person with the ball, and then dropping back to cover the hole-man, has been somewhat negated by the "shoot after foul outside 5-meters" rule. Dropping after the foul will give the uncontested free shot on goal to the player who was fouled. It is probably best to stay in front of the player who has been fouled, and hold up an arm to try and block the shot. Back up the required distance and match arms with the shooter, using the same technique as described above in "zone blocking".

INSIDE FIVE METERS

"Foul and drop" can be a useful strategy inside five-meters in order to prevent the shooter from taking a shot on goal; and also to drop in and prevent the pass to the center-forward. A defender can use the "foul and drop" anywhere on the perimeter, including the wings, anytime there is a possibility of a player shooting or anytime there is a possibility of the ball going into 2-meters. As mentioned above, the wing should be fouled any time the center forward is being fronted, in order to keep the ball from going inside to the center forward for a possible 5-meter penalty call.

THE DELIBERATE FOUL

There are times during the game that you will have to deliberately foul a player. The most obvious is to foul a player inside 5-meters who is about to shot the ball. Water polo is the only team sport where you can "foul to prevent a goal" without suffering a penalty. This is a difficult concept to teach young people learning the game, because they are taught not to foul in other sports. Players must be taught the correct way to foul so that they do not commit an exclusion penalty for too hard a foul. They may hold with one hand, and reach and grab for the shooting arm with the other hand; so that the person with the ball cannot take the shot. The defender must stay under control and reach, rather than come down hard on the arm.

Defenders may also decide to foul during the counterattack, or on the perimeter of play, in order to disrupt the player with the ball; giving your teammates a chance to cover up on defense. The same technique as described above should be used, while also pushing the player down under the water with one hand and giving a little push (12-15 inches) of the ball with the other hand. Your team can gain some time to cover, because the player with the ball will take several seconds to come up and retrieve the ball. A foul of a perimeter player will also give your 2-meter guard time to swim back in front of the hole-man, while the player is retrieving the ball.

PRESS AND STEAL

A situation that occurs frequently in games is when a team finds itself losing a game by one or two goals, with only a few minutes left in the game. It is imperative that the team that is behind not let the other team control the ball, and let the time run out. In order to get the ball back during the leading teams possession, it is often necessary for the team that is behind to go into a "press and steal" defense. Players must press hard and make an effort to steal or foul the ball on every pass.

There are two ways that a player may steal the ball when on defense. One way involves intercepting a pass that is thrown under pressure. The defender who is guarding the man "receiving" the ball must play on his side, in a shoulder-to-shoulder position. As the ball is in the air, the defender takes a stroke and gives a little tug on the arm or hip with his inside arm, and then slides into the passing lane to intercept the ball.

The other way of stealing the ball is to take the ball from a player who is holding the ball in his hand and looking to attempt a pass. The defender slides to the right shoulder of the right handed passer, as the player puts in hand on the ball in preparation to pass it. The defender then puts his right hand on the side of the passers right shoulder and pushes him a little to the left. At same time, he slides his left hand over the shoulder, takes a stroke and grabs the ball, and then just keeps swimming towards the goal at the other end of the pool. If the passer is holding the ball, the referee should not call a foul in this situation. If the steal is not successful, then the player with the ball must be fouled in order to stop the clock. (See Pictures 8-L and 8-M below).

Picture 8-L: Preparing for steal.

Picture 8-M: Push with right hand, steal with left hand.

AVOID THE KICK-OUT OR 5-METER WHEN FOLLOWING BEHIND

There are two situations that occur on defense when the defender finds himself following behind a player, with and without the ball. The first occurs during the counterattack, after the defender has been beaten down the pool. There is no need to foul the offensive player in the backcourt, or try and get around him. He is not a threat in the backcourt, so why foul him? Doing so will only result in an exclusion on the defender.

It is best to simply get to one side (inside position towards center of the pool) and follow right behind him, or next to him, all the way down the pool. If the defender stays in that position, the player with the ball will not be able to pick up the ball and shoot, and will be forced to take an off-the-water low percentage shot. If the offensive player, with or without the ball, falls backwards to draw an exclusion, the defender must immediately lift both elbows and hands out of the water to avoid the foul. (See Picture 8-N on next page)

Picture 8-N: Avoid the kick-out at mid-court by putting hands up.

The second situation is similar and occurs inside five-meters. Again, resist the temptation to reach over the shoulder for the ball. The penalty for reaching is a 5-meter penalty shot. As in the counterattack, follow behind him, on an inside shoulder, and force him to take the low percentage off the water shot. With the goalie towering in front of him, and the defender playing behind, the chances of scoring are very low. Much, much lower than the chances of making the 5-meter penalty shot. If the center forward turns the defender, and is facing the goal with the ball, he should immediately put both hands and elbows in the air to avoid the penalty. (See Picture 8-O below)

Picture 8-O: Avoiding the 5-meter penalty foul.

CHAPTER 9

PASSING AND SHOOTING SKILLS

Making accurate and safe passes is essential for ball control and for scoring goals. Passing is a skill that must be practiced under game conditions. Passing the ball with defensive players present forces the passer to learn how to pass under pressure. How to shoot the ball is an important skill to know in order to score a goal; but when to shoot and where to shoot are skills that are just as important for a player to learn.

PASSING AND RECEIVING THE PASS AGAINST THE PRESS

PASSING UNDER PRESSURE
The first thing a player must do, before he even thinks about passing the ball, is to look and see who he is going to pass to. If the passer waits to find the person he will pass to, after he picks up the ball and turns, it makes it easier for the defender to stop him from making the pass. Before he picks up the ball to pass, the passer's other shoulder should be perpendicular to the defender, and he should be controlling the ball at arms reach with his fingertips. He should not put his hand on the ball unless he is ready to pass, as this will make it easier for the defender to steal the ball or push it under water.

LAYOUT PASS-PASS THE BALL UNDER PRESSURE
Players have to learn to pass the ball under pressure from a defender, and not rely on drawing the foul to get a free pass. First the player with the ball has to separate from the pressing defender. A hard scissor kick and quick turn to a layout position, and away from the defender, should put him in good position to pass. One way to free himself from the defender is to pick up the ball and make a quarter turn to his left, as if to pass. When the defender uses his hands to try and stop him, he should drop the ball, forcing the defender to put both hands up. He then quickly picks up the ball again, rolls to his back, and makes the pass before the defender can grab him. (See Picture 9-A and 9-B on next page)

An alternate way of separating from the defender is to give the ball a small push with the left hand and then take a stroke with the right hand to the ball. Again, a scissor kick along with the stroke is recommended for good separation.

Picture 9-A: Step out and separate   Picture 9-B: Layout and pass

PASS WITH YOUR LEFT HAND IF NECESSARY

If the defender is very aggressive in guarding the passers right arm, he must learn to turn the opposite way and pass with the left hand. This is an important skill for right-handed players who are playing in the frontcourt, and are playing on the right side (left-handers side) of the pool at the 4 or 5 perimeter positions. Players in these positions cannot make a pass to the 1, 2 and 3 positions by using their right hand; because they will have to draw the ball across in front of their face before they make the pass, putting the ball in a position for the defender to take it away. They will have to put their left hand under the ball and make a scoop or side-arm pass to their teammates on the other side of the pool. Players should practice passing and catching the ball with either hand.

DRAWING THE FOUL

Trying to pass the ball under pressure can make it difficult to complete the pass. It is a lot easier to make the "free" pass after you have been fouled. A player can take advantage of the referee who is trying to help the ball down the pool, as most referees seem to be doing these days. A player under pressure can draw the foul by picking up the ball, making a quarter turn to his left as if to pass, and then dipping his other shoulder into the defender while dropping the ball. (See pictures 9-C and 9-D below)

Picture 9-C: Pick up ball to draw foul   Picture 9-D: Drop ball and dip shoulder

The player must be careful and keep the arm that is holding the ball extended in front of him, so that the defender cannot steal it. When the defender grabs him, he drops the ball, struggles a little, as if he is being held. The referee will usually call a foul in this situation, especially if the defender has a hand down. A player may have to try several times before he is awarded a free pass. If the defender puts both hands up in order to avoid the foul, then the passer picks up the ball, separates from the defender, turns and makes the pass.

IT TAKES TWO PLAYERS TO COMPLETE A SAFE PASS

Against a pressing defense, on the counterattack or on the perimeter, most passes should be made on the water (wet). The player passing the ball has to observe the position of the defender who is guarding his teammate that is receiving the ball, and look for the spot that is "safe" to pass to. The pass should always be made so that it lands in a spot that is away from the defender, and only accessible to the person receiving the pass. It helps to complete the pass if the man receiving the ball is moving or releasing towards the ball, while blocking out the defender at the same time. He is "making himself available" for the ball and at the same time "helping" the ball to advance. It takes two players working together to complete a safe pass. Eye contact between the two players is essential for a safe completion.

RELEASE AND HELP

Releasing is necessary when a player is being tightly pressed. Releasing to "help the ball" can best be accomplished by making a move towards the goal, getting the defender to move forward, and then hooking back away from the defender and at an angle towards ball. Timing is essential in completing the pass. The receiver must not make his release move until the passer is ready to pass the ball. The best time to release is after the passer is fouled and is picking up the ball to pass. If the defender does not "bite" and go with the driver on the first move toward the goal, then the driver does not release back for the ball; but simply drives past the defender toward the goal.

ZONE PASSING AND RECEIVING THE PASS

SET THE GOALIE

Most passes against a zone defense, in the frontcourt or on the extra-man, are usually dry passes. The principals are the same for both situations. The person making the pass must first set the goalie by aggressively moving forward in a high shooting position, while looking at the goalie, and faking as if to shoot. He then must turn, look at his teammate, and make a deliberate pass to a spot high above his teammates shoulder and into his hand. The pass must be made so that the teammate can catch the ball and shoot all in one motion. "Look away" or "no look," passes are discouraged, and usually result in an overthrown ball or bad pass.

ZONE PASSING-NEAR SIDE AND OFF-HAND

A pass to a right-handed player from the right, or to a left-hander from the left, only needs to be placed high above the shoulder to be successful. (See Picture 9-E on next page). The pass from the opposite side, the player's off-hand side, needs to be placed a little more accurately to succeed. The ball must be thrown with a little less velocity and must arrive at a position high and in front of the receivers face.

The person receiving the ball must then reach up in front of his face to catch the ball; and then draw the ball back by rotating the shoulder and arm back into a shooting position. This off-hand pass is usually a more difficult ball to catch, and consequently more difficult to shoot quickly, because the shooter has to draw the ball back first. (See Pictures 9-F and 9-G below)

9-E: Catch dry pass from right   9-F: Catch dry pass from left   9-G: Draw back, ready to shoot

2-METER PASSES

Passing into 2-meters from a perimeter player should not be made against the zone, unless there is a safe area in front of the hole man to make the pass. Two perimeter players (after a third player has driven thru to a wing and cleared out a defender, passing back and forth to each other, can create an open area in front of the hole-man. The person who has the ball must penetrate forward in order to be a threat to shoot. If he is a threat, the defenders have to honor the shooter by moving out and away from the hole man and towards the shooter. After several passes and threats to shoot, an open area should be created for either shooter to pass the ball into 2-meters. If the defender does not honor the shooter, or doesn't want to leave the 2-meter man open, then an outside shot has to be taken; preferably by shooting "off the pass".

WET PASS INTO 2-METERS

The pass into 2-meters must be wet and land about one and one half feet in front of the hole man's shoulder, and opposite the side that the defender is playing on. A good "rule of thumb" to follow when passing into 2-meters, is that the ball should be passed in from the side that the hole man is facing, opposite the side the 2-meter defender is playing on. If the pass doesn't land where the hole-man can handle it, then the referee will not make a call. This is called "not paying off the bad pass."

The referee will allow the hole defender to steal the ball if it passed to the same side the defender is playing on and both the defender and the hole man have an equal chance at the ball. The pass must have a little arch, and has to be soft enough so that the ball will not skip into the hole man's face. Passers must take into account that the ball landing on the water will bounce 6-8 inches after hitting the water, depending on how hard it is thrown. The passer must throw the ball from a high body and arm position, and over the top or around the defenders arm.

LOOK FOR THE BALL WHEN SWIMMING

ON YOUR STOMACH OR BACK?
It is critical that a player be able to see the ball if he is to receive it when he is swimming on his stomach. On the counterattack, and also when driving towards the goal, an offensive player must "look for the ball" that is being passed to him, by looking over his shoulder as he takes a stroke on the side that the ball is on. On the counterattack, it might be easier to see the ball when he is on his back. The only drawback to swimming on the back is that the player has to slow down a little when swimming backstroke; unless he only takes a few short strokes while on his back.

Good swimmers should not lose too much speed when swimming on their backs for a few strokes. As the ball is thrown in front of him, the counterattacking player simply rolls to his stomach and continues down the pool.

ON YOUR STOMACH
Another option is to stay on your stomach and look back over the shoulder for the ball. The player can look back over his shoulder as he is pulling his arm out of the water to take a stroke. As the arm goes forward to enter the water, the face also will go forward. Players must practice the "look swim" so that they can look back for the ball without slowing down. Throwing the ball to a player who is not looking for it will usually result in a bad pass and subsequent turnover. Players must never put their faces in the water in these situations.

SHOOTING SKILLS

WHEN TO SHOOT
Players have to know when to take a shot, and just as important, when not to take a shot. A player should shoot the ball when his team needs a goal and he is in good position to take the shot. Both his position in relation to the goal, and having his body in a stable and balanced position to shoot, are important for a successful shot.

WHEN NOT TO SHOOT
A player should not shoot if the game situation does not warrant it, or if the shot that he takes puts him and his teammates in a poor position to cover up on the counterattack. Bad angle shots that a goalie can easily block are not a good idea at any time during the game, and usually result in a counterattack by the other team. Situations that occur at the end of a game when the team has a lead sometimes do not warrant a shot.

Players should not take a shot when their team has a lead, unless it is a high percentage shot, or there isn't a chance of getting countered. An ill-advised shot from the wing at the end of the 30-second shot clock, for example, has little chance of success; and puts the shooter in jeopardy of getting beat on the counterattack.

SITUATIONAL SHOOTING

A player can take a shot at the end of the 30-second shot clock, but only if he is in a good position in front of the goal; and he can get off a good high and hard shot that the goalie might block out of bounds. If he cannot get off a good shot he must "dump" the ball in the corner.

A weak shot that the goalie can control will only feed the other teams counterattack. Remember, the shooter is not necessarily trying to score in this situation; he is mainly trying to gain a new 30-second shot clock. Shooting as described above is called "situational shooting." A surprise lob shot is sometimes warranted in this situation as long as the goalie is playing out, and it is not a direct "pass" to the goalie. It is better to lob too high over the goal than too low and into the goalies hands.

PRACTICE DIFFERENT SHOOTING SITUATIONS

A coach should have his players practice all the possible shooting scenarios that could come up in a game, otherwise, he can't expect his players to do the right thing when a "situation" occurs. Players who are well coached will know what to do in different situations. It should not be necessary for a coach to call a time out to instruct his team every time a difficult situation comes up.

Players should learn what to do in "end of the quarter" or "end of the game" situations, and when their team has a lead or is behind. Practice these situations so that you will know what to do in a game. Under the new playing rules, a player who is fouled outside of 5-meters can take a shot on goal. This is probably the best shot to take, especially at the end of the 30-second shot clock. You probably won't get a better shot in this situation.

WATCH FOR THE FOUL AND COUNTER

The shooter has to be careful in the situation when he is fouled by a defender whose team is losing, and is desperate for a goal. The defender will deliberately foul the person with the ball outside 5-meters, and then take off down the pool. The defense is in essence giving you the shot, hoping that you will miss it, and they will have a free man at the other end of the pool. The best thing to do in this situation is to direct someone to cover the free man before you shoot the ball; or dump the ball someplace where it will take the other team time to recover it, while you cover up the free man.

Dumping the ball in the corner is good if the goalie is the closest player, and it will take him several seconds to get to the ball. If you can, place the ball where the free man who has left you has to recover it; somewhere near the side of the pool. If he has to detour over towards the side of the pool to retrieve the ball, you can easily catch him.

WHERE TO SHOOT

Where to shoot the ball is just as important, if not more important, than how to shoot the ball. Choosing the correct shot to take and where the ball should be placed depends on the position of the shooter in relation to the goal, the position of the goalie, the position of the goalies hands, and the position of the defender. It is up to the coach to expose his players to as many different kinds of shots as they can possibly encounter in a game. Players need to develop a variety of shots that they can use in all of these situations. Players can practice shooting on their own, but the coach must provide opportunities in practice for the players to develop their skills. Defense should be included as much as possible in shooting drills to make the drills more realistic to a game situation.

READ THE POSITION OF THE GOALIE

In order to be effective shooters, field players need to understand what the goalie is trying to do. All goalies will try to put themselves in the best position to block the ball. They cannot take away all of the 10' x 3' goal, so they take away the part where the most logical shot will go. In doing so they will leave part of the goal open. Shooters have to "read" the position of the goalie, find the opening and then take the appropriate shot.

GOALIE PLAYING OUT

Goalies will position them-selves to do two things to gain an advantage over the shooter. First, they will come as far out of the goal as they can in order to take away the "shooting angle" of the shooter. The further out that they play in front of the goal, the more open they are to a lob shot over their heads. Goalies are sometimes willing to concede the lower percentage lob shot, and take away the higher percentage hard shot from outside. Lobs can be a very effective shot when the goalie is out of the goal. Players have to recognize this situation and take the lob when it is given to them.

GOALIE TAKING AWAY THE ANGLE

Goalies will also play on the same side of the goal that the shooter is on, so that they can shorten the distance that they have to travel to block the near side shot. By playing on one side of the goal, goalies are taking away the high percentage shot, near side, shot knowing that most shooters will take that shot. Goalies will also show the shooter the near side space, hoping that the shooter will shoot there, and jump into that space when the shot is taken. This is called "baiting" the shot. Taking away the near side leaves the goalie open for the "cross cage" shot, one of the most effective shots in water polo. Players who practice and take "cross cage" shots can effectively score a lot of goals that might otherwise be blocked. The lob shot to the far corner is also open in this situation. (See Diagram 9-1 on next page)

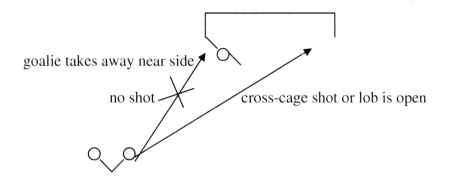

goalie takes away near side

no shot

cross-cage shot or lob is open

Diagram 9-1 Goalie overplays near side, shoot across the goal.

READ THE POSITION OF THE GOALIES HANDS

The standard position for the goalie is sitting in the water with his hands in front of him and resting lightly on the surface of the water. (See Picture 9-H below) The type of shot taken in this situation depends on the goalies ability to quickly get his hands out of the water and block the shot. If the shooter is within five yards of the goal, he should shoot around the goalies head. The shot will arrive too quickly around the goalies head and he will not have time to get his hands to that area to block the shot. This shot is called a "bunnies" shot, as in bunny ears.

A shooter that is positioned 4 to 8 yards from the goal can try to beat the goalie to a high corner, skip the ball, or shoot low under the goalies arms as he comes up in an "iron cross" position. A perfectively placed shot to the high or low corners can usually beat the goalies hands to those spots. Many times a low shot is more effective than a high shot, especially against a goalie whose first reaction is to bring is arms up and out of the water in an iron cross position. (See Picture 9-I below)

9-H: Hands in water, shoot high or "bunnies". 9-I: Iron-cross, shoot low under the arm-pits

As the shooter gets closer to the goal, most goalies will hold their hands out of the water in anticipation of the quick shot, sometimes even holding the hands high above the head. If the goalies hands are being held over his head, the shooter can shoot low, or lob to the opposite corner. When the hands are over the head, the goalie cannot push off the water and get to the back of the cage to block the lob. (See Picture 9-J below)

Picture 9-J: Goalies hands up, shoot low or lob.

SHOOTING-STARTING POSITION

When shooting from a vertical position in the water, the right-handed shooter should use a rapid egg-beater kick, with his left hand in a sculling motion in the water to get up as high as he can. At the same time, he should have his body in a perpendicular position in relation to the goal, with his non-shooting shoulder pointing towards the goal and his shooting arm holding the ball high above his head.

The shooter should bend his trunk at the waist so that his left shoulder is positioned lower than the right shoulder. Lowering the left shoulder and holding the ball higher increases the lever arm; consequently helping the rotation of the arm around the axis of the spine. (See Pictures 9-K and 9-L below).

Picture 9-K Shooting position

Picture 9-L Ball higher, longer vertical axis.

ROTATE AND FOLLOW THROUGH

A player taking the overhand shot, similar to throwing a baseball, must use correct mechanics to get the most speed on the shot. The forward motion starts by first rotating the right shoulder forward and bringing the arm forward at the same time. (See Pictures 9-M and 9-N below) As the arm moves past the shoulder, the forearm extends forward and the wrist snaps as the ball is released, with the fingers pointed towards the goal. (See Picture 9-0 below) As the arm is coming forward, most shooters will give a quick thrust downward with both legs (especially the front leg) to help provide power for the shot.

9-M: Shoulder rotation   9-N: Bringing arm forward   9-0: Arm extension

COMMON SHOOTING MISTAKES

The most common mistake in shooting is to put sidespin on the ball instead of the required backspin. If on the follow through, the hand turns sideways and ends up hitting the water in front of the opposite shoulder, then there will be side-spin on the ball; and the shot will curve to that side. To correct sidespin, the shooter must point his fingers forward as he releases the ball, and the hand must end up in front of the shooting shoulder; resulting in a straight shot at the goal. Remember to point the fingers toward the spot that you want the ball to go.

SHOOTING AGAINST THE ZONE DEFENDER

Shooting against the zone means that the shooter has to shot around an arm that is being held in front of him. The shooter must be in the same high vertical position as described earlier. In order to keep the ball from being blocked, he must shoot to the left or right around the arm. For the right handed shooter, shooting to the right requires that the shooter drop his elbow down and "wrap" or "sweep" the shot around the shooters arm. Shooting to the left requires the shooter to eggbeater to his left and then lean his body to the left to shoot around the arm. (See Pictures 9-P and 9-Q on the next page)

Picture 9-P: Wrap around right

Picture 9-Q: Lean left

CATCH AND SHOOT

The most effective shot in water polo is the "catch and shoot." The person receiving the high and dry cross-pass should shoot the ball immediately, before the goalie and the defender have a chance to set on him or get an arm up in front of him. A shooter who receives the cross-pass should always shoot high to the same side that he is on. Doing so will allow him to beat the goalie, who will dive to that side to make the block. A goalie diving across the goal to beat the cross pass usually will dive low; so the shot should always be placed in the high corner. Another way to beat the goalie is to hesitate slightly before taking the shot, let him dive to that side, and then shoot to the other side of the goal that he has left open.

FAKING

Faking the shot is a good way to commit the goalie early, opening up a better shot for the shooter. To be effective and to get the goalie to commit, the fake must be believable. It has to look to the goalie that the shooter is going to shoot the ball. Simply waving the ball and faking with his head will not get the job done. It is also important that the shooter get into a high shooting position when making the fake. The shooter must bring his elbow forward with the ball, similar to the shooting motion described above; and then suddenly stop the ball when the arm is parallel with the shoulder. This is called a "hitch." One or two fakes or "hitches" are all that are needed to commit the goalie. Once you get him to jump, you can take a more effective shot.

SHOOTING THE LOB SHOT

The lob is a good way to score a goal, especially against a goalie that comes out of the goal to take away the shooters angle (most goalies do this). In order to succeed, the shooting motion for the lob must be the same as if the shooter is going to shoot a hard shot. This is very similar to a baseball pitcher using the same motion for a "change-up" pitch as he does for a "hardball" pitch. As the shooters arm comes forward and in front of his shoulder, he drops his hand under the ball, and pushes it in a high arc over the head of the goalie and into the far corner of the goal.

The ball has to start from a high position above the water in front of the shooters face, and go high enough so that the goalie cannot reach up and intercept the ball. Another effective shot is the "spinner" lob, in which the shooter puts side-spin on the ball as he brings his arm forward; thus curving the ball high and into the far corner of the goal. This shot is very much like the "curve ball" pitch in baseball.

Lobs can be a very effective way to score goals, because most goalies come out of the cage to block the shot. Guys have to get over the "macho" image that "real men" don't lob. Tony Azevedo, one of the top players in the world, has a wicked lob shot; and he has scored countless lob goals. I have seen him score on a lob against the Serbian team, after he was fouled outside 5-meters. The goalie was completely fooled and the shot won the game for he USA.

SHOOTING THE SKIP SHOT

The "skip" shot is another shot that can score against a good goalie, because of the unpredictability of the trajectory of the ball. A player with a decent arm does not need to "try" to skip the ball. He simply aims for a spot on the water in front of the goal. Most balls will skip. Remember that the angle of the ball as it hits the water will be the same or close to the angle that it leaves the water to skip over the goalies arm. The further away from the goal where the ball hits the water, the steeper will be the angle; consequently causing the ball to skip over the goal. Shooters should aim for a spot fairly close to the goal, causing a smaller or flatter skipping angle and a better chance to score. (See Diagram 9-2 below).

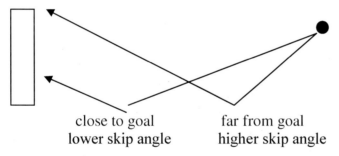

close to goal
lower skip angle

far from goal
higher skip angle

Diagram 9-2: Skip-shot physics

SHOOTING FROM A HORIZONTAL POSITION OFF THE WATER

Any time the defender is directly behind the shooter, he cannot pick up the ball to shoot from a vertical position. He must stay horizontal in the water, protect the ball with his body, and then shoot the ball "off the water." The shooter must keep his hips up to deter the defender from taking the ball. He can also rotate his front shoulder away from the defender and straighten his arm, in order to keep the defender at more than arms length away from the ball.

Putting his hand under the ball gives the shooter the opportunity for a variety of shots. He can pull the ball back in a screw motion, rotate his thumb under the ball, elevate his elbow out of the water, and then shoot with an upward push of the ball towards the goal.(See Picture sequence 9-R on the next page).

Picture sequence 9-R: Off the water shot. 1) Start position, 2) pull back and rotate thumb, 3) push with fingers and thumb, 4) extend and follow thru.

OTHER OPTIONS OFF THE WATER

Remember, the off-the-water shot is probably the lowest percentage shot in water polo, because the goalie is looming over the shooter in front, and the defender is directly behind the shooter. A higher percentage shoot in this situation is actually a lob shot over the goalies head and to the far corner of the goal. With his hand under the ball, the shooter simply lifts the ball and pushes it over the goalie. Most goalies will come out of the goal to take away the angle, leaving them open for the lob. The goalie will probably have his hands out of the water at this time, and will be unable to push off and get to the lob over his head.

Another option when in front of the right post (when facing the goal) and the defender playing on the right (outside) shoulder, is to move the ball to the left and across the goal, and then take the side arm shot around the slower moving goalie. Players should develop an off-the-water shot that they can perform well and consistently score in this situation.

SCORING A ONE-ON-NOBODY

It is embarrassing when a player beats his man down the pool, opens up a 2-3 body-length lead, and then blows the shot. One-on-nobody shots should be scored a high percentage of the time, especially those in which the defender is far enough behind that the shooter has time to pick up the ball and take an overhead shot. Having to take the shot off-the-water considerably lessens the chance of scoring.

A right handed shooter should swim toward toward the left post (to his right) as he approaches the goal. He should glance back before he picks up the ball and see how closely he is being followed. He should pick up the ball on the 3-4 yard line. Any closer than that and he will lose his shooting angle. He then will get into a vertical position, face the goal, and start moving across the goal to his left. This will open up more of the goal, and increase his chance to score, depending on the goalies ability to keep up with him and stay up to block the shot.

TAKING THE PENALTY SHOT

The penalty shot has become more difficult now that it is taken from five-meters instead of four-meters. The extra meter in distance makes it even more important to execute the shot using the correct fundamentals. The starting position for the shot should be facing the goal with the shooter holding in ball in front of him, with his hand underneath the ball and a few inches off the surface of the water. Putting the hand on top of the ball is not recommended because it adds an unnecessary movement of pushing down on the ball before the shooter lifts it to the shooting position. It also makes the ball more difficult to control and to handle.

The shooter should not look at the referee just before the shot, unless it is too loud to hear the whistle. He must also not look at the spot that he will shoot to. Upon hearing the whistle the shooter lifts the ball up and in one motion brings it back into the shooting position. Then, without pause or hesitation, the shooter brings the ball forward and places the ball in the area that the goalie has vacated. (See Picture sequence 9-S below).

Picture sequence 9-S: Penalty shot. 1) Starting position, 2) Bringing ball back, 3) Ball all the back to shooting position, 4) Without hesitation start forward shooting motion.

Most goalies will commit to one side or the other, or sweep forward and low, or simply react to the shot. The action of bringing the ball back before he shoots gives the shooter the opportunity of seeing what the goalie is committing to. A goalie move to one side requires a shot to the opposite side. A sweep by the goalie requires a high corner shot. He will be too low in the water and his hands to far forward to stop the high shot. If the goalie waits for the shot, anything around the head should go; because the goalie cannot get his hands to that area fast enough to make the block.

THE DIRECT SHOT AFTER FOUL
Rules introduced in 2006 to open up the offense, allow for players who are fouled anywhere outside of five meters distance from the front of the goal, to take an immediate shot at the goal. The player who is fouled, once he re-gains possession of the ball, is allowed to pick up the ball, look at the goal, and then shoot immediately at the goal, without undue hesitation and without faking. This shot is especially a good one to take if the player is fouled at the end of the shot clock or end of the quarter. He is probably not going to get a better shot in that situation. This shot will require the shooter to shoot around an arm in order to score. (See Pictures 9-P, wrap around right, and 9-Q, lean left, above)

Players need to practice this type of shot by using a defender who fouls, and then puts his hand up to block the shot. Players also need to learn how to draw the foul that leads to the free shot. The player must be a threat to shoot the ball in order to make the defender have to foul him. He has to absorb the foul and at the same time drop and control the ball, ascertain whether he is outside the five, then immediately pick up the ball and at the same time eggbeater up to a high position to take the shot. The shooter can drop his elbow and shoot around to the right side of the arm; or lean to the left and shoot over the defender's shoulder.

CHAPTER 10

PLAYING AND DEFENDING THE

2-METER POSITION

Besides the goalkeeper position, the 2-meter/center-forward/holeman position is the most specialized position in water polo. Because of rule changes and what defenders are allowed to do, the 2-meter position has changed over the years. In the past, 2-meter players where a threat to shoot, because of their close proximity to the goal; or draw the normal foul and feed drivers with the subsequent free pass. Now, however, the purpose of the position is to draw exclusion fouls, and also to turn and face the goal for the shot; or to turn inside and draw a penalty shot. Defending 2-meters is the most specialized defensive position. Both positions are difficult to play and require special physical and mental abilities in order to play them.

PLAYING 2-METER OFFENSE

PHYSICAL ABILITIES

Size is the first thing that you notice about the 2-meter player. Many times he is the biggest player on the team. Along with size comes upper body strength and leg strength. Just being big and strong in the upper body can help the 2-meter player at the age group and high school levels, because he is usually bigger than everyone else. As the 2-meter player progresses to the collegiate and international levels, he will find that he is being guarded by players who are just as big and strong as he is. He will lose that size advantage unless he also has good leg strength. Many times leg strength will be the deciding factor in the success of the 2-meter player as he progresses to higher levels.

Swimming ability, endurance and speed are also critical factors in the success of the 2-meter player. Because he has a bigger body, 2-meter players are sometimes less mobile than other players. Many teams will try to take advantage of this fact, especially in the counterattack. A big and physical player, who can also swim well, can be very valuable to his team.

The 2-meter position is the most physically demanding in water polo, requiring both endurance and strength. The hole-man must be in the best condition of anybody on the team. He must swim the length of the pool to get to his position, he must be constantly fighting to get and hold his position, he must absorb very physical punishment by the defender, he has to control the ball, and then he has to chase the 2-meter defender down the pool on the counterattack. In addition, he may also be asked to defend the other team's 2-meter player at the other end of the pool.

ABILITY TO GET POSITION

In the physical game that is presently being allowed at 2-meters, the ability to get position and hold it is critical to the success of the hole-man. A player, first of all, needs to have the mobility to quickly get down the pool, all the way down to the 2-meter line. He then must turn his back to the goal, positioning himself in front of the defender, and then keep the defender behind him. If the defender is playing in front of him, he must find a way to get front position without committing an offensive foul.

Under today's rules, this part of the game can become very physical, and almost anything is allowed. Upper body strength and leg strength are essential to getting and holding position. There is a lot of holding going on between the two players, with pure strength being the only thing separating the players. Once the 2-meter player gets front position he must do everything he can to keep the defender behind him. Reaching back and holding the defender is usually the method employed by most 2-meter players in today's game.

SPIN TO GET FRONT POSITION

The most effective method is to gain side position first by spinning away from the defender, and then try to muscle to the front. The fronted 2-meter player must first find the side of least resistance (the side that the defender is not overplaying), face the defender, and make contact underwater with the hand that is on the same side that he wants to end up on. In Diagram 10-1 below, the side of least resistance is on the left; so he must make contact with his left hand underwater, and then make a complete 180-degree move backwards and to his right, spinning away from the defender. He should end up with his back to the defender and facing to the front-left side of the pool. Once he gets to that position, he can try to muscle his way to a complete front facing position, or simply hold that side and have his teammates get the ball around to that side. The worst thing he can do is to constantly change his position, so that his teammates have no idea where to put the ball. (See Picture sequence 10-A on next page)

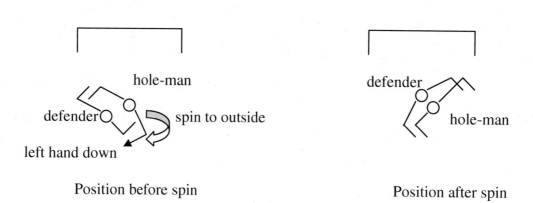

Diagram 10-1: Spin move to get front position

Picture Sequence 10-A: Spin to the outside to get front position.

Once the hole-man gets side or front position, he must hold that position and keep the defender behind him. He can do this by holding his arm out to the side, place his elbow under the defenders arm-pit, reach down and hold the defender's forearm, or reach up and hook or grab the defenders arm between the elbow and the shoulder. He can also slide his body to the left or right, forcing the defender to swim over his shoulder and commit an exclusion foul. He must be careful and keep his elbow and arm under water while holding the defender behind him. If he visibly holds the defenders arm while he has the ball, he will be called for an offensive foul.

If the 2-meter player losses position by being pushed outside the 2 to 3-meter line, and out to 4 or 5 meters, he has to regain position. It is best in this situation not to try and "muscle" his way back to the 2-meter area; but simply to go around the defender and "swim" back to the two. Swimming over the shoulder and/or head of the defender to gain position constitutes an offensive foul. He may loose front position when swimming back to the two; but it is better than setting on the 4-5 meter line, where he is not as much of a threat and can easily be dropped on from outside defenders. Trying to back into position by using the arms in a backstroke motion is also not a good idea; and will usually be called an offensive foul.

FACE TO THE OUTSIDE

In order to receive a wet pass from his teammates, the center forward must face the passer and create an area in front of him for the ball to land. Some 2-meter players will face the defender in order to hold and keep him behind. Then they will turn and face the passer as the ball is coming in. There are several reasons not to do this. First of all, recent rule interpretations do not allow facing the defender and holding him when the ball is coming in. Secondly, by facing the defender, the hole-man cannot see the ball coming in to him, and the passer does not have a target area in front of the hole-man to throw the ball to. Lastly, turning away from the defender and facing the passer as the ball is coming in, can be considered as a push off and offensive foul. 2-meter players have to learn to keep the defender behind without facing and holding him.

2-METER DECISION MAKING – FOUR OPTIONS

THE BALL'S IN FRONT OF YOU... NOW WHAT?

Once the ball has landed in the water in front of the 2-meter player, he does not have a lot of time to do something with the ball. Typically, defenders from the outside will be dropping in on him to steal the ball. He must quickly decide on one of the four options that are available to him; draw a foul, "kick" the ball back outside before he is fouled, turn his defender, or shoot the ball. The longer he holds the ball, the better chance the defense has to steal the ball. The center must always keep his head up and be aware of where defenders are coming from and the position of his own teammates. The center forward in water polo probably has less time than a football quarterback to make the right decision. Plus, the quarterback doesn't have a big defender holding him from behind.

No matter what he decides to do, he must be in a good solid position in order to perform any of the options mentioned. He must be in a "seated" vertical position with his legs slightly in front and under him, his head an shoulders must be above the water at all times, he must have control of the ball, he must be looking to see the position of his teammates and the defenders in front of him, and at the same time know or feel the position of the goalie and defender behind him. He must read the situation and make an instant decision on what to do with the ball. As in football, holding the ball too long by the "quarterback" can result in turnovers (or sacks) by the other team.

DRAWING THE FOUL

One of the most critical factors in order to draw a foul is a high position in the water. Not only the head, but also the shoulders have to be above the water. A referee many times will not reward a center forward who is in a low position in the water. Being low in the water also allows the defender to easily reach over and foul or steal the ball. As the ball lands in the water, the center forward must turn his left shoulder towards the defender as he reaches for the ball with his right hand. He should put his hand under one side of the ball and make a slight turn to the left, away from the defender on his right shoulder.

Depending on what side the defender is playing, the hole-man must turn away from that side, using whichever hand is free. The threat to shoot or turn should cause the defender to grab the center. At that point, simply dropping the ball should draw the call from the referee. It is up to the referee to decide if it is a normal foul or an exclusion foul.

NORMAL FOUL OR EXCLUSION?

One of the main reasons for passing the ball into the 2-meter player is to draw an exclusion against the defender. The main reason for an exclusion call is that the defender is holding, sinking, or pulling back the center forward. Because of his excellent position in front of the goal, the interpretation of the "advantage" rule says that the defender is taking away the center-forwards chance to score; so he should be excluded. If the 2-meter player losses his "chance to score" for any reason, the referee will probably call a "normal" foul instead of an exclusion.

Circumstances that can cause the 2-meter player to lose his "advantage" are bad passes that don't land directly in front of his shooting arm, passes that are made so that the defender can steal the ball, high passes, 2-meter player not in a good position in front of the goal (too far in front of the goal, or too far outside the side posts), and the defender coming around the side and getting a piece of the ball, or stealing the ball.

KICKING THE BALL BACK OUTSIDE

Time is the critical issue in this situation. If there is no crash coming in on the center forward, he will have time to draw the foul, turn, or take the shot. If there is a defender crashing in, he will not have time to do anything but get rid of the ball, either by passing or shooting quickly before the defender can steal the ball. The best and quickest way to pass the ball is first to break the hold of the defender, immediately put his hand under the back of the ball, pull it back slightly, rotate his thumb under the ball, and then lift and push it up and over the dropping defender to his teammate on the outside perimeter. If the 2-meter defender has hold of his arm, he must try to break the hold by turning his shoulder, or use his forearm, wrist, and hand to flip the ball up. If the defender is not holding his arm, he should be able to lift the ball up and out of the water and then make the pass.

TURNING AND FACING THE GOAL

Turning and facing the goal for the shot attempt has now become the most popular option for the center-forward, mainly because this now becomes an opportunity to draw a 5-meter penalty shot. It also allows the center to take the ball away from the pressure of a dropping defender. Hole men have to be able to turn in either direction, and with either hand, depending on which side the defender is playing. An over aggressive defender, who over-plays one side, can be turned in the opposite direction. Some center forwards will hook the guard with his leg; or use his other hand on the hip or elbow under the armpit for leverage.

If the defender aggressively goes around one side for the steal, the defender does not need to use leverage to turn. He can make the turn in the opposite direction by using his arms and legs to make the move around the defender. Once he makes the turn, he must gain control of the ball and try to make a shot attempt. The worst thing he can do is to turn, and then stop and do nothing, waiting for the 5-meter penalty call from the referee. He will usually not be rewarded unless it looks like he is trying to score.

SHOOTING WITH BACK TO THE GOAL

THE DISAPPEARANCE OF A SCORING THREAT

The hole-man shooting with his back to the goal has almost become a lost art. You just do not see as many shots taken in this position as you did 20 or 30 years ago, even ten years ago. The reason for this is that 2-meter defenders are allowed to be much more aggressive when fouling the 2-meter player. In addition, defenders are coached to give up the exclusion foul, and have their team play a man down, rather than allow the 2-meter man to score. Sweep shots, where the hole man sweeps the ball around with his arm held straight, are not taken at all anymore; mainly because 2-meter defenders usually play on the same side that the sweep shot is to be taken. For a right-handed hole-man, that would be playing on the left side to take away the sweep. (See Diagram 10-2 below)

BACKHAND

You do see the backhand shot attempted a lot more than the sweep-shot. This has also become a difficult shot to make because the goalie usually positions him self directly behind the backhand side of the shooter. For a right-handed 2-meter man, this would be on the right side. The hole-man can still take this shot; but the best chance for success is to shot the ball cross-cage, away from the goalie that is directly behind him. (See Diagram 10-2 and Picture sequence 10-B below).

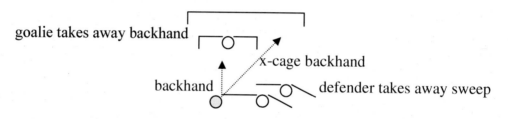

Figure 10-2 Backhand shooting angles. Cross-cage has better chance of scoring.

Picture sequence 10-B: Backhand shot cross-cage.

STEP OUT AND SHOOT

The step out shot, where the center-forward picks up the ball, turns his other shoulder towards the defender, and then steps out away from the defender for the shot, is also not as common as it used to be; for many of the same physical reasons cited above. However, if an outside player, or 2-meter player, can create a physical mismatch in size with the player who is guarding him; and then "post-up" that defender at one of the post positions, he can also take this is the kind of a shot. The "post" player can simply over power the defender because of the possible mismatch in size, and the fact that the defender is not used to guarding a player in that position. The shooter in this situation should pick up the ball, turn and step out and away from the defender, without pushing away from the defender with his other arm. (See Picture 10-C below).

Picture 10-C: Step-out and take shot

STEP OUT AND SHOOT FROM THE DRY PASS

With many teams playing zone defenses, a shot that is similar to the step out has opened up. Because the perimeter players against the zone are free to pass the ball, the 2-meter player can turn his shoulder to the defender, step out and receive a dry pass from the perimeter player for the shot. A right-handed 2-meter player will usually receive the pass from players at positions 03, 04 and 05; or from the opposite post player in the double-post offense. As he turns with his shoulder perpendicular to the defender, he has to be careful and not to push-off with his left arm, or he will be called for the offensive foul. He must use his legs, go straight up to receive the ball, and not push away from the defender to get position. (See Diagram 10-3 on next page).

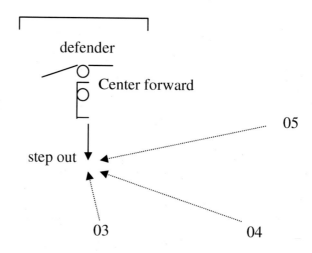

Diagram 10-3: Step out to receive pass

BACK DOOR MOVE

Another type of shot that has become commonplace, because of the availability of the free pass from the outside, is the "backdoor" shot. This situation can occur when the hole-defender plays in front or overplays the left shoulder of the right-handed hole-man in order to prevent the pass from coming in from the left side of the pool. As his teammate at 03 or 04 is fouled and receives a free pass, the center forward simply makes a move toward the opposite post, where he receives the pass for the shot. It is important that the hole-man takes his first stroke or two away from the defender on his stomach, and then pop up high to receive the pass. Any move away from the defender on his back is usually called as an offensive foul for pushing off. (See Diagram 10-4 below).

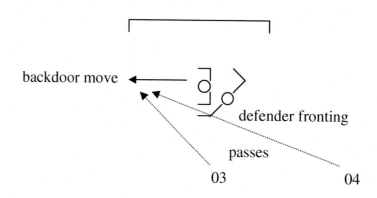

Diagram 10-4: Back door move when fronted

THE 2-METER PLAYER MUST MAKE THE FIRST MOVE IN TRANSITION

A fact of life that the center-forward has to live with, is that he will be countered at every opportunity. It is critical that he make the first move back towards the other end of the pool when the ball turns over to the other team. If he sits still while the shot is being taken, it allows the defender to pull by him and get front position on the subsequent counter. After the initial stroke by the center forward, he must keep sliding in front of the defender as he is swimming; and not allow the defender to get around him.

If by chance he does get beat on the counter, he must resist the temptation to grab the defender and get back in front position. Referees are looking for this situation in the game. The 2-meter player must do everything he can to avoid the exclusion, including stopping and putting both hands up if necessary. Teams will purposely try to get their opponent's center forward excluded from the game, with three exclusions, during counterattack situations.

It is not smart for the center forward to get excluded in the back-court, especially when the defender still has to swim 20-meters to get into scoring position at the other end of the pool. Teammates should always be looking to help out their hole-man in this situation. They should try and switch with him, so he doesn't have to swim all the way to the other end of the pool to play defense.

PLAYING 2-METER DEFENSE

PHYSICAL ABILITIES

The 2-meter defender must first of all have the size to defend the center forward from the other team, who is usually the biggest player on the team. Size and long arms are especially important when playing behind the center forward. Smaller players who get stuck guarding a bigger center should try to play in front of the center, while his teammates press on the outside. Probably the most critical physical attribute that a 2-meter defender can have are strong legs. A defender without strong legs will lose the physical battle with the center every time. The defender should also be a strong swimmer so that he can counterattack the center forward every time the ball turns over. Not only will he gain a free man advantage, but also he will tire out the center forward so that he becomes less effective as the game goes on.

Because of the way the game is being called today, the center-defender should expect to get excluded whenever the ball comes into the 2-meter player. This will happen no matter how good a job the defender does, unless he can steal the ball or have an outside defender steal the ball. It is the price he has to pay in order to keep the center forward from scoring. He can avoid an exclusion foul when his teammates are crashing in to steal the ball, by holding both hands and elbows up and backing off a little.

POSITIONING BEHIND THE CENTER FORWARD

The most common mistake that defenders make is to play directly behind the center forward and directly on top of his shoulders. The defender will lose this battle every time or get ejected in the process. A defender will be much more effective by staying low in the water, with his hands on the shoulder blades of the center-forward, and with a little space between his chest and the center forwards back.

At the same time he must over-play one side of the center forward. He can then move to the other side by using the "lat" area under the center forward's arm-pit, or the outside of the arm, to pull himself from side to side. Playing on top of the center forward's shoulders limits the mobility of the defender and his ability to move from side to side. Playing behind and on top also gives the center forward the advantage; because he knows exactly where the defender is and easier to control. (See Picture 10-D below).

Picture 10-D: Never play directly behind the center-forward!

POSITIONING AND FOULING

Playing on one shoulder or the other will help the defender to foul or steal the ball without getting kicked out every time. Playing on the side allows the defender to reach around the side for the ball instead of going directly over the shoulder. Reaching over the area between the neck and the outside of the shoulder almost always results in the exclusion on the defender. When trying to stop the shot, the defender must reach around for the ball, or at the very least grab the center forward's forearm. This greatly reduces the chances of being ejected. (See Picture 10-E on the next page)

A pass to the center forward from the same side that the defender is playing on is considered a "bad pass." In many of these situations the referee will not pay off the bad pass, and will allow the defender to foul or steal the ball without being ejected, as long as he goes around the side and not over the shoulder.

Picture 10-E: Play on the same side as the ball is on. In this case the right side.

POSITIONING AND CONTROLLING THE SHOT

If the defender is playing on one side of the center forward, the goalkeeper must play on the opposite side. Most passes will arrive to the center forward on the opposite side that the 2-meter defender is on. In most cases, this is a difficult pass for the offense to make, and the slougher can steal the ball. In this situation the goalkeeper has a clear path to the ball for a possible steal, or can position himself for the shot from that side. The ideal situation is for the defender to play on the left shoulder of the right-handed hole man, taking away the power turn or sweep from that side; while the goalie plays directly behind the right shoulder, thus taking away the backhand shot and the possibility of stealing the bad pass. This is not always possible, depending on the position of the ball. (See Diagram 10-2 and Picture 10-B on previous pages).

POSITIONING FOR THE "CRASH" ON 2-METERS

The defender will typically position himself on the shoulder on the same side of the 2-meter player that the ball is situated on. He must play far enough around the side of the center forward, so as to be in position to steal the ball if it is passed in to that side. Doing this will cause the player with the ball to pass it to the opposite side of the center forward. It is on that side that the crasher will come in from to make the steal. This whole sequence has to be coordinated between the center forward and the outside "crasher". If the ball is on the right side, so is the defender; and the crash will come from the left side. If the ball is on the left, so is the defender; and the crash will come from the right side. An example of the latter is shown in Diagram 10-5 on the next page).

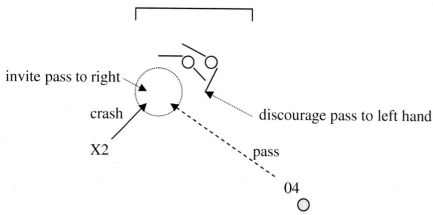

Diagram 10-5: Ball and defender on left side, crash from right side

POSITIONING FOR THE COUNTER

By playing on the side of the hole-man rather than the back, the defender has an easier path to take when he counters the hole man. Playing behind the hole man means that he must get around him before he can start the counter. Playing on the side of the hole-man, with a little tug on the arm as he swims, insures that he will beat the hole-man on the counterattack every time down the pool.

Once the defender gets in front of the 2-meter player he must do everything that he can to get him out of the game by drawing the exclusion foul. If he is pulled back, or even touched by the center forward, he must show the referee that he is being fouled. He can do this by falling back slightly. It is important that he not fall back so much that the move looks to be exaggerated; or that he losses his front position to the hole-man.

DO NOT ALLOW A GOAL

The bottom line for the defender is that he must not allow the hole-man to score. The hole-man is usually the biggest threat on the team, because of his size, his ability, and his position directly in front and close to the goal. The defender must do everything that he can to keep the center forward from scoring, even if that includes getting ejected. The idea here is that your teammates have a better chance of defending the other teams 6 on 5, than keeping the hole-man from scoring a goal. Many European teams rely on this defense because they have such a good extra-man defense. They loose a few 2-meter defenders with three fouls, but they do not allow any goals out of 2-meters. When fouling to prevent the shot, it is important for the defender to grab the forearm of the hole-man, so that he cannot get a shot off.

KEEPING THE BALL AWAY FROM THE HOLE-MAN

Defensively, this is the area of water polo that has seen the most improvement and has become more sophisticated over the years. For most offensive teams, everything revolves around the hole-man. The whole offense is based on the ball getting to him. If a defense can keep the hole-man from getting the ball or delay the ball getting into the "hole", they don't have to worry about getting ejected or the hole-man scoring a goal. To do this takes a team effort and coordination between the 2-meter defender, the goalie, and the outside defenders. Defensively, teams have to decide whether to play behind or in front of the hole-man, or do both.

PLAYING IN FRONT OF THE CENTER-FORWARD

Playing in front of the hole-man is probably the most effective way of keeping the ball from getting to him, or at least delay the ball from getting to him; thus reducing the amount of time the offense has to work with. The center-defender first must allow the hole-man to get to the center position, by giving him an easy path to the goal, following him, and then sliding in front. In order for this to be effective, the ball must be under pressure; so the 2-meter defender doesn't have to worry about a pinpoint pass coming into the hole-man. (See Picture 8-E in Chapter 8, "Essential defensive skills)

The defense must also not allow the ball to get to the wings for an easy pass inside to the hole-man. This can best be accomplished by the wing-defenders playing in front of the wings. If the ball does get to the wing, it must be fouled; thus allowing the goalie to come out of the goal, or the wing defender to drop back to discourage the pass into the hole.

STAYING IN FRONT

Playing in front of the center-forward is the only effective way to keep the ball out of 2-meters when a team is playing a press defense. All players on the team must learn how to guard in front and stay in front position. It is inevitable that any player could be taken into set by the center forward in order to create a mismatch. The player who is fronting must keep his hips up, face the 2-meter player, and constantly be moving to stay between the ball and the center forward. This movement is accomplished by moving the hands and swimming a stroke or two if necessary, and also swinging the legs and hips around and always pointing towards the ball. It is important that the defender keep his hands free and moving, and not wrapped around the hole man's shoulder and neck. (See Diagram 10-6 below).

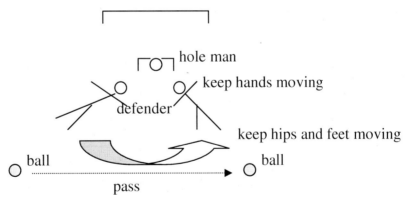

Diagram 10-6: Defender moves around in front by using his hands to take a stroke, keeping his feet and hips pointed toward the ball, and staying between hole man and ball as it is passed around the perimeter.

LET THE GOALIE GET THE OVERPASS INSIDE TO 2-METERS

The goalie must also be in position and ready for the overpass into the hole. This should not be too difficult to accomplish, because the hole-man is so preoccupied with wrestling with the defender, that the goalie has a better chance of getting to the ball than the center does. If the ball does somehow find its way inside and into the center forward, he doesn't have a very high percentage shot; especially with the goalie looming over him and the defender on his back. No problem or 5-meter penalty as long as the defender keeps both his hands up and does not commit a 5-meter penalty foul. Positioning in front of the center is much easier in water polo than in basketball, because in water polo there is a goalie present to discourage or steal the inside pass.

COORDINATING THE WING DEFENDER AND 2-METER DEFENDER

It is the goalies decision on what he wants to do when the ball is passed to the wing. He must first look at the position of the 2-meter defender as the ball is being passed to the wing. If the 2-meter defender can get all the way around to the side of the ball, and take away the passing lane into 2-meters; then neither the wing defender or the goalie have to do anything. If this is done properly, then the wing player will have nowhere to pass the ball. (See Diagram 10-7 below)

If the 2-meter defender cannot get all the way around to the side of the ball, then the goalie must call for a foul on the wing, and then either a drop from the wing defender or the goalie coming out of the goal to take away the pass into the 2-meter player. (See Diagram 10-8 below)

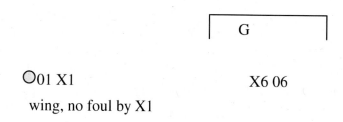

Diagram 10-7: X6 playing ball-side prevents pass into 2-meters. No wing foul needed.

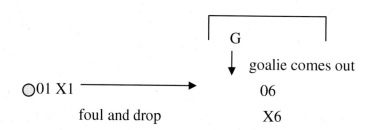

Diagram 10-8: X6 in front. Wing foul and drop, or foul and goalie

DEFENDING SHOTS FROM THE HOLE-SET

COORDINATED EFFORT

The best defense is to not let the center forward get a shot off at all; or completely deny him the ball by playing in front or stealing the ball. If all fails and the center-forward does get off a shot, the best chance of stopping the shot is by a coordinated effort between the goalie and the hole-defender. The ideal situation as described in Diagram 10-2 above and involves the center-defender taking away the sweep or strong-side shot while the goalie takes away the backhand shot. If this cannot happen because the defender is stuck on the wrong side, then the goalie must take the opposite side that the defender is on.

DEFENDING THE BACK DOOR

Playing on the side or in front of the 2-meter man means that he can take off and swim to the opposite post for an easy shot. The 2-meter defender cannot allow this to happen. He must keep control of the center forward, holding him if necessary, so that he cannot make a move to the post. At the very least he has to stay close to him as he makes this move.

If the hole-man makes this move on his back and gives a little push-off, the defender can easily draw the offensive foul by giving a little fake backwards, as though he were pushed off of. The referees are looking for this type of offensive foul from the center forward. If the defender can stay close to the center-forward as he makes his back-door move, then all he has to do is look back and put his arm up to deny or intercept the pass to him.

DEFENDING THE STEP-OUT

The hole-man usually telegraphs this move by turning his shoulder into the defender before he makes the move away from the defender. He then steps out and away from the defender to receive the pass or take the shot. The defender can discourage or intercept the pass by positioning himself in between the passer and the center-forwards face. The defender can also try to hold the hole man underwater by the arm, or try to draw the foul as described above, but he cannot let the hole man get away from him. He definitely cannot push down on the shoulder without risking a 5-meter penalty. (See Diagrams 10-9 and 10-10 on the next page).

A small fake to draw the push-off foul is more effective than a more dramatic backwards flop. If it doesn't work, the defender is still close to the center forward. Once he has the ball in his hand and is attempting to shoot, the defender is allowed to climb his frame, go for the arm and try to sink him in order to throw off the shot.

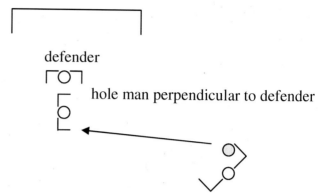

defender

hole man perpendicular to defender

Diagram 10-9: 2-meter defender in poor position to intercept ball or prevent shot

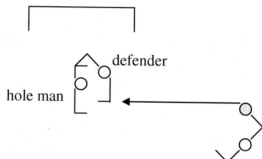

defender

hole man

Diagram 10-10: 2-meter defender in best position to intercept ball or stop shot.

DEFENDING THE INSIDE WATER TURN

First the defender must play one shoulder while the goalie plays the other; forcing the hole man to turn to the side the goalie is playing. The defender must not allow him to turn away from the goalie. Once the hole-man has turned and faces the goal in possession of the ball, there is not much that the defender can do. He must not panic and try to get the ball back, as this usually results in a 5-meter penalty foul.

Rather, the defender must stay calm and "immediately" get his hands up, so that the 2-meter man cannot pick up the ball for a shot. By making him shoot the ball "off the water" (take a wet shot) you are putting him at a disadvantage. The chances of him scoring this shot are much lower, especially in comparison to his chances of scoring the resulting penalty shot. Both hands and elbows must be up in this situation, and the defender must resist the temptation to reach over the shoulder for the ball.

CHAPTER 11

EXTRA-MAN OFFENSE AND DEFENSE

THE DIFFERENCE BETWEEN WINNING AND LOSING

There are many aspects of the game of water polo that are important for players to master in order for teams to win games. In many competitive hard fought games, however, the difference between winning and losing comes down to the success of a team's extra-man offense and defense. There is no guarantee that because you are a man-up you will score a goal, or if you are a man down that you will be scored upon. The game has evolved to the point where if you score 50 percent of the time on your man-up situations, your team is extremely successful. This situation is similar to the sport of ice hockey, where natural goals are hard to come by, and most of the goals scored are in penalty situations. In both ice hockey and water polo, a high percentage of the goals scored in games are from the man-up situation.

DIFFICULTY IN SCORING

Over the years it has gotten much more difficult to score on the man-up situation. Most teams, even at the international and Olympic level, only score about 25-50 percent of the time, and many times less than that. Teams, in most games, get anywhere from 6-12 extra-man opportunities per game. The more times that you can score and take advantage of the extra-man, the more games your team will win. Teams that play good man down defense would much rather play a man down, than to allow the center forward or outside shooter from their opponent's team to get a wide open shot from right in front of the goal. The percentages are in their favor.

TIME ADVANTAGE TO THE DEFENSE

Time allowed for a team to execute is a critical factor in success of the extra-man. Years ago, exclusions were 35 to 45 seconds, and teams had time to pass the ball, run special plays, and wear out the goalie and defenders, until they scored. Now with a 20 second exclusion, teams must set up quickly, make good passes, and look for an opportunity to score against a forest of arms in front of the goal. If a team makes one bad overpass, they quickly lose the opportunity to score. Fear of the overpass forces teams to make less difficult shorter passes, which are easier to defend. The offensive team can easily get into a situation where they run out of time and have to shoot. This gives the defense the advantage, because they know that you have to shoot the ball at that time, and can more easily defend the shot.

SETTING UP THE EXTRA-MAN OFFENSE

THE QUICK

Teams must take advantage of the situation immediately following the exclusion call by the referee. This is when the defense is weakest and most vulnerable. The defense has not had time to drop back and cover up, and is still in the process of moving into defensive positions. This is when the offense should look for the "quick" shot on goal, especially if the excluded player has left someone open in front of the goal. If the ball is at an outside position when the exclusion occurs in front of the goal, it must immediately be passed to the open man. If the man in front of the goal has the ball when his defender is excluded, he can immediately pass the ball outside and then get it back again before he can be covered by the defense. Outside players have to be alert and ready to receive this pass, and then quickly get it back to the open man.

SETTING UP-POSITIONS
Players must take a few extra seconds to get to the positions that they are assigned to, and the ones that they have practiced. Getting all six players in correct position is more important than the few seconds gained by players going to the positions that they may be closest to. The extra-man chances of success improve dramatically if players are in the right position.

SETTING UP IN FRONT OF THE GOAL, THE 4-2
Normal positioning in front of the goal usually calls for four players just outside the 2-meter line, two post players in the 2 and 3 positions, and two wing players in the 1 and 6 positions. The two outside players, 4 and 5, usually line up on the 5-meter line, opposite the two post players. (See Diagram 11-1 below).

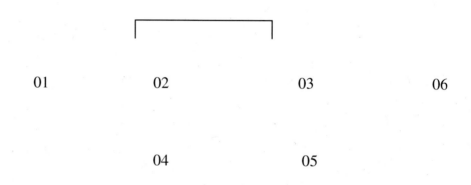

Diagram 11-1: The 4-2 Man-Up Offense

FOUR IN A ROW
Four players, positions 1, 2, 3, and 6, that are lined up on the 2-meter line doesn't always work. It makes the long pass between the 01 and 06 players more difficult, because the ball has to go over the heads of five players, three of them defenders. A team can counteract this problem by putting either the 01 player or the 06 player into the pocket area 3-4 meters from the goal, making for a safer open passing lane between them. This is also a good strategy if you don't have a left-hander to play the 06 position. Putting a right-hander in the pocket at that position gives him a much better shooting angle, and it also makes the 1-6 and 6-1 pass easier to complete. (See Diagram 11-2 on next page).

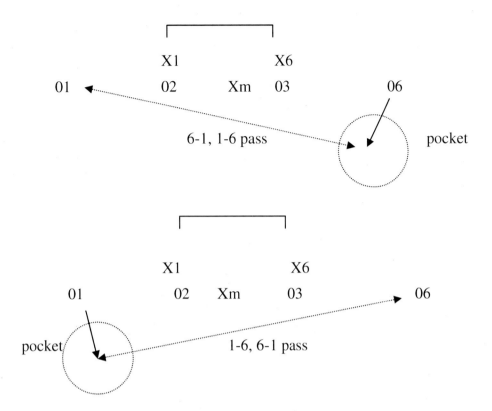

Diagram 11-2: O6 or O1 moves into the pocket to open up the passing lane

SLIDE THE OUTSIDE PLAYERS

A situation that occurs in the normal 4-2 set up is that the O4 and O5 outside shooters don't have good shooting lanes to the goal, mainly because they are directly in front of the X4 and X5 defenders. Moving O4 and O5 to the left or right, puts one of them in the center of the goal, giving him a much better shooting lane to the goal. The players at O4 and O5 move left or right depending on which player O1 or O6 is in the pocket. The shift can be initiated by either O1 or O6 with the ball, moving into the pocket, or inside the 2-meter line. The other three players without the ball simply follow the lead of the player with the ball. They all move together and in the same direction that the player with the ball moves.

An example of this is shown in Diagram 11-3 on the next page. O1 moves out into the pocket, O4 and O5 move with him by shifting to the right, and O6 moves down to the 2-meter line, if he isn't already there. The key player in this situation is O4, who is now in the center of the goal, with much better shooting angles then he had before, when he was directly in front of the X4 defender and the O2 post player.

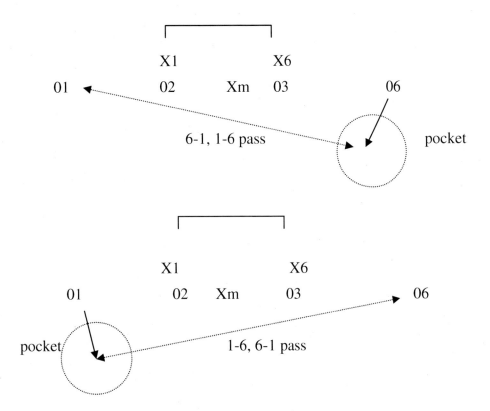

Diagram 11-2: 06 or 01 moves into the pocket to open up the passing lane

SLIDE THE OUTSIDE PLAYERS

A situation that occurs in the normal 4-2 set up is that the O4 and O5 outside shooters don't have good shooting lanes to the goal, mainly because they are directly in front of the X4 and X5 defenders. Moving O4 and O5 to the left or right, puts one of them in the center of the goal, giving him a much better shooting lane to the goal. The players at O4 and O5 move left or right depending on which player O1 or O6 is in the pocket. The shift can be initiated by either 01 or 06 with the ball, moving into the pocket, or inside the 2-meter line. The other three players without the ball simply follow the lead of the player with the ball. They all move together and in the same direction that the player with the ball moves.

An example of this is shown in Diagram 11-3 on the next page. 01 moves out into the pocket, 04 and 05 move with him by shifting to the right, and 06 moves down to the 2-meter line, if he isn't already there. The key player in this situation is 04, who is now in the center of the goal, with much better shooting angles then he had before, when he was directly in front of the X4 defender and the 02 post player.

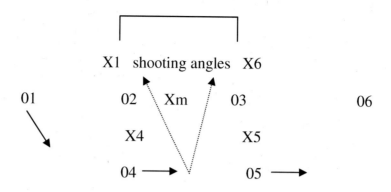

Diagram 11-3: Shifting right improves shooting angle for 04

As shown above, the players at O1 and O4 have dramatically improved their shooting angles at the goal. O5 has not helped his position or shooting angle, especially if he is a right-hander. A position wide right of the post for a right-handed player at O5 makes it a more difficult shot. We can solve this problem in two ways. Option 1 is to have O5 penetrate forward and towards the center, after he receives the ball, in order to help his shooting angle. The other option (option 2) is to shift 05 to the left, and at the same time move O4 to his left. It is better to have the right hander at O4 shooting from a spot that is wide-left of the goal, than to have a right-hander at O5 shooting from a spot that is wide right of the goal. The latter solution also helps your team if you have a right-hander at the 06 position. Moving 06 into the pocket will also help his shooting angle. (See Diagram 11-4 below).

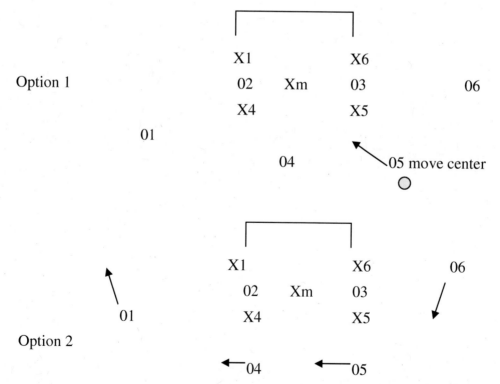

Diagram 11-4: Moving 05 to the left for a better shooting angle in the middle of the goal.

DEFENDERS HAVE TO CHOOSE
Another benefit of shifting O4 and O5 to the right and left, is that it takes the defenders X4 and X5 out of position. If they want to block the outside shot, they have to shift out of their normal position, to a position in front of the shooter. This will take them away from directly dropping back and guarding the post players. It makes it a little more difficult to guard both the outside shooter and the post player; because of the greater distance that the defenders have to travel between them. (See Diagram 11-5 below).

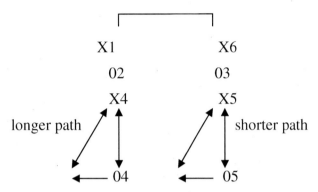

Diagram 11-5: Moving 04 and 05 to the left will force defenders X4 and X5 to move to a less advantageous position.

WHAT KIND OF PLAYERS AT EACH POSITION?
Players should play positions that they are best suited for. The correct position for a particular player has to do with his physical abilities like leg strength and size, his ability to shoot or receive the ball, or whether he is left or right handed. Many times, however, you must place a player in a position that he is not suited for, because you don't have anyone else to play that position. For instance, a right-hander might have to play the 06 left-handers position if no left-handers are available. Players should learn to play two positions well, one on the outside and one on a post; but players should be ready to play any position in an emergency. This also gives a coach the flexibility to move players to different positions in order to confuse the defense.

BASIC POSITIONING
Basic positioning calls for the best shooters and passers to play the four outside positions 1, 4, 5 and 6. Taller players with the best legs and ability to handle the ball can play the two post positions, 2 and 3. The player at the 02-post must have excellent leg strength and long arms, more so than the post player at 03. The player at the 01 position must have the ability to shoot quickly, and also be able to shoot a variety of shots that are available. He has the quick shot to the near corner, the wrap around shot to the near side, and the cross-cage shot to the other side of the goal. The player at the 06-wing position must possess the same qualities as the player at 01; but he should be left-handed. Because of the possibility that the other five players will be right-handed, the 06-player has to make the right decision on whom to pass to at the other five positions. This position is more of a "passing" position than the other five positions.

TWO BEST PLAYERS OPPOSITE EACH OTHER

Most teams put their best right-handed shooter at the 04 outside position. At the same time they can put their biggest player with the best legs at the 02-post position, directly in front of the shooter at 04. This puts a lot of stress on the X4 defender, who has to play between the two biggest threats to score on the other team. Rotating the 04 player towards the center of the goal, gives him a better shooting lane, and also gives the 02-post player room to "pop" out into the open space vacated by the 04 player. See the "2 out" play under special plays. The right-hander at the 02-post position can receive the ball from 06 when he pops out; or the inside pass from 01 for the backhand shot to the opposite corner. The pass from 01 is thrown high and firm. The 02 player simply changes the path of the ball with his hand turned inward, and directs it to the back corner of the goal.

LEFT-HANDER AT 2, NEAR SIDE TRIANGLE

A great alternative is to put a left-hander at the 2-post position, opposite the best shooter at 04. This puts even more stress on the defender playing between 02 and 04. When 04 has the ball the defender must honor him. A pass from 04 to the 01 position, and then a quick pass to the left-hander at 02, cannot physically be covered by the X4 defender. He simply cannot get back fast enough after guarding 04 for the shot. In this situation teams are forced to cover the 02-post player with the middle defender Xm, thus leaving the 03-post open. A pass from 04 to 06 and then a quick pass to the 03-post should be open in this situation. (See Diagram 11-6 below).

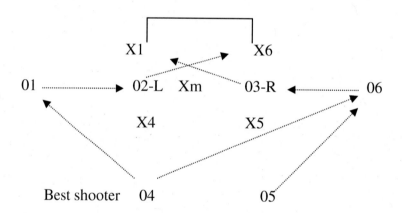

Diagram 11-6: Left-hander at the 02-post and right-hander at 03-post.

The pass from O1 to the left-hander at O2 should be made when O1 is on the 2-meter line. If the pass comes from O1 when he is in he pocket, it takes too long for O2 to turn around and take the shot; and he will be covered by the defense. O2 should shoot the ball cross-cage, because the goalie is set on O1, and covering the near side of the goal. The passer must determine how close the defenders are before he makes the pass to O2.

The same situation as above occurs on the other side of the goal at the 5-6-3 triangle. The right-handed player at the 03-post does not have to be as big as a right-hander player at the 02- post, but he also needs good legs, and the ability to handle a pass from 06, turn and shoot around the goalie. The player at 03 is usually right-handed. His shot should also be taken x-cage and away from the goalie who is playing directly in front of him.

OVER THE TOP

Many times in a 6 on 5 situation, as the ball is being passed around the outside four positions; openings will occur at the 02 and 03 post positions when O4 and O5 have the ball. This situation occurs all of the time because defenses are concentrating on the possible shot from O4 and O5. Since many teams put their best shooters at the O4 position, defenses will try to "knock down" the player at 04 by using the X4 defender. When this occurs, the player at O2 should eggbeater out a short distance towards O4, with his shoulder perpendicular to the goal and his hand up to receive the pass. The player at O4 with the ball should back up and try to draw X4 as far out as he can. He then can pass the ball "over the top" of the X4 defender to O2 for the shot. This same pass can be made from 05 "over the top" of X5 to 03 post for the shot. (See Diagram 11-7 below).

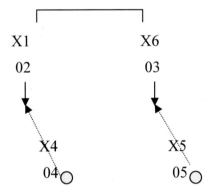

Diagram 11-7: Over the top, 04 to 02 and 05 to 03.

4-2 VERSUS A 3-3

Some teams like to run a 3-3 offense instead of a 4-2, mainly because it is easier to run and only requires three players to handle the ball. This may be true for very young players; but players at the high school level and above should be able to handle a 4-2. To me, it is a no-brainer. The 4-2 offers so many different opportunities to score, and every player is a threat. Passes to the posts from every outside position, and shots from every outside position in the 4-2, together produce twelve different options to score; versus only 3 scoring options from the 3-3 set-up. One problem with the 3-3 is that the position of the two outside defenders, playing in the gaps, gives them a greater opportunity to get free on the counterattack.

BASIC 6 ON 5 FUNDAMENTALS

SET THE GOALIE - When passing the ball around the perimeter, make sure that   each player stops the ball and "sets' the goalie. The player with the ball must make the goalie and the defender set on him, by either giving one fake; or at the very least looking at the goalie. Just passing the ball rapidly around the perimeter does nothing to get the goalie to stop and "set" on you. The man with the ball must look like he is threat to shoot the ball. More than one fake is also not necessary.

DELIBERATE PASS - Once the goalie is "set", the man with the ball should make a deliberate pass to the next offensive player, who has the option of shooting, setting the goalie on him, or passing to another player. Deliberate means that you must look at the person that you are passing to. A blind "look away" or "no look" pass sometimes does not get to the intended target. The passer usually ends up surprising his own teammate and ends up throwing it over his head.

SHOOT OFF THE PASS - The player receiving the ball should "shoot off the pass", before the goalie and defender can set on him. This means that the player should shoot as soon as he receives the ball; without making any fakes. Holding the ball for a period of time, and then taking the shot, usually results in a missed or blocked shot.

STRONG SIDE PASS - The best shot to take is after the right-handed shooter receives the ball from his right side or a left-hander from the left side. This type of shot can be taken much quicker, because the shooter does not have to take the time to draw the ball across the front of his face and bring it back before he shoots.

PASSING OVER DEFENDER - The easiest pass to make is to the person next to you, because there is no defender between you. The 1-5 or 6-4 pass is more difficult to make because the ball must go over the X4 and X5 defenders, with the chance of being intercepted. The 1-6 and 6-1 passes move the goalie and the defense the most; but are harder to complete because of the distance that they have to travel. Shorter passes are easier to execute, but they also do not move the defense and goalie as much as longer passes do. Players have to use caution when making longer passes over defenders by putting a little more arc on the pass.

TAKE WHAT THE DEFENSE GIVES YOU - A defender that comes out of his zone to attack a perimeter player will usually leave a post-man open. For instance, if the 04 player is attacked, then the 02 player will be left open. In this case, either 04 should make the pass directly to 02, or pass the ball to someone else who can get the ball to 02. Where the ball is passed depends on what the other defenders do in order to cover 02.

BE READY- Post players should be ready to receive passes from any of the four outside players, and execute shots off of any of those passes. A post player must always be "ready" to receive a pass from any perimeter player, by always turning and facing the person with the ball, and putting his hand up as a target.

MOVE THE DEFENSE WITH SPECIAL PLAYS

There are two ways to move the defense, by moving players and by moving the ball. Either way will cause defensive players to move within the zone that they are playing. In doing so, the offense is trying to take advantage of a defender that has moved or is slow to react to what the offense is doing. Remember that when the defensive player moves to cover up a movement or pass that you have made, he is leaving somebody open. Every pass or movement that you make should have a purpose in mind.

Players have to learn how to read the situation that they have created, find the open man, and get the ball to him for the shot. This should be a coordinated team effort to find the open man. Players must also learn how the defense will create an opening by react to a pass or movement one of the offensive players. Then they must learn how to take advantage of that opening.

SUCKER PLAY

The easiest play to execute is the sucker play. This play involves the 2-post player, who simply moves out away from the 2-meter line to the 3-meter line. He is trying to "suck" the X1 defender out with him, thus creating an open shot for the 1 player. (See Diagram 11-8 below).

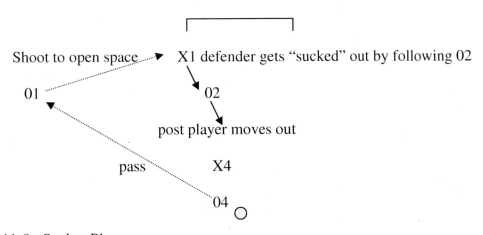

Diagram 11-8: Sucker Play.

2-OUT PLAY

Similar to the sucker play, but pre-planed and with options. This play doesn't take a lot of time in order to succeed. The 01 player must stay down on the 2-meter line, so he won't interfere with the play. The 04 player with the ball, and the 05 player both shift to the right, leaving an open space in front of the 02-post player. The 04 player moves forward with the ball, drawing the attention of the X4 defender. As X4 moves out towards 04, the 02-post moves out into the open area and receives the pass from 04. (See Diagram 11-9a on next page).

If X1 follows 02 out, then 05 passes to 01 for the shot. (See Diagram 11-9b below). If Xm follows 02 out, then that opens up 03. In this situation, 04 passes to 06, who then passes to 03 for the shot. (See Diagram 11-9c below). The last option is for 04 to shoot the ball if X4 does not cover him.

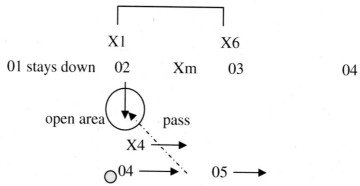

Diagram 11-9a: 2-out play. 1st option

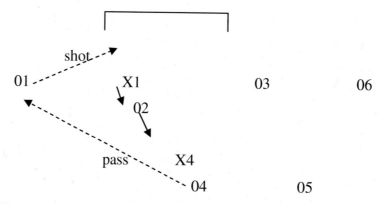

Diagram 11-9b: 2-out play, 2nd option. X1 follows 02, 04 passes to 01 for the shot.

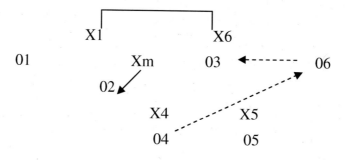

Figure 11-9c: 2-out play 3rd option. Xm follows 02, O4 pass to 06, pass to 03 for the shot.

INITIATION PLAYS
The next two plays are basic movement plays used to initiate the 6 on 5 offense. The "6-in play" was introduced to the USA National Team by Coach Ratko Rudic, and was used as the basic 6 on 5 formation for the 2004 Olympic games. The only drawback to the play is that it takes the right-handed player at 05 wide right of the goal, making him less of a scoring threat. It also requires a left-handed player at 06. A right-hander at 06 will not have a good shooting angle unless he is in the pocket.

A solution to the drawbacks of the "6-in play" involves 01 moving inside the 2-meter line to initiate the play instead of 06. This is called a "1-in play" and was used by the 2008 US Olympic Team. It results in moving 05 to a better shooting position in the center of the goal, and also moving 06 into a better position in the pocket. (See Diagrams 11-10 below and 11-11 on next page).

6-IN PLAY
This play is initiated by the 06-wing player, preferably a left-hander. The ball should go to him almost immediately. He will initiate the play by taking the ball inside the 2-meter line. At the same time that he moves inside the two, the rest of his teammates move with him. The 01 player will rotate out into the pocket, the 02 player will go inside 2-meters and move towards the 3-post, the 03 player will move a little outside the 2-meter line, while 04 and 05 will shift to their right. O6 will have several choices on where to distribute the ball depending on how the defense reacts to the movements of the offensive players. (See Diagram 11-10 below).

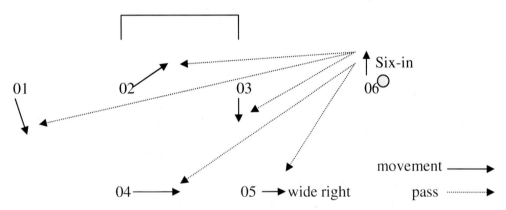

Diagram 11-10: 6-in play

1-IN PLAY
This same play can be run from the other side of the goal with 01 going inside the 2-meter line with the ball and all players shifting towards him. It is not necessary; but a left-hander playing at the 02-post position or the 03-post position would facilitate the execution of the play. Every player is in a good position to execute a shot on goal. (See Diagram 11-11 on next page)

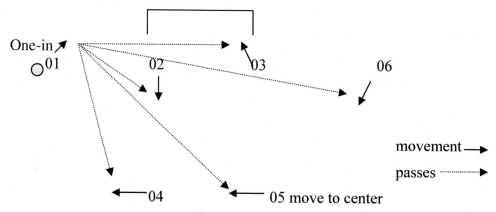

Diagram 11-11: One-in play

One-in

01   02   03   06

movement ⟶

passes ·······▶

04   05 move to center

EXTRA-MAN DEFENSE

ADVANTAGE DEFENSE

The 20-second exclusion under today's rules actually gives the advantage to the defense. The shorter time allows the defense to put pressure on the ball, and perhaps cause a bad pass or hurried shot, and also cover the post players. This fast-moving mobile defense can easily be maintained for 10-15 seconds, than for the 30-seconds required under the old rules. The situation where the offense must take the shot or run out of time comes up quickly, thus giving the defense the additional advantage of knowing when and where the shot is coming from.

SKILLS REQUIRED TO PLAY EXTRA-MAN DEFENSE

SHOT BLOCKING – FIELD

The most essential defensive skill is the ability to block shots with one arm. In most situations the defensive player holds an arm up in front of the shooter, trying to take away the shot to the near side of the goal, while the goalie takes away the cross-cage shot. In most situations the defender will hold up the arm directly in front of the shooting arm. Against a right-handed shooter the defender raises his left hand, and against a left-hander he holds up his right hand. (See Figure 8-4 and Pictures 8-J and 8-K in Chapter 8).

The only time that a defender does not match hands is at the X1 and X6 corner defender positions. As the X1 and X6 wing defenders swing back to cover the shot from 01 and 06, they must first put up the arm nearest the goal post to defend the quick shot to the corner. At the X1 defensive position, the player must swing back and hold up the right hand; and at the X6 defensive position, he must swing back and hold up the left hand.

Once the defense has stopped the quick corner shots, then both defenders will switch arms and hold up a matching hand; at the same time moving slightly right or left to cover the shot to the corner. For X1, that would be the left hand, and for X6, that would be the right hand. Covering the corner leaves the goalie free to block the middle of the goal and the cross-cage shot. (See Diagram 11-12 below and Pictures 11-A thru D on next page).

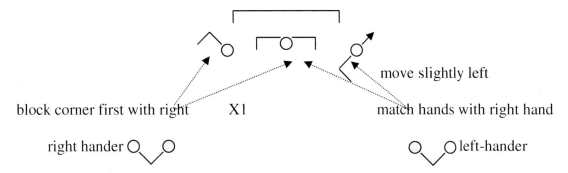

block corner first with right   X1   match hands with right hand

move slightly left

right hander   left-hander

Figure 11-12 X1 is blocking corner first with right hand. X6 has switched from quick left hand to right hand, while moving slightly to his left to block corner.

Pictures 11-A, B: Guarding the left corner. First the left hand up, then switch to right hand.

Pictures 11-C, D: Guarding the right corner. First the right hand up, then switch to left hand.

ROTATING OVER THE HIPS

The other basic skill required of the extra-man defender is to be able to go from a vertical shot blocking position to a horizontal position and then back to a vertical position again. This requires mobility by the defender, and the ability to rotate his body "over the hips" in going from one position to the other. The defender is required to perform this skill in going from a vertical blocking position to defend the outside shot, back to horizontal position to defend the post, back to a vertical blocking position, and then going horizontal to swim out and "knock down" the shooter. This skill is covered in Chapter 8 on "Essential Defensive Skills".

BASIC PRINCIPALS OF THE MAN DOWN DEFENSE

1. TAKE AWAY THE QUICK - Take away the "quick" shot immediately after the exclusion. Recognize when there is an exclusion, communicate who is excluded, and drop back quickly to cover the players closest to the goal. If the player who is excluded was guarding the 2-meter player in front of the goal, while the ball was in an outside position; then the 2-meter player must immediately be covered to keep him from receiving the ball from the outside. If the situation occurs where there are too many defenders in front of the goal, then the first player who arrives will have priority, and must direct the other players to go back out and cover the outside shooters or the other post player.

2. COVER TWO PLAYERS - A defender is responsible for covering two players, the person behind him on the post and the outside shooter in front of him. Be willing to work hard to stop the offensive team from scoring. Know when to drop back and take the post player. If the ball is at O6, and O2 and O3 post players are right-handers, then X4 and X5 must drop back to take away the right shooting arm of the post players. If the ball is passed to 04 or 05, then X4 and X5 must leave the post-man, pivot over your hips as described above, and then get into a vertical blocking position. Communicate if there are any left-handers playing a post position so the outside defender knows when to drop back on the left arm. If the ball is at 01, then the two outside defenders do not have to drop all the way back to the post players; because their right hands are on the inside facing the goal.

3. TAKE AWAY THE STRENGTHS OF THE OTHER TEAM - Knock down a good outside shooter and drop back against a weak shooter, thus "giving him the shot." You especially want to encourage right-handers at the 5 and 6 positions to take the shot, rather than right-handed shooters at the 4 or 1 positions. This is because 5 and 6 are weak shooting positions for right-handers.

4. CHANGE DEFENSES - Playing the same defense all of the time allows an offense to practice against it. Come out with a defense that your opponents are not prepared for. A good time to do this is after the other team has called a time out to set up their offense. You can surprise them with a knock down type of defense, or go man to man on their best player, forcing someone else to shoot the ball. At the very least it will disrupt their planned play. If it is towards the end of the game and you are behind by a goal or two, then some kind of gap defense will put you in good position for an easy counterattack goal.

5. WATCH THE EYES - The key to pressing and "knocking down" the man in front of you is to anticipate the ball coming to him. This can easily be done by watching the eyes of the player who is passing to your man. The passer will always look at the person that he will pass the ball to. Start moving towards your man as the ball leaves the passers hand, and arrive as the ball arrives.

6. KNOCK DOWN – "Knocking" down players down requires a lot of energy and can wear out the defensive team. It is difficult to keep up this type of pressure defense for the full 20-second exclusion. Since most teams will want to "move" the ball and rarely take a shot early in the possession, it is better to wait until 5 or 10 seconds have gone by before you start knocking players down. By putting the offense in a "must shoot" situation, you are increasing the pressure on them and can force them to commit passing and shooting errors.

MAN-DOWN BASIC DEFENSIVE SCHEMES

FULL ZONE

A full zone defense requires shot blocking skills as discussed earlier. The advantage of this system is that field players can block a shot and help out their goalie by taking away part of the goal with their arms; or channel the shot to an area where the goalie can make the block.

The two outside defenders X4 and X5 must position themselves half way between the post and the outside shooter, and only drop back when the ball can be passed to the posts O2 and O3, from O1 and O6. The two corner defenders X1 and X6 must drop back in an arc, so that their bodies are lined up next to the goal post. It is a mistake for the corner defenders to move out toward the shooter, rather than move back towards the goal post. The middle defender Xm must move between, and also guard the posts O2 and O3 when the ball is at O1 or O6; and also get his hand up to help the goalie block the outside shot from 4 or 5. (See Diagram 11-13 below and Picture 11- K on next page).

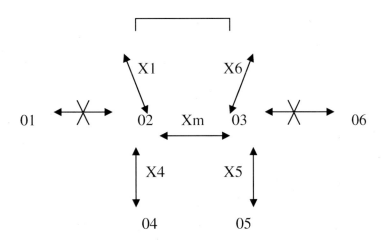

Diagram 11-13: Full Zone

Picture 11-K: 04 shooting. Full zone blocking with four arms (X1, X4, Xm and X6) up or going up. Channel shot to goalie.

PRESS-IN AND OUT

This defense requires mobile defenders who can quickly "knock down" an outside shooter and then get back to guard a post. This defense can be effective in keeping the best shooters from the other team from shooting, and at the same time dictating where you want the shot to come from. This defense also has the advantage of not letting the best shooters on the other team get into a comfort zone, both passing and shooting the ball.

KNOCK DOWN DEFENSE

Very similar to the "in and out" defense described above, except that two consecutive players are knocked down instead of only one player. Knocking down the second player to receive the ball from the first player who is being knocked down really helps to disrupt the passing sequence of the offense. As the first defender knocks down the first shooter, the second defender must anticipate the pass coming to his man, edge out towards him a little, and then explode towards the man receiving the ball as soon as the ball leaves the hand of the first passer. If the defender arrives at the same time as the ball arrives, he can sometimes intercept and steal the ball; or at the very least disrupt the shot.

ALL-OUT PRESS

The all out press is a great defense to surprise the other team when they don't expect it. It requires that all outside players be "knocked down" on every pass that is made. The defender must arrive at the same time as the ball arrives so that the passer is "put on his back", and his next pass or shot attempt is disrupted. (See Diagram 11-14 on next page).

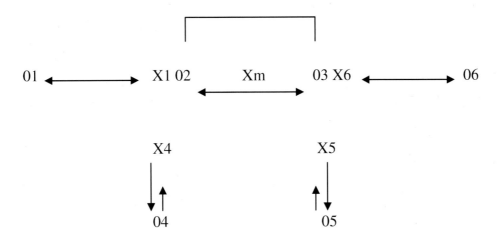

Diagram 11-14: All-Out Press

If enough pressure is put on the man with the ball, his next pass can easily be intercepted, or his shot easily blocked. If a post-position is left open during the passing sequence, then the middle defender usually takes one post and the goalie takes the other post. Once the ball leaves the passer's hand at O4 and O5, the defender drops back off him slightly, so he is in position to attack him again, if the ball comes back to him. This defense requires good anticipation by defenders and constant pressure on the ball.

The all-out press is difficult to maintain for more than 10-12 seconds. Consequently, it should be started in the last part of the 20-second exclusion, instead of the first part. The time to start the press can be set up ahead of time, perhaps during the other team's time-out. Usually it is set up by the coach dictating that the press will start on the first pass to one of the offensive players. Start by "knocking down on the first pass to O6." Defender X6 will start the press by knocking down O6. Every player who receives the ball after that is knocked down, until the ball is turned over, or the teams become even.

ATTACKING FROM THE 'BLIND' SIDE

A lot of teams put their best shooter at the O4 position and their biggest player at the O2-post position, thinking that the defensive player X4 cannot guard both of them at the same time. The defense can counter this move by dropping X4 back on to the O2 post player and bringing X5 over to blind side the O4 shooter. This does leave the O5 player open for the shot; but if he is a right hander there is a good chance of having his shot blocked by the goalie, or the middle defender Xm, who slides over in front of the 3 post player and puts his hand up.

This sequence is also a way for the defense to slide into a 4-1 Gap defense from a 3-2 standard defense. Execute as described above, and also have X1 and X6 go out and guard O1 and O6 to complete the 4-1 defense. It is best executed during the last 5-10 seconds left before the teams become even. Many times X5 can surprise O4 from the "blind" side, causing a turnover and counterattack goal. (See Diagram 11-15 on the next page).

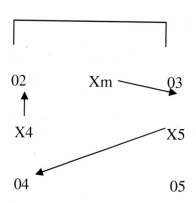

Diagram 11-15: Attack from the blind side with X5

PRACTICING EXCLUSIONS

Players must practice leaving the area of play after being excluded, going to the correct corner, and then coming back in to the field of play after being waved in by the desk or referee; or after his team regains possession of the ball. Any of these parts of the exclusion that are done incorrectly by a player can result in another exclusion, or a 5-meter penalty shot. Players must know the rules and must practice these "exclusion" situations so that they can execute them correctly in a game.

Players who are excluded in practice should always go all the way to the corner, and come back in correctly. The five players on defense must know what to do when the player who has been excluded is coming back into the field of play. The worst-case scenario in this situation occurs when the player who is coming back in, and another defender, both guard the same offensive player; leaving the player with the ball wide open for an easy shot.

CHAPTER 12

COUNTERATTACK SKILLS

WHY COUNTERATTACK?
The counterattack is one of the easiest ways to score a goal. It is a part of the game in which a team can create a good scoring opportunity, and which the opponent and the referees cannot take away from you:

1. It makes players play a more aggressive type of game.

2. If you don't score, it moves the players down the pool quickly; thus giving a team more time to run their offense. This is becoming more important with the 30- second shot clock.

3. Opponents have to be aware of your counterattack. It makes them more tentative; thus taking away their aggressiveness on offense.

4. It tires out your opponent, making them less effective on offense and defense, especially late in the game.

5. It creates an exciting part of the game that is fun to play, and fun for fans to watch.

COUNTERATTACK PHILOSOPHY
How important is the counterattack in the overall scheme of things? At Stanford the counterattack was emphasized more than any other part of the game. The counterattack became a "way of life." This was partly because of the above reasons, partly because it was a good fit for our smaller, faster players, and partly because we decided that it would become our identity as a team.

We found that it was easier to score on the counterattack than in the frontcourt offense. This was especially true when water polo got away from the driving game that favored our faster and quicker players, to a more physical game that favored the bigger athlete. So, we created an attitude and a style of play that favored our players, and that our opponents had to worry about every time they had the ball.

INGREDIENTS FOR SUCCESS
Almost everyone believes that speed is the most important ingredient in the counterattack. If that is true then you can take a competitive swimmer and make a great counterattack player out of him. I have observed some very fast world-class sprinters that played water polo; but did not know how to counterattack. Speed is important, but how you use your speed is even more important.

Anyone can be trained to swim fast for the short distance that is involved in the counterattack. A very fast competitive swimmer has only a very slight advantage over a well-trained water polo player over the 15-25 yard counter attack distance. Good positioning, anticipating the ball changing hands, and quick reaction can overcome any speed deficiencies that a player may have.

"REACTING TO EVERY CHANGE OF POSSESSION EVERY SINGLE TIME, AND COUNTERING HARD EVERY SINGLE TIME, ARE THE KEYS TO A SUCCESSFUL COUNTERATTACK".

POSITIONING FOR THE COUNTERATTACK

COUNTERING FROM A PRESS

A good counterattack starts with good positioning by the defensive players. Players should position themselves so that they have an open lane to the other end of the pool, without having to go around the offensive player. It is easier to counter from a press/lane defense because of the position of the defenders. Playing to the side of drivers and in front or to the side of wings and the hole-man, gives the defender an open lane to start the counter. The defenders have an added advantage in that they are already facing the other end of the pool, and can start the counterattack by immediately swimming in a forward direction, while the offensive players have to turn around before they start swimming back. (See Diagram 12-1 below).

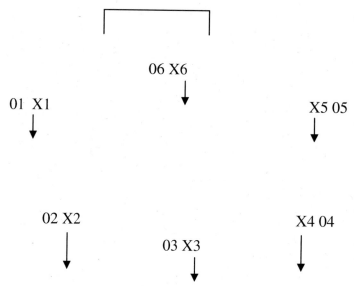

Diagram 12-1: Countering from the press defensive position

COUNTERING FROM A ZONE DEFENSE

The kind of team defense that your team is playing can increase your chances of getting free on the counterattack. It is generally recognized that it is easier to counterattack from a pressing defense than from a zone. Playing in a zone requires the front line defensive players to take several strokes before they are even with the man that they are guarding; and then they still have to get past him.

Teams in a zone will usually get their free man from the back line wing defenders or hole defender; because they will be even up or slightly in front of the offensive wing or hole man. If the free man comes from the wing or hole guard positions, the best that you can hope for is a 4 on 3, 5 on 4, or 6 on 5 advantage; which is more difficult to score from because of the number of people involved. It is important that when the free man is coming from the back line, that the players ahead of the free man, X2, X3 and X4, swim fast and stay ahead of him; and that they penetrate all the way to the 3 or 4 yard line. (See Diagram 12-2 below).

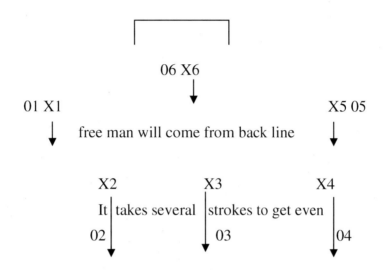

X2, X3 and X4 must stay ahead and penetrate to the 2-4-yard line

Diagram 12-2: Countering from a zone defense

COUNTERING FROM A GAP DEFENSE

A gap defense is the best defense to counterattack from, because playing between offensive players gives the defenders a great position to gain an advantage on their man. When defenders are playing in a gap between offensive players, they should get free every time the ball turns over. There is virtually no one between the gap defender and the other end of the pool. Again the offensive players are at a disadvantage, because they have to turn around before they can chase the defender down the pool. The defender has a straight line shot to the other end. (See Diagram 12-3 on next page).

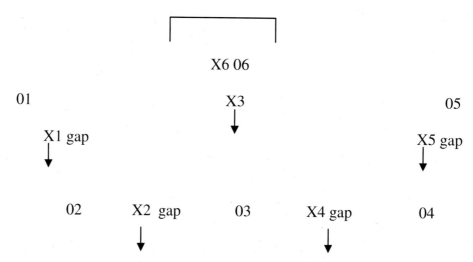

Diagram 12-3: Countering from a gap defense is the easiest.

PRINCIPALS OF THE COUNTERATTACK

Because not all counterattacks are the same, it is difficult to have set patterns for players to follow. It is better for players to learn basic principals that can be applied to any situation that develops. Following the principals and practicing the counterattack everyday teaches players how to react to any game situation. Because the counterattack is so unpredictable, it allows for the most creativity in the game. The counterattack is broken into three different phases, 1) Initial reaction, 2) Advancing the ball, and 3) Finishing. Each phase allows as much creativity as possible, so long as simple concepts are followed.

INITIAL REACTION PHASE OF THE COUNTERATTACK

OBJECTIVE

The initial reaction by the defensive player is to gain an edge over the offensive player, and to beat him to the other end of the pool. It is not easy for players to learn this phase of the game; but without it there is no counterattack. This part of the game must be encouraged at every opportunity, and practiced until it becomes an automatic reaction. Defensive players can take advantage of the fact that offensive players that are involved in executing their team's offense are not in the best position to cover up on a counterattack.

There are many opportunities in a game to initiate a counterattack. Defensive players should take advantage of any turnover of the ball by immediately reacting towards the other end of the pool. Situations like shots on goal, intercepted passes, offensive fouls, little or no time left on the shot-clock, players not involved in the offense, and players not in position to take a good shot, can all help initiate the counterattack.

DON'T LOOK BACK

Looking back at the goal after a shot is taken is probably the biggest mistake that defensive players make when initiating the counterattack. Not looking back is the "key" to initiating a successful counterattack. When a shot is taken by the other team, a player must react immediately on the counterattack, without looking back to see if the ball has gone into the goal. Have faith in the goalie and assume that he has made the block and/or gotten the rebound. The time it takes for a player to turn and look back at the goal, is the time that will give him the jump on the person he is guarding; and the same time will free him for the counterattack.

The defensive player doesn't really have to know if the goal has been scored. The defense should react the same way whether the goal is scored or not. Most teams only make 20% of their shots at best, so the defenders are going to be right 80% of the time. If the ball goes in the goal, you have only wasted a few hard strokes down the pool. Look back as you are swimming down the pool, after you have already reacted. If every player on your team reacts to every shot by the opposition, think of how many extra goals you can score on the counterattack. Not only will you create a free man, but also you will put tremendous pressure on the offensive team.

COUNTER THE SHOOTER

Always counter the shooter. He will be leaning forward as he takes the shot and then he will have to turn around and chase you after he takes the shot. A shooter taking the shot from a bad angle, or from the wing position, is even easier to beat; because the defender has a better angle on him. Count on your goalie to make the block and for players in front of the goal to get the rebound. I would always instruct my players to react to the shot or turnover without worrying about what was going on behind them.

If any of my players were "burned" because our team did not control the rebound, I would take full responsibility for any goals scored by the other team. This situation only occurs very rarely in a game, if at all. A new rule that allows the defense to counterattack if a field player blocks the shot out of bounds, should add many additional counterattack opportunities to each game.

TAKE ADVANTAGE OF PLAYERS WHO ARE NOT INVOLVED IN THE OFFENSE, OR ARE NOT A THREAT TO SCORE

The easiest players to counter are the wing players. Because they are not a big offensive threat from the wing position, they can be fronted and countered when the ball changes hands. If the offense makes a mistake and gives the ball to the wing with only a few seconds left on the shot clock, it makes it even easier to counter; because the wing has to get rid of the ball or take a bad angle shot (which the goalie can block) before he can chase you. The defender should just take off down the pool and leave the wingman holding the ball. You can play off a right-hander on the left-handers wing even more, because he is even less of a threat than a left-hander at that position. (See Diagram 12-4 on next page).

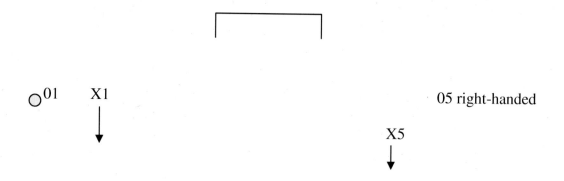

Diagram 12-4: Less than 5 seconds on shot clock. Counter the wings.

If you are guarding any player not involved in taking the shot, you can counter that player if you are playing a side position as diagramed in Diagram 12-1 above. Always counter a shooter who has inside position on you, and always counter the hole-man, especially if he shoots the ball. The hole-man usually is in a vertical position and has a difficult time getting started back on defense, especially if the guard gives him a little push as he goes by him. In addition, the bigger bulk of most 2-meter players make it even more difficult to chase down the pool.

COUNTERING THE MAN WITH THE BALL
The man with the ball can also be countered, especially if there is little time left on the clock, if he is in a position where he has to shoot or get rid of the ball, and he is not in a good position to shoot the ball. The defender can counter the shooter as he is taking the shot, or he can foul him and counter while he is picking up the ball. The defender has to be careful and not give the shot to person in a good shooting position directly in front of the goal. In this situation he must defend first and then counter.

LEAVING EARLY
If the shot clock only has a few seconds left, and the player you are guarding is not in position to score, you can leave even before the shot clock expires. Leaving early is a skill that can be acquired with practice. A smart player will be aware of the shot clock, and when the player he is guarding is out of position. When the shot clock has less then 5-seconds left, the offensive team has to shoot the ball or turn it over. This is the time that a good counterattack player starts anticipating that he will leave and start the counterattack. (See Chapter 7 "Game Strategies" for more information on "leaving early".

SIX-MAN COUNTER-REMAIN A THREAT
Every player must be involved in the counterattack. There will usually be at least one offensive player out of position that can be beat on the counter. Your team can find him only if all six players react to the turnover and counterattack. The basic principal here is that all players must remain a scoring threat by advancing toward the goal. If a player remains a threat, then this will force a guard to commit to him.

Stopping on the counterattack completely takes that player out of the picture, and also will jam things up by causing the free man to run into his teammate who has stopped. A good defender will leave you if you are not a threat, and help out on the free man.

STAYING AHEAD OF THE FREE MAN
If the free man comes from the defensive wing positions or the hole-guard positions, then his teammates ahead of him on the counterattack must work hard to stay ahead of him. They must maintain a comfortable distance ahead of the free man by countering hard all the way down to the 2 to 3-meter line. If the counterattacking players are too close to each other, it makes it so crowded that it is difficult to get the ball to the free man. A counter- defender in this situation can easily defend two players who are playing too close together, and easily break up the counterattack by disrupting or stealing the ball. A good rule of thumb is to stay at least 5-6 feet apart during all phases of the counterattack, but especially in front of the goal.

ADVANCING THE BALL PHASE OF THE COUNTERATTACK

PASS TO THE FREE MAN
Advancing the ball involves getting the ball down the pool to the free man. The easiest pass is the direct pass to the free man from the goalie. This pass can be safely done if the free man has not passed more than three-quarters of the way down the pool. If he has gone further than this, then there is a good chance that the opposing goalie will come out and intercept the ball, especially if the free man is going down the center of the pool.

It is much easier for the goalie to make the direct pass in a 30-meter pool than in a 25-yard or 25-meter pool. In a small pool the player who first gets the ball on the turnover must look immediately down the pool for the free man, before he runs out of space. In a larger pool, the player who first intercepts the ball should pass the ball to the goalie, so that he can make the pass to the free man. The goalkeeper is usually not being guarded and is trained to make this pass. Most intercepted balls in the frontcourt of a long pool should be thrown back to the goalie, unless the interception comes at half-tank.

RELEASING FOR THE BALL
If the goalkeeper cannot get the ball directly to the free man, he must pass to an intermediate player somewhere near half court, who can then make the pass to the free man. This is usually a safer pass because it will come into the free man from the side, rather then a more difficult over the head pass by the goalie. The player releasing for the ball, can flare slightly outward toward the wall to receive the ball from the goalie. The ball must be thrown slightly and to the outside hand of the release man. The closer the defender is to the release man, the further to the outside the ball must be placed. At no time must the player receiving the ball come to a complete stop or turn around to get the ball from the goalie. As soon as he does so, the defender will leave him and take the free man. (See Diagram 12-5 on the next page).

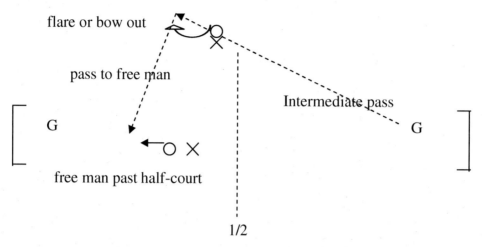

flare or bow out

pass to free man

Intermediate pass

G

G

free man past half-court

1/2

Diagram 12-5: Releasing for the ball, 30-meter pool.

SMALL POOL

In a small pool, a half court hook or square-out 90 degree move can be used to get some distance from the defender who is closely pressing the release man, and get a quick pass to the free man who may already be past 3/4 court. (See Diagram 12-6 below) If the player defending the release man leaves him to help on the free man, then the release man must immediately, and without any hesitation, take the ball, turn and keep going toward the goal. He has now become the free man. Anytime there is little or no defensive pressure on the release man, he should continue swimming down the pool and receive the pass over his head as he is swimming.

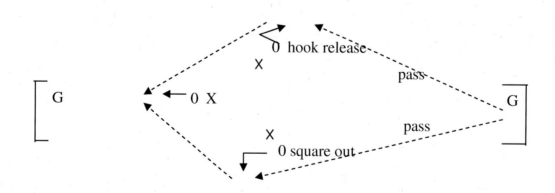

0 hook release

pass

G

0 X

G

pass

0 square out

Diagram 12-6: Moves to create space for the release in a 25-yd pool

LOOK SWIM

The players receiving the ball down the pool must look back as they are swimming so that they can see the ball coming to them. Looking back over the shoulder as the player takes a stroke is an essential skill a counterattacking player must learn. Players can also get on their backs for a few strokes in order to see and receive the ball; but only if they don't loose speed and their advantage over the player who is chasing them. Eye to eye contact between the passer and receiver is essential for the success of the release pass or the pass to the free man. The goalie must not pass to a player who is not looking back for the ball.

PASSING TO THE LAST MAN DOWN THE POOL

In some counterattack situations where a defensive player has beaten a wing player or the hole-man, the free man might very well be the last player swimming down that the pool. It is imperative that he receives the pass from the goalkeeper. A pass to a release player ahead of the free man could be easily intercepted in crowded conditions, or by a good defensive play. The result will be a counterattack in the other direction, from the player who was trailing the free man. When the free man is the last player down the pool he must swim on his back to receive the ball dry. If he stays on his stomach the ball will be passed in front of him, usually an easy interception in the middle of the pool by any defender in the proximity. (See Diagram 12-7 below).

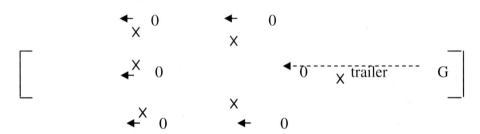

Diagram 12-7: Passing to the "last man" on his back.

SETTING UP A SHOT FOR THE LAST MAN DOWN THE POOL

A shot from the last man down the pool is a low percentage shot, and is usually not recommended; because the trailing player will get an easy goal at the other end if the last man misses the shot. A well-coached team can, however, get a good shot when they have a 6 on 5 counterattack, and still cover the trailer.

The best opportunity for the free man to get close to the goal, and get a good high percentage shot, is for his team to set up a 4-2 offensive formation. This means that at least four players that are ahead of the ball must get all the way down to the 2-meter line, while the last player without the ball must stay even with the player with the ball. As the player with the ball penetrates forward to take the shot, his teammate playing on the other side of the pool, and the player next to him, should start peeling back on defense to cover the trailer. After passing the ball to the last man, as shown in Diagram 12-7 above, the rest of the team must set up in front of the goal in a 4-2 formation. (See Diagram 12-8 on the next page).

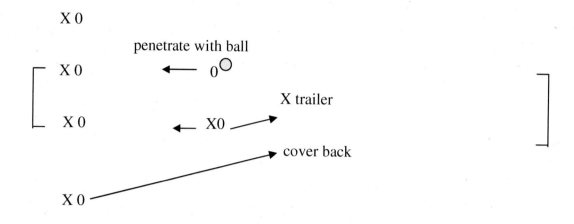

Diagram 12-8: Setting up 4-2 formation to allow last man down to shoot

FINISHING THE COUNTERATTACK

Ideally you want the free man with the ball to take the ball all the way to the goal and take the shot. He should not give up the ball unless a defensive player attacks him. If he is attacked, he must get control of the ball, and be ready to pass to a teammate, before the defender gets to him. Once he is under attack, he must learn to absorb the foul, protect the ball, and then quickly make the pass.

DO NOT PASS UNLESS PRESSED
The free man with the ball is similar to a point guard in basketball. He has to learn when to take the ball to the goal, and when to distribute the ball to an open teammate. He has to know where his teammates are, and where the defenders and goalkeeper are located. A basic principal of the counterattack is that " the more passes a team has to make, the less chance that team has to score".

Following this principal means that one pass from the goalie to the free man is the easiest way to score. More than one pass will slow down and stall the counterattack, and give the defense a chance to catch up. A pass down the pool is much better than a pass in front of team's own goal, because it advances the ball towards the goal. Very rarely should the goalie pass to a teammate on his side of half tank. He should get the ball down the pool as far as he can on the first pass.

SCORING ON THE COUNTERATTACK
Scoring a goal on the counterattack is one of the easier ways to score in water polo; but only if you take high percentage shots. Good defensive teams will force the free man to bring the ball down the right side of the pool, the weak-side for a right-handed player. Taking a bad angle shot from the right side of the pool that is easily blocked by the goalie, will usually result in a free man in the other direction. You can improve your angle by getting the ball up early in a vertical position and aggressively moving a cross the goal to improve your angle for a better shot.

If you don't have time to take the outside shot, you can put the ball on the water and take it inside for an off the water shot, or try to draw a penalty shot. You must take advantage of the situation, and be aggressive in moving towards the goal. If you don't have an opportunity for a high percentage shot, than you have the option of setting up your frontcourt offense. In all counterattack situations, teammates who are not involved in shooting the ball, or committing a defender, should cover back on defense.

LEARN TO SHOOT WHEN YOU ARE TIRED
After swimming all out for 25 meters down the pool to free yourself for a shot, you must have the energy, and will power, to get off a good shot. I have seen players who are so tired that they stop in front of the goal, and hope that the referee will reward them with a penalty shot or exclusion foul. Players must train to be able to shoot when they are tired, especially off the water shots.

CROSS PASS
You can take advantage of defenders who play in between two offensive players by picking up the ball, setting the goalie with a fake, and then throwing the cross pass to a teammate on the other side of the pool, for an easy shot into an open goal. A perfectly executed cross-pass for a goal is one of the most rewarding plays in water polo. You are giving up your chance to score for your teammate, who has an even better chance to score. This is because the goalie is set on the player with the ball; and the cross-pass will beat the goalie to the other side of the goal. (See Diagram 12-9a below)

You shouldn't force the cross pass, however, if your teammate is covered. If the defense is giving you the shot, than you must take it. Even if your teammate is covered, the attacker with the ball could fake a pass to the other attacker to get the goalie to move, and then shoot immediately after. Learn when to pass the ball across to a teammate, or take the shot yourself. (See Diagram 12-9b below).

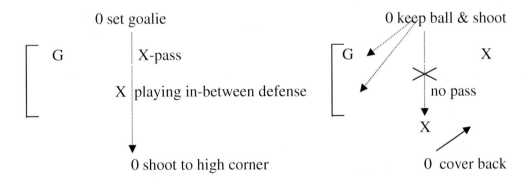

Diagram 12-9a: Set the goalie and pass across.   Diagram 12-9b: Shoot when x-pass is covered

SETTING UP IN FRONT OF THE GOAL-WITHOUT THE BALL

What the players without the ball are doing is just as important as what the player with the ball is doing. Basic principals for finishing the counterattack for players without the ball can be applied in any counterattack situation:

1. Players ahead of the ball must penetrate quickly all the way down to the pool to the two-three meter line.

2. Players without the ball must remain a threat and in scoring position, so that a defender cannot leave them and take the man with the ball.

3. Players must spread out in front of the goal, so that one defender cannot easily guard two players at one time. Keeping two yards apart is a good rule of thumb to follow. There is not room for more than three players spread across the front of the goal. Any additional players must stop around the 4 to 5 meter line, but still remain a threat.

4.When the ball is coming down the side of the pool, players must rotate away from the player with the ball, so that he can get a better shooting angle. Rotate across the front of the goal so that you remain a threat, and not towards the wing where you are not a threat. While moving across the goal, be ready to receive the cross-pass if your defender picks up the free man. (See Figure 12-10 below).

5. As the shot is being taken, players not involved in the shot must release back to protect against the other teams counterattack. Remember that when your team is a man up on the counterattack, then the other team is a man up in the other direction. (See Diagram 12-10 below).

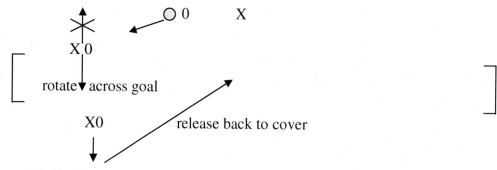

Diagram 12-10: Rotate across and cover back. 3 on 2 counter

SETTING UP IN FRONT OF THE GOAL

Since most teams will not allow the ball to come down the center of the pool on the counterattack, setting up in front of the goal relies on the ball coming down the side of the pool. A two-on-one counterattack usually ends up with a player on each post with the ball in one of the player's hand.

A three-on-two counterattack has three players spread across the front of the goal, all about 2-meters apart, and all a threat to score. (See Diagram 12-10 above)In this situation the ball is with the player on the right side of the goal.

A four-on-three counterattack looks like Diagram 12-11 below, with the ball coming down the side and with three players rotating across the goal. The player on the far side from the ball rotates back to cover the trailer following the free man.

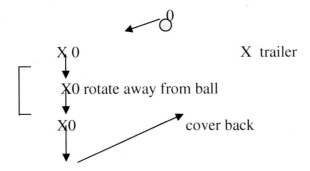

X 0   X trailer

X0 rotate away from ball

X0   cover back

Figure 12-11: Four on three counterattack

5 ON 4, 6 ON 5 SET-UP
Shooting the ball with anything more than a four-on-three man-advantage is discouraged by a lot of coaches, because the chances of scoring are not good; and the other team can easily gain a free man in the other direction. A smart team, however, can score on a 5 on 4 or a 6 on 5 man-advantage if they set up in front of the goal in a formation that allows the man with the ball to penetrate close to the goal, and take the shot while his teammates cover for him.

A team with a 5 on 4 man-advantage should set up in a basic 3-2 formation in front of the goal, while a team with a 6 on 5 advantage should set up in a 4-2 formation. If one of the two outside players is allowed to penetrate close to the goal with the ball, he can take the shot while his teammates cover. As he is about to shoot, the player next to him on the 4-2 and the wing player furthest from the shooter should start peeling back. If the player with the ball cannot get close to the goal, he must pass up the shot and set up a frontcourt offense. Well-coached and well-drilled teams who understand the consequences of taking the shot, and how to set up the formations, can many times "steal" a goal in these situation. (See Diagrams 12-7 and 12-8 above).

BALL CONTROL DURING COUNTERATTACK
It is extremely important that you take care of the ball when your team is on the counterattack. When your team is a man up, you are extremely vulnerable to a counterattack by the other team. Consequently you must make safe passes, and take high percentage shots. A turn over on a bad pass, or a risky bad angle shot, may result in a goal in the other direction. Making the safe pass is especially important for the goalkeeper. The player receiving the ball, and the goalkeeper, must have eye-to-eye contact; especially on long passes down the pool. The goalie must be careful and watch out for defenders doubling back, or jumping into the passing lane for a steal.

DEFENSE OF THE COUNTERATTACK

"YOUR ACTIONS WHILE YOUR TEAM HAS THE BALL ARE MORE IMPORTANT IN PREVENTING THE COUNTERATTACK THAN YOUR ACTIONS ONCE THE OTHER TEAM HAS ALREADY GAINED A MAN-ADVANTAGE".

Once a team gains a "free" man on their counterattack, there is not a lot that you can do to stop that free man from getting a good shot on goal, and perhaps scoring a goal. However, there are numerous things that you can do, while your team is still on offense, to prevent your opponent from gaining a free man in the first place. Your team actions while on offense have a direct effect on whether the other team gets a free man, or not. All the counterattacking team is doing is taking advantage of the situation that the offense presents to them. Players on offense have to learn to recognize and not put themselves in situations that can give an opponent a chance to gain a man advantage.

Following are situations on offense that players must be aware of that can give the other a man advantage in the other direction:

DURING YOUR COUNTERATTACK-The situation when you are most vulnerable to a counterattack is during your team's counterattack, when you are a man up, As covered above, you must protect and control the ball, make good safe passes, and take high percentage shots that have a good chance of succeeding. If you are not directly involved in your teams counterattack, then you must cover back on defense. Remember that a six against five counterattack opportunity for your team is a one on nobody counterattack in the other direction. Let the shooter know that you are covering up before he takes the shot in this situation.

TURNOVERS-Any front court situation can cause a turnover, including bad angle shots, outside shots that don't score, shots by the hole man, drivers with inside water, bad passes, steals by the other team, offensive fouls and shot clock violations. You can usually anticipate a shot by your teammate and cover up for him. However, it is difficult to anticipate bad passes, steals and offensive fouls. Offensive fouls, in particular, are difficult to cover up. It is a lot easier to cover up for a driving or shooting teammate if you are not driving or shooting yourself. Multiple drivers at the same time can "over commit" the offense, and can create a counterattack situation for the other team that is very difficult to recover from.

GAP DEFENSES-Learn to recognize when the other team is in a "gap" defense of some kind, whether it be in the frontcourt or man-down situations. Playing in the gaps can give a team a tremendous advantage in creating a free man because the "gap" defender has open water to the other end of the pool. The most common "gap" frontcourt defense is the "M" zone and the common man-down defense is the 4-5 split on the top two players. Learn to recognize these situations and practice covering up for players that are burned.

END OF THE SHOT CLOCK-Your team has to be able to control the situation that occurs at the end of the 30-second shot clock. Always be aware of the shot clock, and learn when to shoot or when to "dump" the ball in the corner at the end of the 30-second shot clock. If you have a chance to take a high hard shot from the front of the goal that the goalie might block out of bounds, then shoot the ball. Otherwise, if you are in a bad position (like a wing or at a bad angle), or your defender has already left you and taken off down the pool, then dump the ball into the corner and chase back. A good place to place the "dumped" ball is somewhere along the side of the pool, where the free man has to change course and swim over a get the ball; because he is the closest player to the ball. (See Diagram 7-2 "Dumping the ball" in Chapter 7 "Game Strategies".

CHERRY PICKERS-Watch out for defensive players leaving early. In both cases, always send someone back to cover up the free man. Teams that are behind at the end of the game, will many times send more than one player back early in order to try and get a free goal. Cover them at all times and do not shoot the ball, especially if you have a lead and do not need a goal. I have seen teams miss the "sure" goal at one end of the pool and give up the goal that ties the game at the other end. If you are shooting at an empty goal, swim the ball into the goal rather than attempt the so-called "easy" shot that might hit the bar and not go in.

TAKING THE SHOT-Players who are not directly involved in the offense are the best ones to cover back for a teammate who has been burned on the counterattack. There is no reason to stay on offense when a teammate is about to shoot the ball. You have to assume that your teammate who is taking the shot will be countered. All players but the man shooting the ball and perhaps the hole man, should start "peeling" back or going back on defense to cover up for the shooter. The more players that are back on defense, the more your team can "mess up" the other teams chance to score on the counterattack.

PRINCIPLES OF COUNTERATTACK DEFENSE

1. When your team is on offense, anticipate when the ball is going to be turned over, and start leaning or going back in the other direction for defense.

2. React back to defense just as quickly as you react on the counterattack.

3. Cover up for teammates that are committed to offense or are shooting the ball.

4. Learn when "not to shoot" the ball, especially if your shot creates a counterattack opportunity for the other team.

5. Avoid being a spectator to see if your shot or your teammates shot has gone in the goal or not. React back to defense first and then look back.

THE OTHER TEAM HAS A MAN-UP

PLAYING CATCH-UP
Once the other team has created a man up situation there are a few things that you can do to keep them from scoring. In all of these situations you are basically trying to delay the ball from getting down the pool to the free man, until your teammates can catch up to him.

ALWAYS PRESS THE BALL

Try to press the person with the ball. Press hard, without fouling, trying to keep him from making a pass to the free man. Pressing the ball should be done most of the time to help stop the counter. If the defender can stall the ball for just a few seconds it can help his teammate cover the free man. The only time that you would not press is when you are positioned so that you can take the free man yourself. Most of the time you will not be in a good position to take the free-man. If the free-man is even with you, or already past you, or on the other side of the pool, and you cannot possibly get to him, press the ball. 90 percent of the time a defender will not be in position to help back and cover the free man. So press!!

PRESS WITHOUT THE FOUL

Pressing without fouling is probably the most effective tactic on counterattack defense. The reasons for this, and the technique of showing both hands to the referee to avoid the foul, has been thoroughly covered in previous chapters in this text. Suffice it to say that this tactic, along with playing the passing lanes, and fronting the hole man, is an integral part of an effective pressing defense.

FORCE THE OTHER TEAM TO PASS THE BALL, BUT NOT IN FRONT OF THE GOAL.

A basic principal of man down defense is "the more passes the offense must make, the less chance they have of scoring." Going back and forth between two players, and faking as if you are attacking the ball, is called stunting. If done properly, it can slow the ball down, or force a player to make a pass. This should only be done as the ball is coming down the pool, and if the defender is ahead of and playing between two players.

As mentioned above, if the free man is already past you, attack the ball. Attacking the ball without the foul will stop the ball there; or force that player to pass, depending on when the defender arrives at the ball. Anything that the defense can do to stop or slow down the ball will give the team time to catch and cover the free man.

Never stunt in front of the goal. Doing so gives up the cross-pass to the man that you have just left open, making it much easier for him to score. In the situation in front of the goal, the defender should stay on the man without the ball and let the goalie take the man with the ball. The goalie should direct the defender on which man he should take and which man the goalie wants to cover. Whatever you do, do not give up the cross pass! (See Diagram 12-12 on the next page).

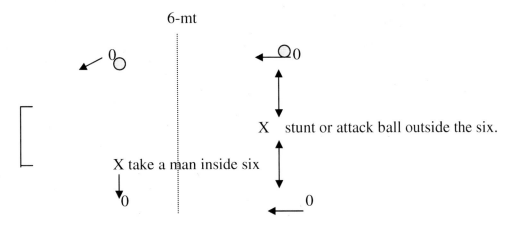

6-mt

X   stunt or attack ball outside the six.

X take a man inside six

Diagram 12-12: Force the pass outside 6-meters; take a man inside 6-meters.

DELIBERATE FOUL

You may foul the man with the ball and drop back to the free man, only if you are in position to help back. If you foul in this situation, reach for the arm and push the ball away a short distance, while also pushing the passer underwater a little; so that he has to take a few seconds to recover the ball. If this foul is too intense, or if you push the ball away too far, be careful that you are not excluded for delay of game. If the defender is not in position to drop back, he must stay on the passer and get a hand up to keep him from making the perfect pass to the free man.

Some teams will foul deliberately in this situation, with as hard of a foul that they can get away with under the rules; hoping that the rest of the team can cover while the passer has to retrieve the ball. Using this tactic is a coach's decision. If you are not in position to drop back and cover the free man, it is best to press the ball without fouling.

FORCE THE BALL TO A RIGHT HANDER GOING DOWN THE RIGHT SIDE OF THE POOL

If you have a choice on which side to press once the ball gets into the front court, press the left side of the pool, and make a right-hander take the shot from the right side facing the goal. This is an easier shot for your goalie to block, than from a right-hander on the left side of the pool. An even lower percentage shot for the shooter is an off the water shot. You can force this shot by chasing the man with the ball, and getting right behind his shoulder, so that he cannot pick up the ball for a shot; but instead must shoot "off the water."

CHAPTER 13

GOALKEEPER TACTICS AND TRAINING

The position of goalkeeper in water polo is unique in that it is completely different than any other position, both physically and mentally. Mainly it is a defensive position that requires stopping the other team from scoring. But, it involves much more than just blocking the ball. The goalkeeper is involved in all aspects of the game. Communication skills are just as important as physical skills. A goalie is the only player not being guarded by someone from the other team, and is a unique position to see everything that is happening in the pool. He must take command and direct his teammates, especially the defensive players.

On defense he must control where the shot is coming from, he must direct the positioning of his defensive teammates, he must come out of the goal if necessary to break up an offensive play, and ultimately he must stop the ball from getting inside the goal. On offense he must help to initiate the counterattack, he must make the outlet pass he must inform his teammates about the time remaining and the game situation, and he must find the open man and direct his teammates where to make the next pass. In many respects it may be the most critical position on the team. A weak goalkeeper can lose games for your team, while a strong goalkeeper can win games with his play.

PHYSICAL SKILLS
If you want to be a goalkeeper, hope that you were born with great legs. That is obviously the most important physical attribute that a goalie must possess. If you grew up as a swimmer and were successful as a breaststroker, you probably have the legs necessary to be a good goalie. Long arms are also important in order to get to the corners of the ten-foot wide goal. However, a smaller goalie that has good legs, is quick, and positions himself well, can overcome deficiencies from lack of height and long arms.

IT'S ALL MENTAL!
There is a lot of pressure on the goalkeeper to be the stopper, the last line of defense, the person most responsible for keeping the other team from scoring. He stands alone in the goal. The defensive field players can just swim away after the other team scores a goal, knowing that the goalie will be blamed for the ball getting into the goal.

How the goalkeeper handles this stress is key to his success. He must be emotionally balanced and disciplined, maintain a calm demeanor, and especially not show any emotion after he has been scored upon. The opposing team will see this as a sign of weakness and make his life miserable from then on. It is also important not to taunt the opposing players or celebrate after he blocks a shot, because it will come back to haunt him when he eventually gets scored on.

The goalie also cannot criticize his teammates when the other team scores a goal. He must take the blame for a goal scored. Encourage your teammates and get excited when they play good defense in front of you.

PSYCH UP! YET REMAIN IN CONTROL
A goalie has to be aggressive and confident in his abilities and not be afraid of failure. He cannot worry about stopping the shooter from scoring; he has to have the attitude that the shooter must beat him. A goalie must be convinced, in his own mind, that he is better than the shooter who is facing him. Once a goal has been scored, he must not dwell and worry about it; but get himself ready to block the next shot. He must have the ability to psych himself up for every shot, both in practice and in a game, yet remain in control of the situation. He must maintain his "psych" over the shooters by not showing any signs of discomfort, or show that he has been bothered by a goal being scored on him.

MAKE THE GREAT BLOCK ONCE IN A WHILE
A goalie cannot be expected to "save" the team by making block after block. He is expected to make the blocks that he is supposed to make, not let in any easy goals, and once in a while make the "great block that might win the game. He doesn't have to win the game by himself, he just has to try and put his team in a position to win the game by keeping the score low.

Nothing will psych up his teammates more than the goalie stopping a "one on nobody" or blocking a penalty shot, especially if that is the game clincher. Letting in an easy shot that he should have blocked can have the opposite effect on his teammates. During the heat of battle, and especially after a goal has been scored, is not the time for the goalie to get on a field player for a defensive mistake. Wait until after the game, when cooler heads will prevail, and then go over what he should have done in that situation.

TECHNIQUE-BODY POSITION

BASIC POSITION FOR THE GOALIE
The goalie must constantly remind himself about his body position. If his technique and body position are good, then he has a better chance of blocking the ball. His shoulders must always be square to the shooter's release point. His eyes must always be on the ball and he must be ready for a shot at any time. His hands should be sculling lightly on top of the water with his elbows on top of the water at a 90-degree angle. His hips must be high in the water and his legs should be doing a rapid eggbeater kick. He must also show a balanced and calm demeanor above the water. (See Picture 13-A on the next page).

Picture 13-A: Goalie ready position

POSITION IN RELATION TO THE GOAL
The goalie must position himself so that he has the best chance of taking away the highest percentage shot. He must be far enough out of the goal to take away the angle on the hard outside shot, and where it will take a perfect lob to beat him. In this case the outside shot is a higher percentage shot than the lob shot. He also must move to the side of the goal where the ball is situated and take away the "near side" angle shot. A goalie should not use the goal at the other end of the pool to position him self, but constantly glance back at his own goal in order to maintain his position. A common mistake for young goalies is to play too far inside of the goal, so that they do not take away any shooting angle.

COMING OUT OF THE GOAL
The goalie must always be ready to swim out of the goal if necessary in order to intercept an errant pass or to steal the ball from a shooter. He can sneak out of the goal if the person with the ball is not paying attention to him, especially if the ball is on the water and not in his hand. He must anticipate the long pass to a free player coming down the pool and intercept that pass if it is overthrown. He can also come out, after a foul anywhere inside the 5-meter line, in order to discourage or intercept the pass to the hole-set.

GOALIES ROLE WHEN FRONTING THE 2-METER PLAYER
The most critical time to come out is when his team is fronting the hole-man. The goalie has to anticipate the pass coming inside to the hole-man, start moving as the ball leaves the passers hand, and arrive at the ball before the hole man can get his hand on it. After a shot or a steal, he must then swim the ball towards the side of the pool and away from the pressure. If a player goes after him, he has to learn how to protect the ball and draw a foul to get a free pass.

Goalies must practice this skill along with the field players. There is nothing worse than losing control of the ball in front of your own cage, and getting a cheap goal scored on you. Remember that the referee wants to help the goalie in this situation. The shooter has had his chance to score. Once the goalie blocks and gets control of the ball, the referee is likely to call a foul, giving the goalie a free pass.

BLOCKING TECHNIQUE

OUTSIDE SHOTS

For shots that come anywhere around your body, eggbeater up, push off the water; but get your hands up quickly and try to meet the ball with both hands, somewhere in front of you. Absorb the ball, knocking it down in front of you without swinging at it. For balls to either corner, start with a strong breaststroke or scissor kick, push off the water with your opposite hand, explode toward the ball with your head and body, and extend your arm to meet the ball. Again, do not swing at the ball, but absorb it and let it fall in front of you. The goalie should never try to catch the ball, but knock it down in front of him. Attempting to catch the ball sometimes results in the ball going through his hands and into the goal. (See Pictures 13-B, 13-C, and 13-D below)

Picture 13-B High corner block

Picture 13-C Over head block-knock ball down

Picture 13-D Follow the head and hand

FAKES

The goalie should not commit too early on a fake shot. He should come up only part of the way on the fake, and then explode to the ball when it leaves the shooters hand. Learn to distinguish a faking motion from a shooting motion. Most players will just wave the ball in a non-shooting motion when they are faking. The elbow and hand together will move forward when the player is shooting.

ANGLE SHOTS

The worse angle that a shooter has gives the goalie the best chance of blocking the shot. On a bad-angle shot near the corner of the goal, the goalie must position his body near the goal post, square to the shooter, with his hands above his head. His body should block the low shot and his arms will block the high shot. Most shooters will shoot right into the goalies arms, trying to blow the ball through him and into the goal.

BAITING

The goalie should always take away the near side shot, but be aware of lobs or cross-cage shots. An angle shot also gives the goalie an opportunity to "bait" the shot. He intentionally gives the shooter an open shot to the near side space next to the goal post. Then when the shooter shoots the ball toward the open space, he moves over and takes the space away. Most shooters will try to shoot to the near side as much as possible, especially if that side looks like it is open.

OFF-THE-WATER SHOTS

A player who has the ball on the water in front of him actually has a very low percentage shot. Hopefully the defender behind him will not allow the shooter to pick up the ball, and the goalie will move forward towards the shooter while towering above him. Blocking this kind of a shot requires more emphasis on the legs. The goalie will be in more of a vertical position and as high as he can out of the water. Elbows will be above the surface of the water and the hands will be up and slightly out to the side. (See Picture 13-E below)

Picture 13-E: Position to block the off-the-water shot

The goalie must concentrate on the ball, and then quickly get a hand on the ball when it is shot around the head area. Most shooters in this position cannot do much more then shoot the ball straight towards the goalie.

SWEEPING THE BALL
The goalie should think about sweeping the ball away, especially if the ball is on the water and the shooter does not have control of it. The most dangerous shooter is the one who puts his hand under the ball, and then either shoots a hard screw shot or a lob over the goalies head. Because the goalie is playing on one side of the goal, he is vulnerable to the lob to the opposite side of the goal. If the shooters hand is on top of the ball, the goalie should put his hand on top of the shooter's hand and push the ball under water.

LOBS
The shooter will usually telegraph the lob because he will drop his hand and elbow under the ball in order to push it over the goalies head, and into the far corner of the goal. A lob shot off the water should be easier to block because it has to first travel up over the goalies head and then down into the back of the goal. A "spinner" lob is harder for the goalie to detect, because the shooter uses the same motion on the shot and then at the last second puts sidespin on the ball.

In order to block the lob, the goalie must move laterally and backwards across the goal, by first pushing off and then pulling with the hands. He must use his inside hand and legs to scull across the goal, and then extend his trailing hand over and back to the back corner of the goal. He should try to intercept the ball at its lowest point without catching the ball, and then knock it down and aggressively swim it out of the goal. (See picture 13-F below).

Picture 13-F: Blocking the lob shot

BACKHANDS
First the goalie must position himself directly behind the shoulder of the shooter, to take away the shooting angle, with his hands out of the water. For a right-handed shooter he must play directly behind the right-shoulder, while the 2-meter defender plays the left side to take away the sweep shot or turn to that side. (See Picture 13-G below)

Picture 13-G: Position to block the backhand shot.

PENALTY SHOTS

Now that penalty shots are taken from the 5-meter line instead of the four, the chances of the goalie blocking the shot has improved, although the odds are still in favor of the shooter. There are three schools of thought on shot blocking technique. A goalie can choose one to concentrate on, or one that works best for him; or he can use two or three different techniques and change them each time in order to keep the shooter guessing. The different methods are the sweep out, pick a corner, or react to the shot.

THE SWEEP OUT

The sweep out is probably most successful against shooters who shoot low to half way up the goal post. The goalie actually starts back inside the goal in the ready position. When the referee raises his arm and the shooter picks up the ball, the goalie starts moving slowly forward. He tries to time it so that he is out to the goal line when the referee blows the whistle. The goalie explodes out in a sweeping motion with hands out to the side and about a foot out of the water. The shot has to be perfectly placed in a high corner to beat the goalie. Shooters who draw the ball back before they bring it forward for the shot are also hard to beat, because they wait for the goalie to commit before releasing the ball. (See Picture 13-H on the next page).

Olympic and Stanford Goalie Chris Dorst used this technique to block 3 out of every 5 penalty shots in his senior year in college; when rule changes on team fouls required each team 4-5 penalty shots per game.

Picture 13-H: The sweep-out to block the penalty shot

KNOW WHICH CORNER TO PICK
If the goalie has scouted his opponent and has an idea that he might shoot to a certain area, he can dive to that spot when the whistle blows and hope that he has guessed right. He can also play shooter tendencies, knowing that right handed players will usually shoot to the goalies lower right and left handed players will shoot to the goalies lower left. Some players do not like to shoot high because they are afraid of hitting the bar.

READ AND REACT
Some goalies just try to react to the shot and try to block it wherever it is placed. The extra meter in distance gives the goalie just a little more time to react because it takes a little longer for the ball to get to the cage.

MIND GAMES
The goalie can play mind games with the shooter by jumping to a side or coming out of the goal just before the whistle blows, putting doubt into the shooters mind. Of course the referee has to allow the goalie to get away with this stunt. He can usually get away with one early jump before the referee decides to call a second penalty against him.

COMMUNICATION
The goalie is not being guarded and has a view of the entire pool. He must communicate to the field players, who may not know what is going on. Whatever it is that the goalie is trying to communicate, he must do so in a load and clear voice. He must call out the name of the player in order to get his attention, and then tell him what he wants him to do. The goalie must not be constantly chattering in a monotone, or the players will not listen to him.

When directing players where to go or where to throw the ball, he must first get the players attention, give the command, and point if necessary to get his point across. The field players must remember that the goalie is the leader of the defense in the water, and they must do what he wants them to do. The coach of the team should stress to the field players that the goalie has the authority to direct the team in the water.

I never liked my goalie to constantly be telling the players where the ball is located. The field players should always know where the ball is. The goalie doesn't have to tell them. It also takes away from the goalie concentrating on running the defense. "Direct traffic" as necessary, tell players where to go on defense, when to come back on defense, and encourage them to counterattack; otherwise keep quite and concentrate on the task at hand.

FRONT COURT

The most important thing that a goalie can do on offense is to let his teammates know how much time they have on the shot clock. Since his teammates are 25 meters away, he must do so in a loud and clear voice, so that he can be heard. When it looks like his teammates are about to turn over the ball to the other team, he must direct any offensive players not involved in the offense to come back and play defense. This is especially critical at the end of the 30-second possession clock or in a "cherry pick" situation.

COUNTERATTACK DEFENSE

During the counterattack, it is essential that the goalie direct the defensive players. If there is a free man and a defender is in position to help back on the free man, then the goalie should direct him to do so. If he is not in position to help, then the goalie must direct him to press the ball. If a perimeter foul is necessary, he must call for the foul in a loud voice and then call for the player to drop back and help. This is necessary, especially if the 2-meter man is fronted and the ball gets to the wing. Calling for a foul on the wing will allow the goalie to come out and double the 2-meter player. The goalie has to be alert if he calls for a foul on a player outside of the 5-meter line; because that player may now shoot the ball after he is fouled.

If faced with a 2 on 1, 3 on 2, or 4 on 3 situation, he must direct the field players to guard the best shooters or the shooter with the best chance to score, and the goalie will cover the weakest shooter or the shooter with the weakest angle. All of this should be done outside of six meters from the goal. Once the players get inside 6 meters, they must stay with the person that they are assigned to cover, and the goalie will set on the person that he wants to take the shot. This is done so that the person with the ball inside six meters must take the shot, and the goalie can concentrate on him. Changing defensive positions inside the six allows the cross pass in front of the goal, and takes away any chance that the goalie might have to block the shot.

FRONT COURT DEFENSE

The goalie must call for the team to press until the attack has beaten the press. Then he must call players back into a drop defense, depending on what the game plan calls for. If he wants only one player to drop, then he must call out his name and command him to drop in. Dropping off the weakest shooter allows the goalie to concentrate on him and block the shot. The goalie must make sure that his team's best 2-meter guard is guarding the 2-meter position. He must direct the 2-meter defender to switch if a weaker guard is guarding that position. Once the guard is behind the center forward, the goalie must direct him to play on the correct side. He must then be ready for a shot from the opposite side.

INITIATE THE COUNTERATTACK

The goalie helps to initiate the counterattack by yelling for his team to counter when there is a turnover or shot that he or his team will gain control of the ball. Once a player gets control of the ball, the goalie must move towards the outside of the goal and away from the pressure. He then calls for the ball from the field player. He must hold the ball high above his head during the counterattack so that his teammates can see that he has the ball. If he has time he can take a few strokes down the pool to help shorten the distance that he has to throw the ball down the pool.

He must first look deep down the pool and try to get the ball to the "lead break" somewhere past half court. He has to be careful that the man receiving the ball is not too close to the opposite goal, giving the other goalie a chance to come out and make the steal. If he is too far past half court, then the ball must be thrown to an intermediate player near half court, who can make the "safer" pass. A pass to a player going down the side of the pool is much safer than a pass to player going down the middle and already past half-court.

WHERE TO PASS THE BALL

If the player he is passing to is being defended then he must throw the ball to the outside shoulder, away from the defender; being careful not to make the pass too wide, thus taking the player out of the counterattack. If he can do so safely, he must try to throw the ball in front of the field player, so that he can maintain the counterattack by swimming in a forward direction towards the ball. It is critical to the success of the outlet pass that the player receiving the ball makes the correct release move. This usually depends on the length of the pool, where he makes the move, and the proximity of the defender. (See Diagrams 12-5 and 12-6, "releasing in 25 or 30 meter pool" in Chapter 12 on the "Counterattack").

It is critical that the goalie outlet pass be a safe pass. A turnover on the counterattack usually means a free man coming back in the other direction. It is imperative that the field players look back for the ball, and that the goalie has eye contact before he throws the pass. The closer the defender, the further to the outside the ball must be thrown. Most passes should be wet and slightly in front of and to the outside shoulder. A dry pass can be thrown to a player on his back, but only if the defender is not too close.

LAST MAN FREE

If the free man is the last player down the pool, then the goalie must throw him the ball. The free man must be on his back and the pass must be a "dry" one, because a pass thrown on the water in front of him can be picked off by a defender who doubles back. If the goalie throws the ball far down the pool and there is a turnover, then there will be a one-on-nobody coming back right at him in this situation. (See Diagram 12-7, "throwing ball to the last man" in Chapter 12 on the "Counterattack".

Some 2-meter players will purposely "cherry-pick" when they are beat down the pool. The goalie must make sure that the "cherry picker" is covered before his teammates shoot the ball at the other end of the pool. He can do this by calling the closest player back to cover the "cherry picker".

RELEASE PASS

If the goalie cannot make a direct pass to the free man, then he must throw to a mid-court release man and direct him to throw the ball to the free man. If the free man is right handed and swimming down the left side of he pool, then the release pass must go down the right side of the pool. This allows the right-handed free man to catch the cross pass from his right and take the shot directly at the goal.

FIVE ON SIX DEFENSE

USE YOUR DEFENSE TO HELP COVER THE CAGE

Remember that the five defenders will help to take away part of the goal, while the goalie defends the other part. The goalie cannot take away the whole goal. He must trust the field players to help him. Since their backs are to the goal, the goalie must direct them to slide right or left as the situation dictates. When the ball is at one of the outside shooting positions, the goalie will be in a normal defensive position, with his hands light on the water and moving his body from side to side with the ball. Picture 11-K in Chapter 11 on the "extra man", shows four defensive players with their hands up, or about to put their hands up, to help out the goalie on 5 on 6 defense.

A common mistake on the 5 on 6 is for the goalie to play too far back inside of the goal, and thus lose his shooting angle advantage. Also, the more that he plays outside or in front of the goal, the less distance he has to travel across the goal to cover the ball. When the ball is at the corner positions, many goalies will play with their hands out of the water.

CHANNEL THE SHOT

The goalie cannot cover the whole goal by himself. He must depend on his teammates to help defend the goal, and also to channel the shot towards him so he has a better chance to make the block. In a zone defense, or after a 5-meter foul, the defender should put up the arm that matches arms with the shooter. Against a right-handed shooter, the defender must hold up his left arm and take away the nearside of the goal; while the goalie must take away the cross-goal shot. If every field player does this, the ball will be channeled towards the goalie. (See "zone blocking" Diagram 8-4 in Chapter 8 on "Defensive skills").

CORNER SHOTS

6 on 5 shots that come from the 01 and 06 wing positions must be defended differently than the normal zone shot from outside. The X1 and X6 defender must hold up the inside arm closest to the post and take away the quick corner shot. The goalkeeper must take away the cross-cage shot. It is important that the goalie not position himself directly behind the X1 and X6 defenders, because then they will be guarding the same area. The goalie should be in a position closer to the center of the goal, rather than trying to cover the corner. If the field player is not covering the corner, then the goalie must call out and move the defender right or left accordingly. (See Picture 13-I below).

Picture 13-I: 5 on 6 corner defense. Defender takes corner and goalie takes x-cage.

TRAINING THE GOALKEEPER

When training a goalkeeper, there is a fine line, between doing enough work to get him in shape, and doing so much work that you have a goalie with tired or injured legs. The best workout for the goalie is blocking a lot of shots in practice. Between shooting drills, extra-man drills, counterattack drills, and scrimmage, the goalie will be blocking a lot of shots during a 2-2 1/2 hour practice. This alone will get the goalie in shape without piling on a lot of heavy weights or doing hours of legwork.

There is a certain amount of work that has to be done outside of the goal; but that should be done at the beginning of the week in order to give the goalie a chance to rest his legs a day or two prior to a game. You can give the goalie a heavier load during the off-season; but during the competitive season you have to make sure that he has "fresh" legs for games. As a general rule, most of the legwork during the season should be done in the water.

Some dry land exercises can be done for strengthening the goalies legs, with more emphasis on dry land in the off-season then during the competitive season. During the off season in Europe, goalies will get together with several field players and go to the pool on their own, and just shoot for several hours. It is a fun way to train on their own time that will help both the shooters and the goalie to get better.

EXERCISES FOR ENDURANCE AND STRENGTH
1. Eggbeaters with one or five gallon plastic jug filled with water held over the head.

2. Heavy balls-two persons in the water or one on the deck and one in the water passing the ball back and forth- two-handed catch and throw.

3. Eggbeater with surgical tubing resistance.-Tie tubing to a deck fixture and around the goalies waist. Eggbeater away from the side of the pool.

4. Sink Drill - One player pushes down on the other player, hands in and out of the water

5. Walking with hands out

6. Gravity Drill - Explode up with hands out and stay up for specified period of time

EXERCISES FOR SPEED AND TECHNIQUE

High and low corner lunges-Explode to the corner and then come back to the center. Repeat to other corner. 1 set x 10 reps high, 1 set x ten reps low.

Mirror lunges-Two goalies facing each other. One goalie lunges and the other mirrors his movement.

Controlled pull downs-One goalie throws the ball fairly hard above the other goalies head. He reaches up and pulls the ball down to his stomach

5 on 6-Start in the center of the goal. Explode up, then skull to the left and lunge to high left corner. Return to center, explode up, skull to the right and then lunge to the high right corner.

JUMPS

1. Walk from post to post, facing goal, hands above the head, hands explode up over top of goal 5 times. Reverse direction.

2. Walk from post to post, hands in the water, hands explode up over top of goal 5 times. Reverse direction.

3. Four-yard sprint, 2 lunges up right and up left, four-yard sprint, 2 lunges. Repeat across pool.

4. Two-yard sprint, 2 lunges up-left and up right, two-yard sprint, 2 lunges. Repeat

GOALIE DRILL – UNDER PRESSURE

Goalie starts in position in goal. Position a field player on each side of the goal on the 3-4 yard line. Have someone shoot a medium hard shot to the goalies left or right side. After the goalie makes the block the field player on that side attacks him. The goalie must get control of the ball, turn away and protect the ball from the field player, try to move it to the side of the goal, and then try to draw a foul for a free pass. This can also be done by having the coach throw the ball between the goalie and a field player, but slightly closer to the goalie so that he gets there a little sooner than the field player.

GOALIE DRILL - COUNTERATTACK PASSING

Have 2 players swim down the pool, one on offense and one on defense. Create different scenarios by changing the positions of the two players in the pool and the position of the defender in relation to the offensive player. Make sure that the goalie makes the correct pass that the situation calls for. Repeat over and over again with different players in different scenarios. Add a second player going free down the other side of the pool and have the goalie direct the release man to pass the ball to the free man. This drill provides the coordination necessary between goalie and field player to make the counterattack a successful one.

DRY-LAND TRAINING

Plyometrics-Jumping up onto higher and higher wood steps or boxes. Step down.

Box side-to-side lateral jumps- Stand on top of box and jump off the right side with the right leg, jump back up on the box and then jump off the left side with the left leg. 30 reps.

Straddle jumps- A leg on each side of a bench, feet on the floor, jump up on the bench with both feet. Step down and repeat. 3 sets x 20 reps

Step ups-Hold dumbbells in hand, step up on bench, lead with same foot 20 times

Slide board- Slide back and forth on slick plastic board with socks on, like ice skating

Ice/Roller Skating in the off-season trains the muscles used in the eggbeater better than any other land exercise.

Squats- Instead of putting bar on the back of the neck, hold dumbbell weights in hands, squat down, when coming back up, do a shoulder shrug. Vary exercise by pointing toes out to the side. 2 sets x 10 reps

One-legged squats- Holding weights in hands, stand with one leg on platform and one leg bent and hanging off platform. Squat down, one leg at a time. Great for balance and strength. Two sets per leg x 10 reps

Front lunges- Weights in hands, step out in front and bend knee. Alternate legs as you move forward. 2 sets x 20 yards

Side lunges-light weights-Step to side, toes at 45 degrees, and bend knee. Step back. Alternate right and left sides. 1 set x 20 reps

Leg extension/flexion on weight machines. Abdominals and back extension exercises.

Upper back and shoulder exercises – bent arm shoulder raises (side, front and bent over side raise), upright rows, lat exercises, horizontal rowing, triceps exercises.

GAME AND PRACTICE WARM-UP

-Easy swim, free style and breaststroke, easy flutter, breast and eggbeater kicking with ball in water or kickboard.

-Warm-up passing. Start at five yards apart and gradually go to 20 yards apart.

-Pull downs. One goalie shoots an easy or medium speed shot over the other goalies head. The goalie reaches up and grabs the ball with both hands and pulls it down to his stomach. Repeat 10 times, then reverse roles.

-Eight quick high and low explosive lunges

-Take shots. Easy shots from other goalie, and then hard shots from field players.

-Rest and get mentally ready for game

It is important to remember that this is game day. You want to get loose; but you don't need a workout. Focus on the shots during warm-up; but don't get frustrated if some get by you.